BROSELEY

THE PEOPLE AND THE PAST

BY

JOAN GRIFFITHS

FIRST EDITION

Best Wishes
To Charlie Hyland
From Neil and Ann

Joan Griffiths née Beddow

Published by Joan Griffiths
C/O GET Community Publishing, The Old Fire Station, 1 High Street, Bridgnorth, Shropshire, WV16 4DB

broseley@g-e-t.org.uk

First published 2003

ISBN 0-9546663-0-5

Printed in the United Kingdom by Cambrian Printers, Ceredigion, SY23 3TN

DEDICATIONS

I dedicate this book to my family; firstly to my grand-daughter Victoria Robey who was my inspiration to write this book, and to Abigail Griffiths my second grand-daughter.

To my grand-sons Richard Robey; and Steven and Robert Griffiths, hoping they will read and enjoy it one day.

To my husband Les, for his support throughout the years it has taken me to write it.

To my daughter Ann, for helping me with the computer work, without her help I would not have published it.

And lastly to my sons John and Tony, I hope they get some pleasure from reading my story.

Acknowledgements:

My daughter Ann Robey, my husband Les Griffiths, Brian Davies, Elwyn Rickers, Kath (or Kate) Morris, Iris Welch, Joyce Forester, Norah Jones, Bill, Margaret and Neil Beddow, Les Pugh, Ron Miles, Derek Pountney, Carolyn Molyneux, Lol Oakley, all the people who spoke to me on the tapes, Jack Owen, Joyce Coulthard, John Powell, Roger Edmundson, the Churches, National Trust/Benthall Hall, Richard Benthall, Melinda Evans, Claire Roberts, Mike Kaiser, Heads of all the schools, Roy Lane and Pat Long, my late father for the many family photographs and anyone else I have not mentioned.

The photographs I have been given have been innumerable so thanks to all who have given me permission to use them, some of them I do not know where they came from, but I have done my best to get permission for the ones I have used.

Some of the postcards I have had many years and don't know who did them as there are no names to try to contact.

All reasonable efforts have been made to obtain permission to reproduce the photographs in this book, but I wish to apologise if any item has inadvertently been included without permission.

CONTENTS

INTRODUCTION

I have been researching this book for about 12 years. When my seven year old granddaughter asked to borrow an old 'washing dolly' for a Victorian display at school and wanted to know how to use it, I thought it should be written up about how life was lived many years ago, without the aid of the electrical gadgets available in today's world. I started to write about the things I remembered and then began to be interested in the local history, I did not realise then it would lead to a whole book being written. I have done a lot of research, but the information available varies from one source to another in some subjects, so I have done the best with the information I have collected. I have tried to make this as interesting as possible with the information I have used, and hope there are not too many inaccuracies. This is my first book.

I would like to thank everyone who has given me help, encouragement and information, also the people who have given me so many of the photographs of Broseley and the people, and I hope everyone will like looking at them now they are all together in a book. Without your invaluable help I could never have achieved this, and I have been persuaded by many people to print what I have written, there has not been a book on life in Broseley for many years now, so I hope this will be enjoyed by all who read it.

I hope you will all enjoy my memories of Broseley. I must apologise to anyone who disagrees with my views of the town. This is my personal reflection of Broseley that has grown from my love and interest in the area.

On the left, the house we have lived in for 45 years at Benthall, Broseley

MY STORY

The first thing that I can remember in my life was going down to my paternal Grandparents, who lived at 12 Quarry Road, Broseley Wood, opposite The Mines.

My Grandmother - Alice Beddow nee Corfield

My Grandfather – William Henry Beddow

They used to keep fowl and pigs and fed them on boiled potato peelings, which were cooked on the old black lead grate coal fire, they also cooked them in the old copper wash boiler, they had a special smell when cooking and were mixed with meal and grain etc to feed the fowl and pigs.

The way of life then was feeding the animals that eventually fed the family, eggs and meat from the fowl and meat from the pig, was part of the day's work.

I liked to help to do this and collected the eggs out of the hen boxes which were set in an old piece of ground with brambles growing in it, the eggs were still warm when I felt around in the nests for them, I put them into the basket very carefully, making sure they did not break. Neighbours often exchanged these foods for other things, helping each other, as many of them did not have much money in these hard times.

There was a pigeon pen in this part of the garden, fenced off to separate the fowl and the pigeons. These pigeons were the pride and joy of my uncle who was totally dedicated to pigeon racing, they raced as far away as France and won many cups and prizes for him. He started taking an interest in the sport as soon as he could walk, as did his brother - my father. His father and grandfather were pigeon fanciers too, it was a popular hobby in this area then, as it is today.

Most of the pigeon fanciers were a special breed of men and were very serious about their hobby, they could win quite a lot of prize money and paid a lot for these prize birds.

The pigeons had rings on their legs to identify them and were raced in the Spring and Summer months on Saturday afternoons, we were not allowed to play down the garden by the pigeon pen or make a noise as the slightest thing would stop the pigeon from landing. You could see the pigeon flyers waiting at their pens to 'clock in' the first pigeon home, after sending them on a journey in pigeon baskets, by train or other forms of transport to other parts of the country. They were also sent out of the country in big races, to France and Spain. They were then released together and the first one home won the prize.

The 'clock' was usually kept at one of the local pubs, years ago it could have been the Albion, in later years it was the Kings Head in Broseley Wood and the Pheasant in the Square, and now at the Birchmeadow Centre. It had to be reached as quickly as possible by the runners, it wasn't just fast pigeons in those days it was fast runners too, and they weren't above trying to nobble the others, a good runner was worth a few pints then.

One story told was of a man rushing in on his bike to clock in his pigeon, he was so keen to win he fell off his bike, the first concern of the other people there was not if the man was hurt but getting the pigeon ring clocked in. A lot of these men wore red or blue spotted neckerchiefs or mufflers. There were sometimes heated arguments about pigeons that came home, but could not be coaxed into the pen to clock them in, many were threatened with having their necks pulled.

Collecting the eggs with Georgina Dudley 1943

There were 'Presentation' nights when the winners were presented with their trophies at the pigeon supper, a special end of season get together which was usually held, at least in my time, at the Kings Head pub, in the 'Buff' room and some were held at the Town Hall. The cups won during the pigeon racing season were displayed and presented to the winners at this event, and a jolly good night was had by all, the wives and lady friends of the pigeon flyers too, most of them were staunch supporters of their men with this hobby. They were entertained by a local group of men playing piano, banjo, guitar, mouth organ, piano accordion, yukelele, wash board and comb/paper. Perce Beddow (my father), Frank Miles, Harry Holcroft, Bill Harrison, Sammy Oare and many others, all local people who played and sang at these functions.

As the evening wore on and they had all had a few beers, some of them too many, they all joined in with the singing, all the old songs 'You are my Sunshine, It's a Long way to Tipperary, I'll be Your Sweetheart, Danny Boy and many more. They knew the words in those day's as a singsong was family entertainment then.

Pigeon Club Presentation Night 1950's

Many tales could be told of some of the characters around Broseley years ago, one being taken home in a wheel barrow too drunk to walk, and another character found in Simpsons Lane in a drunken state, singing 'I'm Forever Blowing Bubbles', he was arrested by the local bobby and taken to court at Much Wenlock. He was fined by the Magistrate and apologised for the offence, afterwards being taken next door to the pub by local councillors who knew the fellow. They paid for his fine then bought him drinks and he ended up in another drunken state. (Perhaps these tales can be told at some other time, as there are still families of these characters about and it could cause embarrassment to them.)

Pigeon Club Presentation Night 1950's

The pigs were kept in a pigsty at the bottom of the garden, the pigswill was tipped into a trough in the sty. I can remember one day when I was at granny's seeing a wooden bench in the yard and a man was standing there talking to my grandfather, his name was Mr Wallbank and he lived in the row of cottages, now demolished, at the back of the Prince in King Street. I was taken into the house out of the way, but I heard the pig squealing and found out later that the man was a pig killer and he had slit the pig's throat on the bench. The animal was then cut up for food, and the pieces of bacon joints were salted, wrapped in Muslin and hung on hooks in the ceiling. The bacon rashers were cut off these joints for eating as required. I was most upset by this, as I fed these pigs and could not understand that they were bred for eating. We used to play with the pig's bladder, which was blown up like a balloon.

There were geese down the garden too, they were quite fierce and they used to fly at people, hissing, they pecked the ribbon tie of my bonnet when I was small,

Pigeon Club Presentation Night 1950's

I didn't go too near them afterwards. Visitors were very cautious too if the geese were at the gate, they entered at their peril.

We slept at granny's sometimes, a treat for us as we were allowed a small barrel- shaped glass of beer with our bread and cheese for supper, which Grandad fetched from the 'Pitchyard' pub just over the Brook, in a white, blue edged enamel jug. We were told not to tell anyone we had this beer, so that made it rather special, as it was a secret. A lot of people fetched beer in jugs from their nearest pub to drink in the house.

I remember a picture on the bedroom wall above the single bed I slept in. It was of a little girl struggling through the snow with a pony, and it was nice going to sleep looking at this in the light of the oil lamp, a shadowy, flickering light, which was a comforting sort of light or a little frightening if you woke up in the night. I sometimes slept in Granny's bed when I was small but she said I kicked her all night so I expect she was glad when I went into the single bed.

There was a wash basin, soap dish and water jug set on the marble topped table in the bedroom, and a chamber pot to match under the bed, and mats on the wooden floor boards. They were very cold houses as there wasn't any heating in the bedrooms or carpets on the floors or stairs.

The stairs were scrubbed and kept very white, as was the kitchen table. There was a large, polished chest of drawers and dresser in the room too. The beds had iron bedsteads, a spring base and feather or flock mattresses which had to be turned every week, pillows and a bolster, and sheets and blankets. These were very heavy especially in the winter when the extra blankets were needed to keep you warm, and some were lucky to have an eiderdown, for extra warmth.

This was about 1940 and there wasn't any running water in the houses, or sewerage drains at this time, wastewater was carried outside in buckets and thrown down open outside drains. Drinking water was carried in from taps situated in various places in the streets, some of these were called 'lion' taps they had a thick, iron, ridged body and the face of the lion was set on the top. The water came out of the mouth when the handle on the side of the head was turned, there was also a small trough at the base of the tap for the dogs to drink from. There are still a few around today.

My brothers and I used to fetch buckets of water in for our grandparents from a tap along Simpsons Lane, opposite Enfield House, known as the Cross Keys' when it was a public house many years ago. This tap was the main source of drinking water and was used by all the people who lived in the cottages on the lane. The water was poured into pitcher urns and a wooden board was placed over the top to keep it clean, steins were also used for water containers and to make wine in, gauze or net was placed over these containers to keep the contents clean, weighted down with beads sewn in the corners. These, and the bowls for washing and washing up, were kept on the stone setlez, built about 3 feet high, made of brick and built along the walls of the kitchen, local tiles were sometimes used to line the walls and surfaces. There were openings cut out at floor level and shaped into a sort of half circled compartments, which were used for storage. The meat safe was a wooden cupboard, with a white, wire mesh front where the meat, butter and cheese were kept to stop the flies getting at the food, this also stood on the setlez.

Most of the houses had a well of water in the garden, some even had one under the house itself, this was rain water from underground springs in the area, a lot of this area was undermined in days gone by. It was quite fascinating getting the water out of the well, I remember being taught how to tilt the bucket before throwing it into the water and hauling it up by a rope tied to the handle, it was a frightening experience at first as I imagined falling down the well which was very deep. The well was made with a brick wall lining and had a wooden trap door fit over the top, the water came from the underground springs and was very clean and clear.

Most people grew their own fruit and vegetables in those days, many digging pieces of ground called allotments, a common sight then but not seen so often now. The men were very keen and competitive when growing their garden produce, providing their families with fresh fruit and vegetables, some of these were bottled, or salted to keep for the winter.

There used to be 'Vegetable Shows' where people showed off their best prized exhibits of the season, the local show at Benthall was held at the New Inn pub, on Bridge Road or the old Pitts Yard on Coach Road as it was called then. This was called the Benthall Potato Show when it started in 1902, at the time of the Coronation of Edward V11, it was a potato show only to begin with but was later extended to include fruit, vegetables and flowers.

It was one of the annual local attractions and was called the Benthall Potato Show as the members were given a pound of special unnamed seed potatoes, known only to the secretary, which they grew in their gardens. When they were harvested, they were washed and cleaned very carefully after being chosen for size, shape and quality. The show potato class was for quality and seed, other classes were kidney and round.

They were then displayed on plates in different classes and judged by some one qualified, for the prizes. The people who competed were very serious about their products and carefully guarded the secret ways they had of enhancing the vegetables and fruit they had grown, the quality of this was very good.

In the early years when Alice and Will Perks were licensees, the walls of the old stables where the show was held were covered with leafy branches and fern's, trestle tables were lined with old wall paper and were set up for the exhibits. It was a very popular event. The Perks' were very good landlords, who made people welcome, I remember as a child there was always fresh cut bread and cheese, and pickles brought into the pub for the customers.

The waste from the old earth closets were often dug into the soil in the gardens, it certainly made the sprouts etc. grow well.

Group of local men at Pitchyard Show 1925/30's.
Will and Bob Perks, Tom and Fred Corfield, Billy Goodwin, Mr Clinton and young man Arthur Beddow

Families turned up on Saturdays and Sundays to see the exhibits, these included fruit, vegetables, and flowers, Chrysanthemums, dahlias, roses etc. and flower arrangements, there was also a children's class for wild flowers. On Sunday evenings the exhibits were sold off to the people who went there to buy the produce, and the money was given to the children's Xmas party and old age pensioners of Benthall. We looked forward to the show as kids, it was an evening out where we met our friends and had pop and crisps, the old fashioned Smiths crisps with the little blue packet of salt.

In about 1970 the landlord of the New Inn was Reg Hindley, he told the organisers that he did not want the show to be held there. This was very sad, as it was the end of a very old and popular local tradition. Dennis Mason was president of the Benthall Flower Show at the time and he arranged for the show to be held at Broseley Social Club, where it is still running today

There were several shops in the Broseley Wood area, many of which have been closed over the years and lots of houses demolished, some pubs have been closed and converted into houses for people to live in, and some new buildings have been built.

There was a sweet shop on Quarry Road which belonged to Humphries's, in their cottage, and next door to that, there used to be another shop which belonged to Wilkes's, John Wilkes I believe, he sold bread and all sorts of things, - as well as paraffin - like most of the small shops which were about then, my father told me John Wilkes used to say to the mothers who took their babies into his shop and sat them on the counter 'don't put the babies bottoms on the counter, it might taste the bread'. Though paraffin was sold in many of the small shops, it was also taken many miles around the houses in trucks, John Wilkes took his wares in his truck or barrow as far away as Buildwas. He wore a whistle around his neck which he would blow when he got to the bottom of the steep Bridge Bank on his way home, he would stop and wait for his wife to come down and meet him and they hauled the truck up the bank together with a rope. The Goodall family lived in this house when I was a child.

The old Post Office in Simpsons Lane was once a pub called the Cross Keys but is now a private house called Enfield House. This was owned and run as a Post Office when I was a child by Mary Johnson, she was a large lady who wore a long black dress and had her grey hair in a bun at the back of her head. She was a kindly lady and kept a pet bird, a raven, in a big cage in the Post Office, which was also her home. There was a wooden counter in the room on the left hand side of the front door where she served her customers, it always seemed so gloomy in there, but of course there were no electric lights at that time, just oil lamps and candles.

Scholfields was another shop, which sold bread and all sorts of things that people would need for every day use, from bread, groceries, sweets, green grocery, medicines, such as Syrup of Figs (this was the first thing you were given if you didn't feel very well, to clear the system out), aspirins, bandages, ointments, cotton, candles, shoe laces, pencils etc.

Other old remedies were chocolate wormcakes, with bits sprinkled on them, Brimstone and treacle to clear the blood, sugar, butter and vinegar for coughs, goose grease for the chest, blue bags for bee stings, olive oil for earache, oil of cloves for toothache, zambuk for chilblains, basilicon ointment for drawing infections, iodine for cuts, siedletz powders for chills, and calamine lotion for itching skin to name a few.

This shop was in Quarry Road, (it was a pub the Rose and Crown many years ago) and the Post Office was

Benthall Potato Show late 1940's. All local people.
Roly Owen, Bert Weekes, Alice Perks, George Reeves, unknown, Tina Owen, unknown, Dennis Venn.

eventually moved to these premises in about the nineteen forties, a letterbox was built into the brick pillar at the stepped entrance to the shop, and is still used for posting letters today. This shop was closed, about 1975, but was very useful for local people when there was little transport about. It offered a delivery service, and orders were delivered to our homes. I have lived here many years and really appreciated this little shop and the amenities it provided for the local people, it was kept by Mrs Simmonds in the 1950's and later by Mr and Mrs Bedson. I have still got some of the notebooks with my orders in them and the prices that were relevant at that time, it is quite interesting to compare the prices of then and now:

loaf of bread cost 1s/7d – (8p,)	12 Eggs 4s/-d – (20p,)
1 lb Jam 2s/7d – (15 1/2p,)	Toilet Roll 1s/6d – (7 1/2p,)
packet Salt 6d – (2 1/2p,)	All Bran 1s/6d – (7 1/2p,)
stamp cost 4d – (1 1/2p,)	...just to mention a few.

Sliced bread could be bought from about 1930, and toilet paper from 1807.

Converting these prices to the change in pounds, shillings and pence in 1971 to the new money shows how much the prices have gone up today. It was also a place where people met and chatted together, exchanging the local gossip and passing the time of day, there was time to do this when the pace of life was so much slower.

In the winter it was quite nasty when the ice and snow was about and people used the ashes from their coal fires to put on the jitties and lanes, so that they could get out and about without slipping down. There was no road salt provided then. These jitties were short cuts to the paths and houses in the areas.

Nothing was wasted in those days, snow was melted and used for water, rain water was collected in 'boshes' which stood outside most back doors, catching the water running into the gutters from off the roof, and there were wells in most gardens, this water was used for doing the washing, cooking, bathing, washing hair and washing up. Water was never wasted, as it had to be carried in buckets from outside taps, used water was thrown on the gardens. Potato peelings and vegetable stalks were cooked for the fowl and pigs, other left over food was fed to the cats, dogs and any other animals.

Socks and stockings were darned, the cuffs and collars of shirts were turned when they were frayed and worn, sheets were cut down the middle and joined, side to side or top to bottom or middle, to get more wear out of them.

The coal fires were used for heating the house, boiling water and cooking meals and the oven was used for baking and cooking, even the oven plate was used, for warming the bed. Oven bricks too were wrapped in newspaper or a cloth and put in the bed. Some were lucky enough to have stone water bottles that were filled with hot water and had a stopper. 'Spills' were made from strips of newspaper rolled up like a pencil and the top turned down to stop it unwinding, they were kept in jars on the mantle piece above the fireplace for lighting the gas lights and candles, pipes and cigarettes etc. from the fire.

There was an art to lighting coal fires, a lot depended on the way the wind was blowing and a draw plate was often needed to help fan the flames. Sheets of newspaper were twisted and screwed up to look like sticks and placed in the grate in a crisscross manner, then layers of small dry sticks and finally small pieces of coal. Sometimes it lit well and other times it took several attempts to get it going, a newspaper was sometimes used instead of a draw plate to help get the fire going but this was quite hazardous as it could easily set fire to the soot up the chimney. It was important to keep the chimneys swept as many house fires were caused if this was not done regularly, a very dirty job though! I remember on one occasion when we were having the chimney swept, the sweep put the brushes up the chimney, but when he brought them down there were no bristles left on the end, we had not lit the fire in the grate, but the chimney must have been on fire, it was very funny to see the sweeps face.

Mothers Union, Benthall 1950's

The soot was used for the gardens, and it was also used, with salt for cleaning teeth. The ashes from the fire were shaken through a riddle and the cinders were used to 'back up' the fire at night, coal dirt or slack were put on top of the cinders and this was then damped down with cold tea left in the teapot. Most homes had fire guards around the fire, to protect the small children from burning themselves, it also protected grown ups who often had the habit of standing in front of the fire to warm their bottoms and legs, especially the women. There have been some perilous episodes if the fireguard had been removed, as they used to hold the back of their dresses or skirts up to warm themselves, and they sat on the guard itself sometimes, if it wasn't in its place, one could easily topple into the fire. The fireguard was used for drying the washing too, many things were burnt or singed this way if they were not watched carefully. A lot of women had mottled legs from sitting too close to the fire and burnt their legs warming themselves. The toasting fork was another essential item as the bread was toasted in front of the fire, the slice of bread was put onto a three or four pronged metal fork that had a long extending handle, and held in front of the red hot fire bars. This was very tasty, especially with pork dripping from the 'late' pig spread on it, and a little salt, not very healthy according to today's health programme!

Mothers Union, Benthall 1950's

Washday was an epic in itself, it was done in the brewhouse, or "brewuss" as it was called by locals. An early start was required, as the water had to be carried in buckets from an outside tap or well and heated by a coal fire. This wash boiler was a square shape built of bricks, with a round copper or iron tub set in the centre of the top, with a wooden cover/lid. In the middle of the front wall was a small iron door, inside would be an iron grid where the fire was laid to heat the water under the copper tub, this had to be topped up with coal throughout the washing session to keep a supply of hot water. This washing was pre-soaked overnight, having been sorted into 'whites' for boiling, 'coloureds', and the more heavily soiled garments like work clothes and overalls etc, and were washed in that order. The 'whites' were washed in a dolly tub, with a wooden dolly which was used to bash the washing clean, and the soap was blocks of Sunlight soap which may have been 'shaved' by the children ready for washday, it was then rubbed on the wash board, boiled, rinsed, then put in water which had been 'blued' with a Recketts Blue Bag and finally starched. It was then put through the mangle, this was a heavy job, but if done well made the drying of the washing so much quicker.

It was carried outside in the wicker washing basket and hung on the clothes line if the weather was fit for drying it, or hung on lines stretched across the ceilings in the houses, on the wooden clothes horse or on the fireguard around the fire, some had pulley lines which were wooden slats to hang the washing on and they were pulled up and down from the ceiling with a pulley, there were also lines strung across the fireplace front under the mantle piece.

The ironing was done on the kitchen table with cast irons that were heated on the coal fire, and tested before applying them to the clothes, this was done by lightly spitting on the iron to see how it sizzled, if they got too hot the washing could be singed or burnt, there were usually two irons, one to use and one to re-heat and they were stood on an iron stand when not being used.

King Street–on left Kenyons shop, then Thomas's the Painter/Decorator, early 1900's

We lived at Cape Fold from 1935 in a two bed-roomed house, there were six in our family, two boys, two girls and our parents. Mom and Dad had one bedroom and we shared the other one, the two boys in a double bed and my sister and I in a single bed, there was only enough room for one piece of furniture in our bedroom, a table which had a mirror on it, this had a wooden base and frame and the mirror could be swung to and fro, - and of course, the chamber pot (or jerry/guzunder) which was a familiar sight in all the houses. It was put into a bucket to be carried across the yard to the earth closet to be emptied.

View of Cobwell Road, Broseley Wood, before the new houses were built 1959/60

Oil lamps, candles and night lights were used to light the bedrooms, the night light stood in a saucer of water and the candles stood in candle sticks or in jars for safety, as they could be a fire hazard, if they toppled over or were played with by mischievous children.

There was a living room and a back kitchen, with an outside toilet. How families lived in these small houses is hard to believe these days, larger families than ours lived in these two bed-roomed homes. One family in Broseley Wood lived with the husband's parents in a tiny 2 bed-roomed cottage, they and their eight children all slept in one bedroom, the husbands parents slept in the other, living in these cramped conditions must have been very hard for all the family, but they survived.

There were seven families living at Cape Fold, (at the top of Barratts Hill/Cape Street,) of all age groups, lots of the communities in Broseley lived in groups of houses like these. Most of the neighbours helped each other in those days, there was a much closer relationship amongst the people then than there is now. We would pop next door if we ran out of sugar or milk etc, or needed a shilling or some coppers for the gas meter, and the neighbours knew they could do the same. Neighbours would be there to help each other when needed, like one big family really. Of course there were the squabbles, but they were soon forgotten.

There was usually a communal washhouse or brewhouse near the houses, which was shared, and used by each family on different days. The water for the washing was drawn from the nearby well, the nearest tap was on the road at the top of Barratts Hill/Cape Street, this was then used after the washing was done, to scrub down the brick yard or 'fold' in front of the houses.

We were lucky enough to have a gas boiler, which was a round metal tub on three legs, and the top had a hinged lid where the water was poured into the tub. The gas supply came through a rubber hose from the gas pipe in the wall connecting it to the side of the boiler. There was a tap at the bottom of the front of the tub to empty the water out, into a bucket.

There was a brown earthenware sink built into a corner of this crude kitchen but it didn't have a drain for the water to run away, there was a hole in the corner of the sink but waste water ran into a 'slop' bucket, which most of these cottages had, and was carried to the drain outside, the water had to be used from a bowl which stood in the sink. All wastewater was carried in buckets to a drain outside the house.

The brick floors were cleaned, on hands and knees with a bucket of hot water and a floor cloth and scrubbing brush, 'soft soap', a soft brown substance in a pot was scooped out with the fingers, it made the water lovely and soft and soapy. The table was white topped and scrubbed to keep it clean.

Neighbours at Cape Fold, Ellen and Barrie Holcroft, Mabel Colley and my mother Lilian Beddow, in the traditional pinafores they wore.

We had a gas ring for boiling the kettle or saucepan which was kept on the lid top of the gas boiler, some had a two gas rings with a grill under it, but most used the coal fire in the black lead grate, this had to be cleaned with black Zebro polish and a brush till it shone. The brass or iron fender in front of the fire had to be cleaned too with Brasso, some fenders had a box seat at each end, which was used to keep shoe polish and brushes in.

There was a lot to clean up every day from the dust of the coal fire ashes, a companion set stood by the side of the fireplace, this stand held a small brush and shovel, a poker and a pair of fire tongs to keep the fire place tidy, or fire dogs used with the long brass tongs and poker which lay across the fender.

Over the top of the fireplace was a shelf called the mantelpiece, this had a fringe fastened around it, and photographs, ornaments and a clock were displayed upon it. Black beetles could be found scuttling in the hearth and the cupboards.

They were really horrible things and quite frightening, especially if they crawled on you, and another familiar sight was the silver fish quickly darting about everywhere.

We had a large cupboard which was built into the wall to the left of the fireplace, the top part was used for storing food, I remember especially the Pink Emulsion, Virol and Cod liver Oil and Malt being kept in there.

We kept our shoes in the bottom half, along with the gas meter. We had to make sure we had change in the house to feed the gas meter as we relied on it for light, we were often sent round to our neighbours for change for pennies or shillings if we had none. The gas meter had to be emptied by the 'Gasman', who collected the pennies and shillings out of it, tipped them on the table and counted them, then gave the people a rebate.

A friend told me that when she was a child she was watching the man emptying the meter, and she suddenly asked him why he was counting the pennies in piles of thirteen instead of twelve pennies to the shilling, he must have felt quite embarrassed to have been caught out by a child, he said he must have counted the first pile wrong, but then just stacked the other pile of pennies to match it.

My sister Kathleen with her cat and an old fashioned gas boiler.

The cupboard under the stairs was used to store coal and wood for the fire, imagine having the coal tipped in there, and all that dust and dirt in the living room! The stairs climbed up behind the coal cupboard partition which was made of tongue and groove boarding, there was a knot hole missing from one of the boards, when we kids couldn't sleep we used to sit on the stairs and look through this hole at what was going on in the down stairs living room. We watched our parents and their friends some nights, drinking beer they had brought home from the pub after turning out time, and having a singsong in the living room, Johnny and Nellie Cole, Herbie and Nellie Davies and Eric Corfield to mention a few.

We had a daily wash when we were small, sitting on a towel on the kitchen table with a bowl of warm water beside us, we would be washed - hands and arms, face, neck and ears then the legs and feet. When washing the legs we were stood up on the table and our heads very often hit the fragile gas mantle light which hung from the living room ceiling, and broke the mantle, we didn't have a gas globe on our light.

That meant someone running across to 'Snows Shop' to get another gas mantle before he closed at 8 o'clock. Mr Snow's shop was not very big but he sold everything you could need from reels of cotton, groceries, vegetables, medicines, hair pins/combs, pencils, razor blades etc. He used to sit in his chair just inside the counter and do his knitting, a most unusual hobby for a man but he knitted some lovely things. Mrs Snow was a small lady who I remember had a lovely round happy face, her hair was done in plaits wound round to look like wheels and fastened at the back of the head near the neck with hair pins, this was a popular style in those days, hair nets were also worn then.

I remember my father sending my young brother across to Snow's shop one evening for some razor blades, to get him to go quickly he said 'see how long it takes you to go to Snows shop and back', my brother ran as fast as he could and came back, out of breath and asked how long he had been, my father hadn't timed him and just said 'about 3 minutes' to answer his question, this was accepted as alright. My father then said 'where are the blades? my brother looking quite put out, said he had forgotten them - he had run there for nothing! Another funny incident was when he was given a shilling by our uncle to get some birdseed from the shop. He put it in his pocket and promptly forgot about it, later in the day finding a shilling in his pocket he spent it on sweets. Our uncle came up at night and asked for his birdseed, my brother was quite put out, he had lost a shilling, found a shilling and spent a shilling and found the whole thing very puzzling indeed.

View of Benthall from top of Barratts Hill

One regular job we had to do was cleaning our shoes, this was done every day, we never went out with dirty shoes as they had to be well polished.

Another amenity we had was the earth closet lavatories which we relied on then, they were outside buildings, sometimes one on its own, sometimes several in a row, depending on how many houses they had to cater for. They were deep pits with a brick wall front and a wooden seat placed over them with round holes cut out for people to sit on, The ones with a small one for the children and a larger hole for the grown-ups were 'posh', family lavatories, these seats were scrubbed to keep them clean, lavatory paper was newspapers, cut into squares, a hole was made in one corner for string to be threaded through, and hung on a nail on the wall. Lime was burnt in the limekilns and the powder was spread in layers over the contents of the pit to burn it. It was also used in the garden, a trench was dug, then a layer of manure/a layer of lime, then left to rot before planting time. It was frightening going to these lavatories at night, as there were rats about. We used a candle set upright in a jam jar as a light, we let drops of candle fat drip into the bottom of the jar and then stuck the candle into it, then tied a piece of string round the top of the jar and made a long handle. These lavatories had to emptied, sometimes by 'muck-carts' which came round at night, or by people who dug a hole in the garden or waste ground nearby and buried it, again covered with burnt lime. It was sometimes spread over the gardens! Not a very nice job! It's not surprising there were serious diseases about like Scarlet Fever and Dyphtheria. The next day we played on the same ground that our lavatory had been emptied into.

In the 1950's when we got married, we lived in a small cottage with no amenities, just the same as Cape Fold, but we had then progressed to an 'Elsen' pan, a chemical toilet, this was a type of bucket treated with a chemical, which could be lifted out of a container with a toilet seat -but this too was emptied into a hole in the garden. One person who hated this job always left it until it was full to the brim before emptying it, and could be seen with a handkerchief tied around his face and his stomach heaving as he felt quite sick, no one was more pleased to get a house with a flush toilet than he was. Thank God those days have gone.
Bath night was once a week, usually Fridays, consisted of either an oval or oblong tin bath with handles at each end to carry it with. The water was boiled in saucepans and kettles, or boilers if you were lucky enough to have one and the bath was set on the hearth in front of the coal fire, we usually all used the same water starting with the baby!

The floors of these cottages were made of brick or tiles, and the women made 'rag' rugs to put on the floor. They were made from any old clothes, coats, curtains, socks, jumpers etc. which I remember cutting into strips about 4-5" long and 1-2" wide, (the scissors hurt your hand after doing this for some time) these strips were then pegged into a sack bag or piece of sacking with a special pegging tool, by my mother. These rugs were made very attractive by the many different designs and colours used by the individual person making them. They were warm and hardwearing and cost virtually nothing to make. They made warm bed covers too.

There was not much money about when we were young, clothes and shoes were passed down through the family, poorer families were glad to have clothes from other better off people, all handed down as long as there was some wear left in them to others. The girls wore a vest, a liberty bodice, a small fleecy lined waistcoat with rubber buttons, so named as it was the next thing to a corset but was free from the bones, hence the name liberty (designed in 1908), interlock knickers elasticated at the top and legs, and a small pocket at the side above the knicker leg, and a flannelette petticoat, under our top clothes.

Group of workers – Potteries

Lace up shoes and Wellingtons for winter, and in summer a pair of pumps, white or brown T bar sandals. Best shoes, if you were lucky were black patent. We had Sunday best clothes which we kept for going out in, usually got on the large side to make sure we got our wear out of them. Gaberdine macs were worn for school in the winter, and coats were of wool in a fitted princess style, we wore pixie hoods, scarves and sometimes berets, usually knit by some member of the family, as were the jumpers and cardigans, socks and gloves. In the summer we wore bonnets, these were very pretty, and decorated with small flowers and ribbons, some made of straw, or material with ruched shading for the face. The boys wore caps and balaclavas. The women wore crossover aprons, usually of a flowery designed cotton fabric, and turbans around their heads, and a stylish pillbox hat with a short veil was worn for going out. As money was short, and so were stockings, the ladies used to put gravy browning on their legs to make it look as if they were actually wearing stockings, and a fine pencil line was drawn down the back of the leg to look like a seam. A mixture of sugar and water was used for 'setting lotion' for the hair. Rags and pipe cleaners were used for curlers, as well as the metal 'dinky curler' and metal waving clip to pinch the waves into the hairstyle of the day. We later used 'home perms', a more permanent way of curling the hair, these were called 'Toni', 'Twink' and 'Pin-up' perms.

Old woollen garments were unpicked and the wool unravelled and wrapped around a piece of wood, washed and wound into a ball ready to use to knit with again. Sleeves were cut off old jumpers and used for mitts and socks, and buttons and zips were saved.

The clinic for babies and children to be taken to, was held by the doctors surgery along the Wharfage at Ironbridge, the boxes of powdered baby food and bottles of orange juice was collected from there and the Virol

Broseley Square – the lady is Sylvia Edwards

jar was re-filled at the clinic. The school dentist and checks for flat feet were done there too, some had blocks built onto their shoes to correct this and some had to do exercises.

Another job that had to be done regularly was having your head 'looked at' for nits and bugs, especially if the nurse had visited the school and had given children notes to take home to their mothers. This involved newspaper spread on the table with your head bent over it and a very fine toothed steel nit comb pulled through your hair, it was quite a painful process. Then we were kept there while a search was done for the nits or eggs, the hair with the nit on it was pulled out and it was cracked. UGH! Derbac and carbolic soap was used to discourage these mites, and in later years Suleo was used, a much easier solution. But in later years the lice became resistant to these shampoos and doctors have said the best way by far to control head lice is the old fashioned way with the nit comb and conditioner on the hair, done for several days on the trot to catch the eggs as they hatch out.

During the war years everyone had ration books for food and clothing coupons for clothes. Food rationing began in January 1940, which was one of the coldest winters we can remember, and sweet rationing in 1942. The allowance was 3 ozs a head per week. Some children were so hungry they would ask other kids if they could finish their apple cores, and beg a bite off a crust of bread and jam, or a sweet. Cadburys and Nestle's chocolate, Rowntrees Kit Kat's and Smarties, Mars bars, Crunchies and Quality Street were still about during the war, but were rationed. Some people sold their clothing coupons for money or exchanged them for food etc. One of our neighbours sold her coupons so she had money to go to the Central or Plaza picture house, she was a regular film fan.

Eggs were hard to get then and I remember we had a big bowl with what looked like white, solid froth in it and eggs were kept in this 'isenglass' as I believe it was called. Dried egg powder was also used. Other food substitutes were Pom dried potato, Snoek fish food, Prem and Spam to name a few. Meat was very scarce, and recipes were available in magazines and leaflets for meals without meat. Foods used were cabbage, potatoes, cheese, and green vegetables, fruit was used for jam making and fruit bottling. People were encouraged to grow their own vegetables/ fruit in the gardens and allotments.

Many families relied on a rabbit stew for dinner, we never went hungry, my dad would catch a rabbit for us to have a good meal, often poached from the fields around the area, that is a another story though, the poaching. Bread and jam was eaten a lot too. One of the sayings about this food was 'Jam and spam, spam and bloody jam' people were so fed up with having to eat what was available to them due to the rationing.

Instones funeral hearse

We had evacuees here during the war years, children split up from their families and sent from the cities and large towns away from the bombing. They were sent to the country, to live with people who were forced to take them in. It must have been heart breaking for these children and their parents and brothers and sisters, being split up and not knowing if they would see each other again, also for the families having to adjust and cope with these sad children. Some of the children were lucky and got good homes, but others didn't.

Children were evacuated very early during the 'phoney war', when nothing happened they were sent back home, but many were killed when the cities were eventually bombed.

One evacuee who came here with his sister, Tommy and Marian Montgomery returned in the 1990's and told how he came as an evacuee on 1st September 1939, with only his gas mask in a box on his back, and a bag with a bar of chocolate, and a packet of plain and chocolate biscuits, he would not let go of this bag for months, it was all he had of his own, to remind him of his own family. He came here with his sister and they were taken in by two of my aunts, who were very kind people, they were lucky they found good homes.

I remember feeling sorry for another evacuee who stayed in Broseley, having her hair treated and tooth combed because she had head lice, she must have felt devastated and upset having to go through the undignified and quite painful procedure of the nit combing, by some one strange to her. We were lucky here in Broseley to be with our families during the war.

Wartime – scene outside Broseley Town Hall

Old view of The Mines, Benthall from Quarry Road, taken before 1942 when the thatch was taken off number 49, the cottage on the far right.

We had Air Raid shelters, one was in the front playground of Broseley School yard, (now the Health Centre) and one in the back. The one for Legges Hill school was behind the top playground. We also had gas masks, they had round metal bases we could breathe through and a rubber face covering with a 'window' to see through, and straps that went over the head. The babies had a different one, they were much larger and the baby was put inside it and air was pumped in from a pump attached to the side.

Women joined the forces, the WAAF, WRNS, ATS, AFS, NAAFI and the Land Army. These Land girls worked many hours all over the country, harvesting the crops and fruit, and looking after the animals. They also worked as post women, conductors, munition workers and many more roles previously filled by men.

Some of the comics and annuals about at this time were the Beano, Triumph, Tiny Tots, Girls Crystal, Radio Fun, Rainbow, Rover, Wizard, and Boys Own to mention a few. Magazines were Woman's Own, Lilliput, Radio Times, Everybody's, Picture Post, Woman's Weekly, Men Only, Jane's Journal, most containing saving tips for cooking, mending clothes, and knitting and dressmaking patterns. Song sheets were popular then too, as singing and playing the piano were a part of keeping the community spirit up, costing very little.

The gypsies were a familiar sight when we were young, one family particularly remembered were the Locks. Gypsy Lock, as she was known, was a tall thin woman with grey plaited hair, carrying her basket of pegs, lace, shoelaces and lucky charms around the town. She would tell your fortune if you crossed her palm with silver, or so they used to say, but some people were afraid of them and would not answer the door. Others thought it was unlucky not to buy something from her if it was only a few pegs or a bit of lace or elastic, they were a part

The old footbridge by the Boat at Coalport demolished in 1999, replaced 2000

of life here then. There were younger ones around too, very colourful with their dark looks and bright coloured clothes. The pegs were made by the gypsy folk out of willow, just two pieces of shaped wood, fastened together with a narrow piece of tin wound around the top and tacked together, they were very effective. There were several gypsy encampments, one was near the Free Bridge at Jackfield, by the Lloyds, and another was on the Ironbridge Road close to the cemetery. They were the old Romany horse drawn caravans, and their dogs would lie about the camp area, probably used to catch the rabbits for supper, which were hung in a pot over the outside camp fire.

The old Free Bridge, now demolished, new bridge opened 18th Oct 1994

Then there were the rag and bone men with their carts, collecting old clothes etc. house to house. They blew a trumpet and shouted 'Chickens for rags' and gave the children a small yellow chick, (which was kept in a box on the back of the cart) a gold fish or a balloon for any old rags.

There were tramps about at this time too, old men with beards as I remember, and very rough looking, their coats tied around the middle with string, they slept rough, under the hedge rows and in the barns of the local farms, but were usually regarded as harmless characters.

Many stories and tales have been passed around of characters in the town, one was of a Sunday School collection being taken to Balls Lanes to bet on marble games being played there, the 'taw' was lost, the big un,

People standing on the frozen River Severn in 1917

a voice suddenly said "ere's thee taw lad" and it was given back to them. They could hear chains - and ran home frightened (or frittened) to death, they swore they had seen the devil. Then there was the woman, in her curlers and turban, fag in her mouth saying 'If men wore their trousers the way the vicar wore his bloody collar, there'd be no waifs and strays. Another amusing saying was about the families living behind the Albion pub, called the Backs, they were Hall's, Ball's and Everall's.

A tale told of the old Toll on the Ironbridge in 1932, was of when a five year old came home on Christmas night in the family horse and trap from his grandparents farm at the top of Madeley Bank. He was snug under the large canvas sheet, lined with warm tartan wool. They crossed the Ironbridge, paid the old toll-keeper, who was still on duty on Christmas night although it was rainy and foggy. They drove over the railway crossing at the station with its dim gas lamps and past the Hairpin Bend, up through the brickyards and kilns, glowing red in the mist, still at work. He remembers clattering home into the muddy yard and being hurried to bed with a hot drink, while his father stabled the horses and put away the trap.

The winters were very harsh in the early 1900's, the rivers and pools were often used to skate on when they were frozen over, one of the most popular was the Moon pool at Posenhall, and another the one on the Tileries. Christmas was an exciting time, even then, when there was not much money for lots of presents, most had a sock with a few nuts, an apple or/and an orange, books, games or jigsaws and clothes if they were very lucky. Decorations were hung around the house, many were home made, holly and mistletoe and the Christmas tree, this was often a holly tree, cut from one of the coppices, which was dressed up and decorated. We were always dressed in our best clothes and taken to visit our relatives on Christmas morning, what the festive season was really all about, families caring about each other and being together.

Xmas Party held at the Kings Head, many of the children will recognise themselves

Carol singing was popular with the children, who went in groups around the houses singing, and hoping for a few pennies in their pockets or some sweets or other small gifts if they had sung nicely and properly. They were not averse to playing unkind tricks if they weren't rewarded for their efforts.

Home made wine was consumed at Christmas, as well as other occasions, this was usually very potent, especially if it was allowed to stand for a long time. Wine was made from parsnips, potatoes, carrots, beetroot, elderberries, nettles, elderflowers, parsley, dandelions, rhubarb and many other fruits and plants etc. and was very pleasant to taste.

A story was told to me about some apple wine, one year the mother made apple wine that would not be ready until the following summer. On a hot day in July the father was cutting hay in the field with two horses drawing the mower. At midday the mother walked up with his lunch in a basket and a quart bottle of apple wine, knowing the thirsty work. She thought it was the equivalent of home made cider!

The father, sitting on the fresh mown grass, drank the whole of the bottle with his lunch. He dozed off and woke with a splitting headache to hear the Broseley Church strike four o'clock, and see the horses, that had wandered to the top of the field, munching the freshly mown grass.

Ironbridge/Broseley Railway Station

Another tale was of a soldier who volunteered for the army early in the First World War. He was a private in the Royal Welsh Fusiliers and did his initial training at Kinmel Bay in Rhyl.

Before being sent overseas he was given a short leave at the end of which, he was seen off by his family. It was late at night and Ironbridge Station was blacked out. The train drew in and a voice called out "Is George Roberts there"? It was one of his old friends from the same unit. Just before George joined him in the dimly

Old photograph of Broseley War Memorial

lit compartment with its blue shaded lights he passed his silver pocket watch into his brother's hand. He was drowned on the 15th April 1915 when the troopship Arcadian was torpedoed on its way to Salonika. His watch is still with the family today. Many years later they were told by a man in the locality that he was on the ship next in line, and saw the Arcadian torpedoed and sunk by a German U-boat. That soldier's name is on the memorial in Broseley Square.

There were some fascinating buildings in Broseley but many have been demolished over the years, one of these was the Town Hall, which stood where the Spar Market now stands. The Town Hall was built in 1777, it was made of brick and situated in the High Street, it seems there were no deeds to it and it was presumed it belonged to the church, it appears from entries in a Parish Book and from a memorandum in the handwriting of a late curate, that several charity legacies left to widows and the poor were put together and the sum of £380 was lent to the Parish about the year 1777. It was employed with other monies borrowed and raised by subscription in building a market house and shops, from the rents of which it was agreed that a sum, not exceeding £18 should be annually distributed among the poor. This borrowed money was later paid back with the rents collected from these buildings.

As you went up the steps through the front doors of the Town Hall the room on the left was once the library, the room on the right was the boys woodwork room. Through the doors straight in front of you curving iron stairs took you to the top floor. There was a store cupboard at the bottom of the stairs.

At the top of the stairs on the left was the Ante-room, used by the artistes to change into their costumes, there was a door leading to the big room right by the stage. Just at the top of the stairs in front of you were the double entrance doors to the 'big room' where events such as dances, concerts, talent shows and film shows etc were held. Along the corridor on the right hand side were the ladies cloakroom/toilets. Next to this was a small room used for making teas, a kind of small kitchen. At the end of the corridor were the fire doors, which led you down some wrought iron curving steps and out onto the High Street by the side of Hayden Burns Garage. There were also double doors into the 'big room' next to the fire doors. This was the main room in the building, it had a wooden floor and a stage at the bottom end.

There were five large sash windows, which you could sit in, with window boxes outside of them, and the fireplaces were on the opposite wall.

Broseley High Street – pub on left Elephant and Castle

Broseley Town Hall 1963

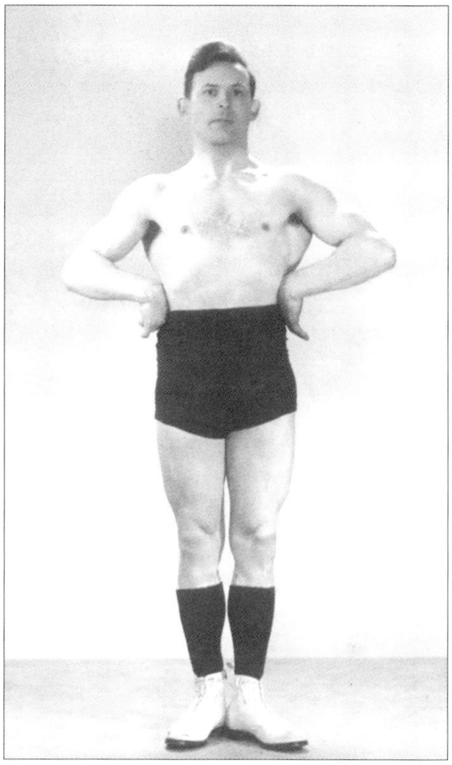

Mr Osborne, Weight Lifter and wrestler, billed on the Boxing poster

The local dances were held there and were very popular with the local people, especially the annual Carnival Dance where the Queen and her attendants were chosen, people waited outside in the street at night to hear who had won the title. There was a travelling Theatre Company, concerts and talent shows held there too, singers, tap dancers, recitations etc. with local people taking part

The Broseley Amateur Dramatic Society performed plays there for many years with the late Mr. Potts a local solicitor, about the 1930's. Travelling shows performed there, shows such as 'Murder in the Red Barn' and 'The Face at the Window'. Mr Osborne the weight lifter and wrestler also appeared there, his name is on a Boxing Bout poster pictured in this book.

There were talent competitions, and some of the locals entertained the public with their recitations, singing and dancing, Vera Colley was one who loved to tap and ballet dance and sing, Lorraine Giles a red haired girl from Coalbrookdale used to sing the song 'Californi-ay, Peg O My Heart was another popular song, Wendy Oakley did tap and ballet dancing, Turley Oakley and Babe Smith sang 'A bike made for two', Norman Miles sang Al Jolsen songs, Jack Harris sang Mario Lanza songs, John Rowbery sang 'Tears run up and down my spine' and John Wase played the piano, just to mention a few remembered for their efforts. Film shows were also held there, I remember watching one called 'The Clutching Hand', it frightened the kids so much one of them fell off his chair.

Old Tyme Dance classes were held there and taken by Mr Sumners who lived in the row of council houses on the Bridgnorth Road or New Road as it was called then, near to Copper Dean our local bobby at that time.

The Catholic Church used it for a time in the 1950's to hold their Church Services. The building was demolished in about 1963.

Broseley High Street early 1900's

There was little traffic about in the early forties and the children used to play in the road. All the children played together, games such as, rounders (with the ball going over the gates of Mr Harrison's, the plumber and decorators at the corner of Padmans Alley on Cape Street, we had to climb up the old gas lamp-post and over the wall to get it back), tracking (with one going off and chalking arrows on the road or walls as they went for the others to follow and track them down, they sometimes used sticks placed in the shape off an arrow). Hide and seek was another popular game. Another pastime was standing on two tin cans, tied with a piece of string which were held in each hand, and trying to walk on them, a bit like stilts.

Top and whip was played on the road, with a wooden top with a stud at the base, this was pressed into the ground or steadied with the hand to stand it up, then the whip which was wound around the stem of the top was swiftly spun off and the top spun round and round. You kept whipping the top to make it spin. We used to make patterns on the tops with coloured chalks which looked really pretty as they spun round. We sometimes used the small black screw tops out of pop bottles.

Ball games were very popular too, I remember playing ball against the back wall of the house of two old ladies who lived opposite us, Miss Teague and Mrs Bagley, tensies, ninesies etc. we must have made their lives very miserable sometimes with the incessant thumping of the balls, usually two or three at a time, a kind of juggling game with the first one to drop the ball out. I don't remember them asking us to stop.

Statues was another game, and playing 'babies cradle' with wool or string threaded around the hand and fingers and lifted off by another person, into another design and repeated until the patterns ran out, not forgetting 'autographs', getting friends to write a little verse or saying into an autograph book and signing it.

Raffia was a popular hobby, winding the strings of raffia around circular pieces of cardboard with a hole in the centre and fastening them together to make mats and bags, the cardboard tops off milk bottles, which had a small hole for the straw to go through, were very good for this work. Pom poms were also made with the same shape of cardboard, but it was doubled, and when the wool had been wound around it quite thickly, the scissors were inserted between the pieces of cardboard and the wool was cut all around, a piece of wool was then tied tightly in between the cardboards pieces, and the cardboards were pulled off. Cork work was done with wool and a wooden cotton reel which had four nails tapped into the top of the cotton reel, the wool was started onto the nails and the wool wound round the nail and the stitch lifted over the top of the nail with a needle, the work was pulled through the centre hole of the cotton reel. Knitting, sewing and crocheting were other pastimes, also useful for clothing the families.

Collecting glossy postcard size photographs of film stars like Clark Gable, Betty Grable and film magazines were a popular hobby at that time, as the cinema was one of our pastimes, the Central at Ironbridge and the Plaza at Coalbrookdale were our nearest. We paid a halfpenny toll over the bridge and bought a batch cake from Miss Robert's shop next to the police station, or a carrot, to eat during the film.

Some families have told me how they tricked the toll keeper, by one child paying and several of the others creeping under the 'window', while he took the halfpenny. He would shout after them 'I saw you, I'll get you on the way back. But he has been known to say 'go on' if there has been a lot of children in the family, he knew that it cost a lot of money to clothe and feed the children, who could not afford many, if any, treats.

The Central Cinema was built and opened in 1912 and was a popular place for entertainment, the first two rows were for the children and the double seats on the back row were very popular with young courting couples, and all the latest films shows were eagerly awaited. Cowboy films-Gene Autrey and Roy Rogers, Tarzan, King Kong, Old Mother Riley, musicals, comedies, cartoons and dramas were all part of the films at that time. The cinema closed about 1960.

The other cinema was the Plaza at Coalbrookdale, this opened 31st August 1931 with the Eddie Cantor film 'Whoopee'. My husband remembers being taken to see it with his mother on the second night's showing. The little shop next door was called the Chocolate Box, and belonged to Mr Russell.

There were problems getting to see films here sometimes because it was closed when the River Severn flooded, the water always came up at the Dale End when there were floods. The Plaza closed about 1968.

Acrobats was another popular game, the girls tucking their dresses up into their knicker legs, the interlock navy knickers with the elastic in the tops and the legs and the little pocket, which were worn for school. Leapfrog, skipping with a rope and hop-scotch were other popular games which were played on the roads. Bowlers was played by bowling a hoop along the road and hitting it with a stick to keep it rolling. Marbles and conkers were played regularly by the boys, marbles were played under the gas lights by men as well as the boys, and many spent hours whittling sticks, and making small toys, catapults etc. Reading books, colouring books and chalk boards to draw on, jigsaws, ludo, snakes and ladders and tiddly winks were games played in winter months, listening to the old records played on the windup gramophone, and to the radio.

The girls had their dolls and if they were lucky, a pram, if not, cardboard shoe boxes were used to put the dolls in, with a piece of string tied at the two front corners to make a handle to pull it along, some used a stuffed sock for a doll if they did not have one. Another game was making 'scent', we would collect rose petals and soak them in water in jars, then drain them off, and keep the lovely smelling liquid in bottles as perfume.

We played in the fields and made necklaces and bracelets of daisy chains, collected buttercups, which were held under the chin, if the flower reflected its golden glow, it was said you liked butter. Cowslips, blue bells, clover and many other wild flowers were picked, and we looked for the 'lucky' four leaf clover, hoping it would bring us good luck, hips from the dog rose, haws from the hawthorn and acorns from the oak tree were collected and used for making necklaces. The blackberry picking, eating the leaves of the hawthorn tree, which we called 'bread and cheese', and the centre of the wild geranium flower we called a 'pancake'. The holly leaf forecast our true love, the thorns saying 'he loves me, he loves me not' as we went round each thorn on the leaf. The roly poly's down the grass banks, the picnics, catching frogspawn and tadpoles in jam jars with string tied round the neck of the jar to make a handle, were just some of the things we were free to pursue in those days.

We liked to 'dress up', we had an old suitcase full of clothes and used to play in the brew-house, we made up all sorts of plays and games, and had quite an imagination between us. We took this case up the Deer Leap, a field next to a coppice not far from where we lived, where all the children around our area met and spent a lot of time playing together. We built 'dens' with a frame made of tree branches, and ferns woven around the branches to camouflage it, we dressed up in the old clothes we took with us and did plays and concerts in the glades, we took sandwiches to eat and really thought it was good fun. Usually ready for bed after a hard days play!

The boys played at being 'Tarzan' and made bows and arrows with sticks and pieces of string, they climbed trees and made tree camps, and dens with branches and ferns for camouflage, played cowboys and Indians, tracking and shooting at each other in the ferny undergrowth.

Children at Cape Fold, all dressed up 1946

They made trolleys out of old pram wheels and pieces of wood, which they rode on the roads, and trucks and barrows, they also loved playing with catapults, which often got them into trouble with windows being broken, or someone being hit. Of course football, cricket and rounders were regular games played by the boys.

We made kites out of brown paper and flour paste, fastened onto hazel sticks tied together like a cross, a long tail was made out of string and small pieces of paper were tied all the way down the string, marbles was another popular boys game and in the autumn they played conkers. We made parachutes out of hankies or a square piece of cloth, string tied to each of the four corners with a stone for a weight tied at the bottom end, which was then thrown into the air to float down.

In winter one of our favourite past-times was tobogganing down the sloping fields covered with snow, the Deersleap and Folly were favourites, snow balling each other, and building snowmen, we used to make icy slides on the roads to slide on, but these were spoilt when the adults put ashes on to them. There was very little traffic on the roads at this time. We went home with our clothes very wet, these would be put to dry on the fireguard and the clothes horse around the fire, once we had got warm and dry, we had a hot drink, oxo's or milk, or tea. We could be away for hours but there was no danger then from strange people taking you off.

The railway station at Ironbridge, Ironbridge/Broseley, opened in 1862, was a favourite form of transport, up the line to Buildwas/Shrewsbury and down to Coalport/Bridgnorth used a lot by the local people and the kids loved the ride. It was closed about 1963 when my children were small and was a sad loss.

One place we were banned from was swimming in the River Severn. We used to build ourselves houses, laying old bricks down in the shape of a house foundation, front room, kitchen etc. then we collected old saucepans, cups and anything we could scrounge to make it like a proper house.

Another pastime was playing with silver paper we got from various places, one place was the old blacksmiths building on the Ironbridge Road, near the bottom of Balls Lane, or the Slip as it was called by the locals, we made silver clothes and Christmas decorations for hanging around the house at Christmas.

We spent many happy hours playing these games costing virtually nothing. In those days there was no television, but we did have a wireless which was on a high shelf in the corner of the small living room, we used to listen to 'Dick Barton - Special Agent' on this, and stood on a chair to get as near as possible to hear every word. Radio Luxemburg was popular then too, so was Donald Peers, his signature tune was 'By a Babbling Brook'. We had to make sure the accumulator was 'charged' as the wireless would not work without it, and the battery. We took our accumulators to Haydn Burns or Will Oakley's garage, both in the High Street, it cost sixpence to recharge the battery.

Ballet and tap dancing classes were held in the 'Buffs Room' at the Kings Head Pub, and there was boxing in a building down Church Street, on the left hand side just past Raddle Hall, it was once the stables to Whitehall, but has been renovated and is now lived in as a house.

The Ironbridge/Broseley Railway Station and Signal Box

Playing in the snow 1947

Broseley Boxing team.
Back.Row: ? Roberts, Butcher Dodd, Fred Jones, Sid Fletcher, Geo. Pritchard, Sid Watkins.
Front Row: Bill Oakley, Les Colley, George Burgess, Harry Gough, Lol Oakley

Fairs and circuses have come to Broseley for many years, with records going as far back as 1811, and maybe before that. Fair days were the last Tuesdays in April and October, and schools gave a half-holiday for the occasion, they were very popular and the children have looked forward to them over many years.

When I was a child in the 1940's the annual Fun Fair visit was an event we all loved to go to, especially after the long hard winters we had then. It was Spring and the days were getting longer and the evenings lighter. The Fair was held on Instones field in Dark Lane when I went to it, but Gerald Instone told me it used to be held in a field up the Bridgnorth Road before that. It usually managed to rain on Fair Day Tuesday, leaving the field very wet and muddy under feet, but this did not people off going.

The owners of the Fun Fair in my time were 'Davies', they had a very attractive, dark haired daughter called Norma, who was admired by the young men of the town. There was quite a lot at the Fair then, a roundabout for the little ones, Speedway and Waltzer for the older ones, Jellywobble, and large and small swing boats.

There were Hoopla stalls, roll a penny, darts and rifle stalls, coconut shy's, candy floss and all the bright lights and loud music to attract the customers. When we were teenagers we were allowed to go on our own, that was where the boys and girls met up, but we had to go with our parents when we were small. It was hard for our parents to spare any money to spend at the Fair, but we usually had enough to go with, aunties and uncles sometimes gave us some pennies too.

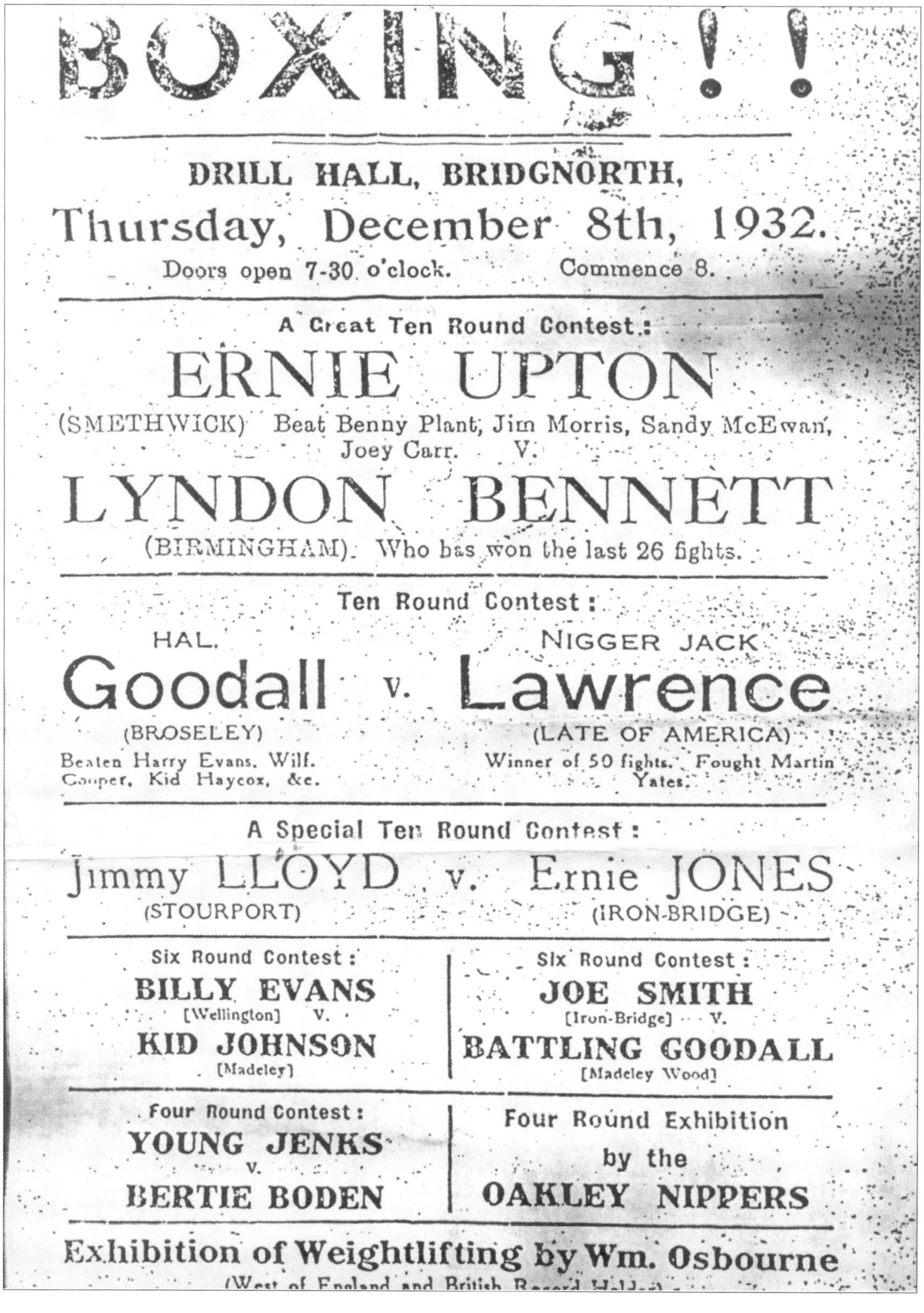

BOXING!!

DRILL HALL, BRIDGNORTH,
Thursday, December 8th, 1932.
Doors open 7-30 o'clock. Commence 8.

A Great Ten Round Contest:
ERNIE UPTON
(SMETHWICK) Beat Benny Plant, Jim Morris, Sandy McEwan, Joey Carr.
V.
LYNDON BENNETT
(BIRMINGHAM). Who has won the last 26 fights.

Ten Round Contest:
HAL. Goodall (BROSELEY) Beaten Harry Evans, Wilf. Cooper, Kid Haycox, &c.
v.
NIGGER JACK Lawrence (LATE OF AMERICA) Winner of 50 fights. Fought Martin Yates.

A Special Ten Round Contest:
Jimmy LLOYD (STOURPORT) v. Ernie JONES (IRON-BRIDGE)

Six Round Contest:
BILLY EVANS [Wellington] v. KID JOHNSON [Madeley]

Six Round Contest:
JOE SMITH [Iron-Bridge] v. BATTLING GOODALL [Madeley Wood]

Four Round Contest:
YOUNG JENKS v. BERTIE BODEN

Four Round Exhibition by the OAKLEY NIPPERS

Exhibition of Weightlifting by Wm. Osbourne
(West of England and British

A Boxing program, with some Broseley competitors - 1932

A carnival picture of my mother about 1920

A Carnival procession in High Street, Tosh Edwards with his pram. Far left Derek Watson, then Dilys Day, Bernice Fielding – far right man Wilf Elcock, Henry Perks and Neil Beddow – about 1950

The carnivals were another event which took place each year, people looked forward to dressing up and parading round the town, some walked and some were on bikes and horse back, and some on the backs of lorry's which were all decorated to represent some theme, nursery rhyme and comedy. A lot of work and time went into making the costumes and decorating the lorries, Many hours were spent collecting ferns, and making paper flowers to decorate the vehicles, as well as painting and sewing material for the backgrounds, a lot of these were organized by housing estates or groups like the British Legion, and pubs. Football teams, the cricket club, and other organizations had 'beauty queen' lorries. There have been as many as twenty 'floats' as they were called, in the parades when they were very popular. The streets were filled with families and people of all ages, kids with ice creams and the pubs were full to bursting with folk out to have a good day, many had a drop too much to drink, and a sore head the next day, but it was enjoyed by all.

The Carnival was led by a brass band, to let the people know the procession was on its way, and to give the event some atmosphere, people loved to hear the sound of the brass bands. In later years processions had a lot of girl dancing troupes some came from away, they came in bus loads and made the carnival very colourful with their pretty costumes, again a lot of effort was put into these troupes making the costumes and head dresses for such a lot of children and young people.

Carnival photo about 1930/40

The children loved performing in these parades. In the evening a procession of people carrying lighted torches walked around the town and lots turned out to watch, others went to the Carnival Dance which was held at the Town Hall and a good day out was had by all. They seem to have started about the time the war ended, I believe there were carnivals before the 2nd World War, and resumed again afterwards, but they faded out during the 1980's, efforts were made to try to start them up again in the 1990's but no one wanted to know. People had cars and were able to travel to the seaside and other interesting places by this time, so there has not been a carnival here in Broseley for some years now.

One of the dancing troupes in a Broseley carnival 1970's

Broseley Ladies British Legion about 1950

A Carnival Queen lorry early 1970's. Queen Mary Oakley, attendants Jane Nutt, Ann Harrison, Margaret Hood, Lynn Oakley, Ann Griffiths, Sarah Whitehouse

All blacked up – a Broseley carnival group about 1930's.
Man 1st left is Jack Cross and Perce Watson is also said to be on this photo.

A carnival lorry 1990's with Sylvia Ball enjoying a drink

Another carnival picture 1990's with Gloria Hislop

A group outside the Albion pub about the 1940's

My dad and brother, part of a musical group in one of the carnivals about 1950

Miss Broseley Rangers Carnival Queen about 1990

Another Carnival Queen lorry – Miss Valentine

One of the special days we looked forward to were the Baptist and Wesleyan Chapel Anniversaries, all the girls were dressed in their best pretty white dresses and wore white socks and sandals, with ribbons in their hair. At the anniversaries at Benthall Church the girls wore a white triangle cloth tied around the back of their heads, and a sweet pea buttonholes. The boys wore short trousers and their best shirts and jackets.

The dress that I remember best was made by my mother's cousin, it was white satin with very pretty smocking across the bodice and I felt really special when I wore it, but I did not go on the Anniversary as I was Roman Catholic, we were not really supposed to go to the other churches, but I went with my friends.

There were two schools in Broseley when I started in 1940, one was in Broseley where the Health Centre is now, and the other one was the Infant School on Legges Hill in Broseley Wood.

The school in Broseley consisted of infants, boys and girls, the classes were not mixed, boys were in the left hand part of the building and girls in the middle, the infants were mixed classes on the right hand side of the main door as you went in, the teachers at this time were Miss Smitheman, Miss Smallwood and Mrs Garbett who was in charge of the infant classes. I remember the first two as nice gentle natured teachers, but Mrs Garbett had quite a reputation for being very strict and having a terrible temper, it was said if she started to go red from the neck up you could look out for the ruler to appear - it was used too, so most of the children behaved, she was known to put children in a cupboard if they misbehaved. She was remembered for warming her legs in front of the school stove, holding her dress up at the back and showing her long knickers, she kept her hankie up her knicker leg.

When a child started school they were allowed a ride on the school rocking horse if they were good, and another treat was being chosen to ring the school bell.

All the children had school milk, it was delivered to the schools in crates and the bottles, which were not very big, were sealed with a cardboard top with a circle punched in the centre that could be pushed out to put a straw in.

The girl's classes were across from the infants. The first class for me there was when I was aged 7, and it was taken by Mrs Wase, before that I went to Legges Hill School in Broseley Wood. She used to read stories to the children and the one I particularly remember was 'Larry the Lamb', she used to draw out 'lamb' in a trembly voice that fascinated me. This was on a Friday afternoon after she had done all her work on the registers etc and she had got the children to tidy and polish their desks, this was done quietly while she worked, she then read the Toy Town Tales of Larry the Lamb to the class. She also taught us double writing and I still do most of my letters as I was taught to many years ago, we used paper with a special line on it and the letters had to be done with the base of the letter in the small line and the tops of the tall letters going to the top line, we had to use pen and ink from the inkwells in the desks which could be quite messy. We had to wash the inkwells and leave it all clean.

Bead threading, fraying material and knitting khaki scarves for the soldiers were some of the things we did in school.

Another teacher I remember was Miss Almond, she was younger than the other teachers and she took Geography, she used a map up on the classroom wall that had small light bulbs that lit up all the different countries in the world. The Headmistress was Mrs Brookes but I didn't go into her class as I went to the High School at Coalbrookdale when I was 11 years old.

During the war years we went to the Rectory for our school dinners, we were taken there by the teachers in a crocodile file from the school down Church Street, and went in through the French windows into the room facing the lawns, where we had our dinners.

Garden fetes were held at the Rectory in the summer and we also did Maypole dancing there on the rectory lawns. It was fascinating to watch the girls dancing around the maypole and the pretty patterns made by the ribbons as they twisted and folded around the pole to the music played on a gramophone.

We had lovely summers then and sat out in the playground at the back of the school on oval shaped raffia mats in the sunshine. We used pumps for our games lessons, these were kept in a large wall cupboard by the back door in the cloakroom, and everyone had to sort out their own shoe size for games.

Maypole dancing Guides and Brownies 1946

Broseley Rangers "Cannibal" carnival float – both pictures

Some of the schoolyard games we played were 'The big ship sails in the Alley Alley Oh', 'Farmer, farmer may we cross your coloured waters', and the 'Farmers in his Den' to name a few. The school toilets were in the playground, they were very small ones, quite low down but just right for the children. There were school allotments for the boys situated next to the boy's playground.

Broseley Wood School opened on Monday 8th February 1892, 25 children were transferred from Broseley School to Broseley Wood. It has been said that it was a workhouse or institution before becoming a school.

There were two teachers when I was there in 1940, Miss Pardoe and Mrs Roberts, the playground attached to the school was very tiny, more like a passageway really, and the toilets were around the back, (we were told the boys competed to see who could aim the highest over the wall), the children were taken over the road at the top of Legges Hill to another bigger playground. It closed as a school about 1966, but is now used as a base for the local Territorial Army Cadets, and there is a bungalow in the big playground over the road.

I enjoyed my school days there, the two rooms were heated by coke stoves stood in the middle of each room, with a large pipe going up through the roof for the chimneys, they were very smokey. The chairs and tables were very small and there were large black boards/easels used by the teachers for lessons.

Some of the children came to this school from the small school held for Benthall children at the Floyer Hall, opened 28 October 1872, situated above the Clay Meadow by Hill Top Farm.

An early 1900's photo of school children dressed up for some occasion

Rummage sales were held at Legges Hill School through the years, the money was used to buy things for the children there. There were pleasant memories there for some children and some not so pleasant for others, as is still the case these days. After the Infants, all children over the age of seven went to the 'big' school in Broseley until the age of eleven, they then went to the Madeley Modern School in 1949, or Coalbrookdale High School, or the Walker Technical College at Wellington.

We went home for dinner, from Legges Hill School, as we lived at Cape Street that was not far away, and I remember going back to school after dinner in a horse driven milk float with Perce Roberts, the farmer from Coneybury Farm who delivered our milk, we really enjoyed that. The milk was kept in large metal churns with a metal measurer which hung over the side, and was also delivered by men, or women, who had 'yolks', wooden shoulder bars, which had chains hanging down each side and a bucket fastened to it. A tale was told to me of someone (who liked his drink of ale) who had several cows and delivered his milk in this way, when he noticed the milk inspector coming after him he fell down to lose the milk, so it couldn't be checked.

Another tale of the milk inspector, was when he was known to be waiting in hiding for one of the milkmen to go on his rounds, so the milkman got a mate to go on the usual route with his yolk on his shoulders, but only water in the buckets, the milkman did his round in peace when the inspector followed the man with the water. They were very crafty in those days.

Opening of Sports Area (running tracks etc) on Birchmeadow 1952

We could get milk from Miss Matthews shop on the corner of Barratts Hill and Harris's Green, she had these milk churns, with metal ladles that hung by over the edge of the churn. She had her milk off her cows she kept by the Baptist Chapel, her brother, Walter Matthews had a farm at Dark Lane.

Towlers shop was on the opposite side on this junction by Harris's Green/ High Street, this was a bakehouse and shop, where they sold bread, cakes and groceries, and many other things. The Cape of Good Hope pub was opposite Towlers and just a bit higher up from the pub in the High Street was another well-known character Georgie Potter Harrison, the barber and canary breeder. He was known to start shaving a customer, lathering his face well, and then getting involved with an argument over his birds, he would leave the unfortunate man lathered up and proceed to prove his point and not finish the shave.

On the junction of Barratts Hill/Cape Street was Cis Harrisons Paint/Plumbing Shop on the left hand side, later a Motor Spares shop and the last business there was a Television Shop. Then there was 'Navvy' Evans the chimney sweep who lived in the cottage on the right hand side, near Cape Fold, he did the gardening for Mr Downes who lived round the corner on the High Street, his wife had a red birth mark on her face and my sister, when she was small, called her the lady with the jam on her face. Further along Cape Street, were two cottages, Braziers and Molyneuxs lived in these, and there was another cottage next door. The last large house on the right was called the Burnt House, this was a gramophone shop that belonged to Mrs Parry, I remember her as a very small lady, and buying gramophone needles from her. The Burnt house was said to have been a workhouse and a public house over the years, and was burnt down at some time hence the name, there were so many of these pubs in Broseley years ago.

A Sunday School party 1897

Across Queen Street, down King Street the first house on the right was lived in by the Hartshorne family, next door to Mr Snow's shop, this small shop sold many things needed for every day use, and the house next door used to be the Blue Bell pub. Then several more cottages before coming to two large houses next door to Southorns Pipe Works. The left hand side of King Street, the cottage jutting out into the road belonged to Annie Lloyd, a little way down was the Capacity Engineering Works, this had a wonderful view of the Clay Meadow and across Benthall. After the engineering company, there was a path leading down to a row of cottages lived in by Becky Mason, the Wilde, Wallbank, and Aston families and three other small cottages. The next cottage on the road was Woods, then another house, (again another pub) called the 'Prince of Wales'. There were two more small cottages next, set down some steps into a dip (there was a well in the yard) and then there was Kenyon's bake house, these were later demolished. Mrs Kenyon had very white hair, fastened, as was the fashion, into a bun at the back of her head, and wore a long pale blue/white striped dress and white apron, this was a long building with a brick fold in front of it, it later belonged to Farlows. Further down the road was Thomas's Paint shop, they sold wallpaper and paint, this too was a pub years ago called the 'Unicorn, this was opposite Southorns Pipe Works, which was a few cottages up from the 'Duke of Cumberland' pub, later demolished.

These shops are in Broseley Wood, still King Street, where two more shops next to the paint shop, James Davies - later Rowbreys, and Harvatts then Hancock's who again sold groceries and Matt Davis's butchers shop, later owned by Stan Harris and then Joan and Dennis Powell, closed some years ago. It was then a greengrocery run by John Hurdley. The walls of this butchers shop were covered from top to bottom with very old decorative tiles, which are still there now.

James Davies Shop, King Street, Broseley Wood now a Guest House

At the top of Legges Hill, the small house on the corner, still there, was once the 'Globe', at the bottom of Legges Hill which was the smallest pub, the 'Nelson. Just before the 'Kings Head' pub was Bowens - another grocery shop and the other side the pub was the Fish and Chip Shop on Quarry Road, this was once the 'Seven Stars' pub. And unbelievably just down Quarry Road was the 'Bell' pub. There were two more pubs down Quarry Road, the old Post Office was the Rose and Crown and the Potters Arms was nearby. Back up to Woodlands Road among the small cottages stood the 'Napoleon' and further down the road was the 'Maypole'. There was a candle factory by the Maypole Green in the early 1920's.

Back up the road on the left hand side, after the Legges Hill schoolyard, was a small garage belonging to James Davies, (he owned the shop opposite) this later became the 'Button Factory and is where BBR Engineering and other small units are now sited. There were still lots of little shops in Broseley in the 1940's, the town being very self-sufficient.

Down the High Street on the right hand side, going down from Barratts Hill cross roads, were several houses and cottages, the last one before the Bank was Dr Whitney's surgery. After the Bank, was the Bank House, which all belonged to the Pritchard family, solicitors at one time, then Owen Jones Shop, now the Star's newsagents, it was a newsagents then, and sold stationery, pipes, magazines etc, he sold chocolates, sweets and ice-cream too but they were in a separate room just as you walked through the door. Thorn Pudsey the solicitors were next door, this was later Pearl's Hairdressers.

The High Street garage belonged to Oakleys, it was adjoining the solicitors and was once the stables to this large building, this was later Robert's and is now Dave Bladen's garage. Next door was Oakleys scrap yard, which also used to be a small grocery shop, it belonged to my grand-parents. The house is a private residence and the yard is now Broseley Tyres.

Down the road across Swan Street, stood the Co-op Stores, later Broseley Fashionware and now a Mobility Shop.

Next to that was Potts, solicitors. This was E C S White (Major White, made suits for the gentry) - tailors till the early 1940's and later on the premises of Mr Hartshorne, then Mr Edge, they were Registrars for births and deaths. It became a grocery/outfitters, but has been W H Taylor & Sons a Ladies and Gents Outfitters for many years now, with nice fashionable clothes, and a friendly service.

Sand's shoe shop was another one I remember well, Mr Sands sold and cobbled shoes, there was a lovely smell in this shop from the leather and polish, we were sat down on a chair in this small dark room, while some shoes were sorted out from the high shelves with rows of shoe boxes for us try on by Mrs Sands, her husband would be mending shoes in another room by the entrance door.

Next door was Listers, a large private house, now flats, the Vaults pub was set back behind the Town Hall, the large building used for all functions at that time which was next to Burn's Garage, this was lastly a shop called 'Allsorts & Collectables', now closed.

Across Carvers Road was Bert Jones butchers shop, now the site for the flats, then the Victoria Hall, and of course, as it is today, the Memorial Green and Monument, and the Pritchard Memorial, well there is only the plinth of that left now. The Vaults, Town Hall and Jones Butchers shop were later demolished, the Town Hall about 1963.

Broseley High Street

A Broseley Race outside the old Cumberland about 1940's

Back up the street, at the junction of Fox Lane/High Street opposite the newsagents, on the left hand side going down was Mrs Powells sweet shop, a little old lady with grey hair used to sit in her chair behind the counter and serve lemon and strawberry kayli or sherbert, and sweets out of a large selection of jars into cone shaped, hand made, paper sweet bags, all these small shops seemed to quite dark inside. This was later to become the Laundrette.

Next door was the Crown pub where many a rowdy evening was passed, singsongs were a regular occurrence, and many a scuffle took place there when some of the local characters had drunk a drop too much ale.

Further down was Potham's the butchers, Mrs Potham, a thin, pleasant lady with the hair style popular at that time of plaited hair coiled in a circular pattern at the side of the ears, held in place by hairpins. She sat in a small glass fronted cubicle, when we paid for our meat we sat on a small stool in front of her.

Benthall Potteries Xmas party 1950's

My Grandmothers Shop,38 High Street.
Betty, Norah, Bill and Lol Oakley where they lived in about 1932

Then there was the Lion pub, still trading today as a hotel, recently very nicely renovated. Next to this, facing down the High Street was the 'Bon Marche' kept by the Roberts family, Mr and Mrs Roberts and their son and daughter Fred and Frieda. It was an interesting haberdashery shop, one of the things remembered was when paying for goods, in the room at the back of the shop, the money was put into a box which was carried along a suspended wire to the till in the room at the front of the shop. The family lived in the house next door. This shop later became Downes Grocery/veg shop, a family run business with a friendly and obliging service, and Bryan & Knott and the Chinese Take Away, which has proved to be very popular, are in the house the family lived in, next door.

Across the road here on the left hand side, at the start of Barber Street was the butchers shop, still a butchers today, a nice family butchers shop catering for all our needs, it is in fact the only butchers shop in the town, except for the meat department in the SPAR market. Down the back was Barbers Row and the public toilets. Carrying on down the High Street was Ezra Milwards popular fish/chip shop. (He served the fish and chips with his cigarette in his mouth, no one bothered in those days.)

Next door was the Elephant & Castle pub, then another shop I cannot remember but I know it was Sweetland's barber shop in the 1960's, and then there was Davis's bread shop, we fetched lovely batch cakes dusty with flour from there and used to go down with a basin to get their creamy yellow ice-cream, still a tasty bakery today called 'Catherines', Catherine Gough was one of Mr. Wedge's daughters (the bakery in Church Street)

The Albion pub was next and the 'wet' fish shop and then the closed up Instones butchers shop kept by three old ladies the last I remember, now a busy wine bar. There was a path down to some cottages behind these buildings on the High Street, (called 'the backs' years ago) between these shops, the next shop was kept by Miss Horton, a small slim lady with grey hair, again, it was plaited and coiled at the back of her head, as was the style in those days. She sold grain and corn, tea, butter etc, and had a small library on the right hand wall as you went through the door, this was another shop which was dark inside. The next shop was Loach's, it sold groceries and vegetables and was later taken over by Roberts, the Bon Marche family.

Across Dark Lane, the chemists shop was still there, then a private house and James Hurdley's shop next which was then Tippen Davies's, it was a real Aladdin's cave in those days, but very dark inside, it's a wonderful Aladdin's cave today, well run by a very obliging local family, and next door was Dixon's Post Office, a very small shop, now a lovely shop of trinkets, paintings, picture frames etc run by Marise. The Post lady then was Norah Jones, and the postman was Mr Powell, they delivered the letters on their bikes.

There were two cottages set back in a dip next and the building before them became the local Fish/Chip Shop, now the only one in the town. How nice they smell when you walk past! The cottages were later on burnt down.

The Miss Taylors had their haberdashery shop in the Square, they sold ladies underwear and sanitary wear, which was served to the customer in a very secretive manner, children were not allowed to see these purchases in those days, it was also told that a close eye was kept on the ladies of the town purchasing sanitary wear, if they missed they were soon marked down for baby clothes next! They sold children's bonnets, baby clothes, wool, embroidery silks, socks etc.

The Garage, High Street. was Oakleys, then Roberts and now Bladens

Aston's cafe was next door, Mr Aston was also a cobbler, the youngsters used to hang out there when we were young, to listen to the juke box. This is now a Stonemasons, which makes fitting gravestones for lost loved ones. Cruxtons sweet shop was next door, now a very good and popular café. A bit further down, in Church Street was Hurdleys greengrocery shop, there were cottages set back on the left from the street here, by the Clenchacre path that led to the Fairfield, these were later demolished and Pritchard House flats were built there. The greengrocery shop became an 'Off Licence' but is now just a house.

Next down Church Street were Instones butchers, sadly closed but now a small general store selling a wide variety of goods, and Molyneaux's sweet and ice-cream shop, where we were sent on a Sunday afternoon for Moms sweets, also closed. Much further down Church Street, opposite Wedges house was a small grocery shop, once belonging to Instones, kept by Arthur Crewe. All closed now.

Next to the Pheasant pub was Wedges bakery, another well known friendly family run shop, with a lovely smell of fresh baking, both these are still here today and just below was another small grocery shop which last belonged to Mr Fellowes, these were once the premises of the old Crown pub. There was a small second hand/antique shop just below this at one time too.

The Miss Taylors Shop/Astons Shoe Repairs /Cruxtons Sweet Shop about 1950's

There was a shop on the corner of the Square/Hockley Road, used over the years for several different businesses, and just past the Duke of York pub (still there) was Gough's small shop, where they sold lots of different things - including sweets.

Pickens had a small shop in Barber Street, which sold groceries, (this later became a house) opposite the Catholic Church and they then moved to the shop between the church and the butchers, this shop belonged to Thompsons who sold mens wear, and overalls etc. in the 1930's. It has since been a hairdressers and barber shop, it is now the Broseley/Much Wenlock Credit Union, where ordinary people can save, small and large amounts, and also borrow money at a very low interest rate.

Norman Jones bike shop was along Duke Street, he was always very popular with the children, and their grateful parents, for repairing the kid's bikes and the general maintenance work he did on all sorts of things, including electrical repairs. Turning off left into Birchmeadow Road, was Elcock's grocery shop, now Carols Hairdressers just before the Birchmeadow Chapel (later the Bladen Club) that was nearby. Back in Duke Street, and leading along to the Wesleyan Chapel and the 'Lord Hill' pub, on the junction of Cockshutt Lane.

Another interesting thing about Broseley is the dialect spoken by the true Broseley inhabitants, dying out over the years as new people come to live here and the old ones passing on. Some of the sayings are very similar to the old Quaker language that was spoken here many years ago. I canna, I dunna, I shanna, I wunna, meaning I cannot, I do not, I shall not, I will not, to just mention a few. A typical example of the way it is spoken is "Bist gooin down the bonk" (are you going down the bank). How bist my wench - how are you my girl.

Carnival Queen lorry about 1952

Queen Joyce Gough, Sheila Marston, Evelyn Hall, Pat Humphreyson, Pat Smith, Audrey Humphreys, Kathleen Beddow.

Crusaders Japanese Float

Carnival float about 1935

Crusaders 1950

Carnival lorry – Wedding of Lilli Marlene

Doreen Finch, Joan Thomas, Joan Beddow, Sybil Pountney, Iris Wilde, Jean Thomas, Alan Thomas, man at the back Percy Beddow

Fancy Dress at Victoria Hall about 1980

CARNIVAL PICTURES ABOUT 1984

Royal Naval Assoc. Broseley branch float

Broseley Lions FC – Raft Race Float

Judy Williams with her horse

Tony Tacchi – Roman Soldier

Another 'Queen' float

Opening of Shirlett Sanatorium by Princess Alexandra of Teck Aug 2nd 1911

Nativity Play – Xmas at Legges Hill School Broseley Wood in 1966

A Broseley Parade – Girl Guides

A Broseley Parade – Nurses

A very old Carnival

MY ANCESTORS

My ancestors have lived in Broseley for many years, on both sides of my parent's families. I didn't know how long ago this was until I started tracing our family history. For several years now I have been going to the Family History Society and the Records Office at Shrewsbury, and have spent many interesting hours looking through the material available there. There is a lot of work involved doing this, but I have found my families so far, going back into the early 1700's.

I have many family photographs on both sides, some going back to the 1800's, and have been fortunate to have people who have named these for me.

I will start with my father's great grandmother, Frances Aston. I have a copy of a drawing of Frances, done in her cottage by her grandson Walter Owen, a local artist, and kindly provided by her great grandson Jack Owen. Frances was born Frances Hill and she married James Aston in 1851. They had eight children.

Frances Hill was the daughter of John Hill and Mary, born in 1831. John Hill was the son of Hiram Hill and Mary, born in 1802, and Hiram Hill was the son of Stephen Hill and Elizabeth, born in 1770. All at Benthall.

Her father John was also the nephew of Stephen Hill born in 1763, and who at one time worked the old Benthall iron foundry and blast furnace at Bridge Bank, they also carried on business as colliery proprietors at Broseley. These premises were later taken over by Maws Tile Works. John's father, Hiram Hill (brother to the above Stephen and grandfather to Frances) occupied a prominent position as mine surveyor under the Coalbrookdale Company at Lightmoor, when the collieries were in full working order.

A Stephen Hill was also a family grocer, tea and coffee dealer on the High Street in 1893, shown on an invoice to Broseley Rejoicing Committee for the celebration of a Royal Wedding.

No one seems to remember any of these family connections, but the first lead I got was when I was told that Frances and James Aston's grave was in Benthall Churchyard. We found the gravestone, in good condition and with all the names and dates readable, so this was a good lead. But on looking around the Churchyard as a matter of interest, we discovered leaning against the wall between the boundary of the Churchyard and Benthall Hall, the headstones of Frances' grandfather Hiram Hill and his brother Stephen, who both had iron head stones, which were made at Benthall ironworks, to mark their graves. Hiram's headstone was quite ornate, and the other one was plain. We also found a marble headstone for Enoch Hill, and one for Stephen Hill jnr who were brothers to Frances' father John.

Frances and James had twin girls who were born in 1862. Liza Ann was my great grandmother and she married Thomas Corfield in 1884, I have a photograph of them together when they were young and one of the Aston twins when they were about 60years old. The other twin Elizabeth married Charles Henry Owen, both of these families still lived in the Benthall area. Elizabeth's son Walter was a local artist, who had an exhibition of his work at Shrewsbury Art Gallery after his death in 1958. Frances's granddaughter Ellen married Harry Southorn, the Broseley tobacco pipe maker, in the early 1900's, her father was James Aston.

There are many photographs of the Corfield family, my grandmother and great grandmother are pictured on the photographs around of getting coal at the Foxholes at Benthall, and on the photograph of the Wake held at the small field on Bridge Road, opposite the New Inn pub, or the Pitchyard as it was called in those days, with her two sisters. There is also an album of photographs put together by Beatrice Corfield in 1921, with a nice collection of old silk cards, glossy birthday cards and one card featuring the lovers at Benthall Edge, and another post card from 'Broseley', pictured in this book.

There is a lot of interest today in tracing family ancestors (this takes my family back seven generations for me, and nine generations for my grandchildren, all Broseley born), and wanting to know how the people lived years ago, a vast difference to the way of life to day.

Some of the family photographs we are lucky enough to have, and the names are as follows:

Frances Aston nee Hill b:1831 (both at 51/52 The Mines) James Aston b:1831

Frances Aston and her husband James, had eight children, these included twin girls, Liza Ann and Elizabeth, born in 1862. There is not a photo of their daughter Isabella.

Thomas and Liza Corfield nee Aston 2 of their children opposite

Arthur Corfield/Margaret Aston Alice Corfield /William Beddow

Liza Ann was my great grandmother, she married Thomas Corfield in 1884, they had seven children. Their daughter Alice Corfield, born in 1887 married William Beddow and they had two sons, the youngest being my father. Arthur Corfield was her brother.

Photo's of Ellen and Beatrice Corfield

Ellen Corfield

Beatrice Corfield

Ellen and Beatrice's brothers Thomas and Fred Corfield.

Thomas Corfield on the right

Fred and Annie Corfield

This photo is of the Aston twins in their later years, and the one on the right is of Liza Ann's grandsons, Arthur and Percy Beddow.

Lisa Ann/Elizabeth Aston - Twins (Corfield) (Owen)

Arthur and Percy Beddow

Two postcards from a collection belonging to Beatrice Corfield dated about 1921

Photo of Beatrice and Ellen Corfield, and Arthur and Percy Beddow

Photo of Alice, Will and Joan Beddow

Group getting coal for their fires from the Foxholes at Benthall
My great grandmother is on the middle row, 1st right, behind the lady with the two buckets.

Another group photo of people getting coal from the Foxholes, Benthall, with my grandmother and her two sisters

The above pictures are of local people getting coal for their fires from the Foxholes at Benthall. The top picture shows my great grandmother standing behind the lady with the two buckets on the right hand side. The bottom picture is of another group also getting coal at the Foxholes, on the back row, second one in with the big hat is my grandmother and her two sisters. The girl in white in front of her is Beatrice, and the girl next to her with the black hat and long hair is Ellen Corfield. The people in Benthall, and Broseley, gathered the coal from the Foxholes, in the Workhouse coppice and carried it home for their fires.

They carried their water in from the Spout in Spout Lane. The Spout has provided water for the Benthall area for many years, it is said it has never dried up. In 1963, the underground water pipes to the houses were frozen and we had to carry water in from the Spout for ten weeks.

When Alice Corfield married William Beddow, this gave me another family name to research, and this family name too goes back into the 1700's. There is a photo of a musical group which shows my grandfather, aged about seventeen playing a pipe or flute on the back row, and on the front row the old man with the beard and the army jacket playing the banjo was his father, born in 1853. The banjo has played a big part in the lives of the men in our family over the years, my father played in the pubs entertaining, and enjoying it, for many years, but even today there is still a skill there, my nephew Ian Beddow won the All Britain tenor banjo in 2002, the silver medal two years previous, and the All Britain mandolin in the year 2001.

Various instruments are played throughout the family today, the piano accordion, mouth organ and piano were once played, and the flutes and pipes, violin, guitar, clarinet and drums are still being played, the sounds have changed very much over the years but the music goes on. Still bringing pleasure to many people.

School photograph of Beatrice Corfield with her fellow pupils about 1910

A musical group about 1905, with my grandfather and great grandfather Beddow, playing a banjo and flute.

Frederick and Jane Oakley

We have also done the family tree for the Oakley's on my mother's side of the family. My ancestors seem to have come to Broseley in about 1810, they were originally a Much Wenlock family going back to about 1730.
My great grandfather Frederick Oakley was born in 1857, fifth of the nine children of William Oakley (teacher and haulier of Leighton) born in 1823, and Harriet Turley (milliner of Lentwardine). Fred married a Jane Challenger of Madeley Wood in 1880 and they had 9 children, 6 sons and 3 daughters.

Frederick Oakley ran several businesses in Broseley, according to advertisements in two programmes I have in my possession these are as follows:

He was a coal, timber and corn merchant, garage proprietor and also had several stables and yards here. The adverts were for Motor charabancs, high class cars for hire, haulage by steam, motor and horse. Funeral and wedding coaches for hire. Threshing tackle for hire and bulk storage. In 1926 the garage in High Street advertised garage with inspection pits with electric lights, accumulators charged, tyres, petrol, oil and petroleum. Everything for Wireless in stock. Agents for Marconiphones. Telephone Ironbridge 23. Still in 1926 Edwin Oakley, my grandfather, at Carvers Road was Agent for Kemberton coals, haulage contractor, Furniture removals, Hearses and coaches, Charabancs for large or small parties. Also best prices given for rabbit skins. Telephone Ironbridge 59. There is an invoice for coal and bundles of stick to Mr F Dromgole from Carvers Road in 1931.

These adverts were in a Broseley United Friendly Society 'Sports' programme dated Saturday 18th August 1923, several Oakley children ran in these races, including my mother, as the entrants are named in each of the races. Another programme is for a Broseley Race Meeting on 17th September 1938, six horse races:

The Ladywood Stakes,	Benthall Stakes,	Kearnewood Stakes,
Wedgewood Stakes,	Caughley Stakes,	Knowle Stakes

There is no mention of where the event took place.
My mother talked of some of the properties the family owned in her time, corner house Fox Lane (part of the laundrette building that is today), garage High Street, 38 High Street and yard, Yard, house and stables Swan Street, 3 houses Swan Street, Stables Carvers Road, 7-8 Carvers Road, Villa and stables for eight horses Carvers Road, April cottage High Street, No.1 Duke Street, and coal and timber yards.

Granny Keay, my great, great grandmother had a shop in Carvers Road, there is a tale told of children being so hungry they ate the candles they were sent to get for lighting the houses, times were really hard in those days, and many families were very poor. Fred Oakley supplied the army with horses in the 1st World War, he also had a contract to damp down the dirty, dusty High Street before it was surfaced. I remember as a small child being taken to the fields down Dark Lane with my mother, where the school is now, and watching them harvesting the hay, in the warm sunshine. We took a picnic with us, and had a lovely day watching the horses drawing the long wooden drays, loaded up with freshly cut hay, while the people worked very hard getting it cut and bundled up ready for the winter.

I remember seeing the Shire horses in the stables at the yard in High Street, the smell of the hay and the leather from the horse harnesses and the horse brasses hanging on the walls, these horses looked magnificent when groomed and decorated with the brasses.

My grandfather used to take us all to Sandy Beach at Buildwas in his car, where we spent the day by the river, taking a picnic with us and paddling in the water, carefully watched by our parents, we could do a lot of outdoor things in the lovely sunny days we had when I was a child, sadly the weather is not so nice now, but on the other hand we do not have the very harsh winters we suffered then, how the seasons have changed over the years!

Frederick died in 1932, and his four sons Edwin, Jack, Fred and Will carried on the business for several years. By the 1940's the only business left was the garage on the High Street and the Scrap yard next door. Walter went to live in London and Ernest became a teacher, he was a Headmaster before he retired to Codsall.

Horses and carriages belonging to Frederick Oakley, The driver on the right is Edwin Oakley, on the far right is Fred Oakley and in the centre is 'Flooky' Sargeant.

The picture of the horses and carriages belonged to my mother, and the coachman on the right was her father Edwin, his brother Fred was on the left and the man in the centre was 'Flookey' Sargeant.

The picture below of the people in the horse and trap, was given to me and I was told it belonged to Oakleys. It was taken on the top of Barratts Hill, the building in the front was the old Cape of Good Hope, with some very old cottages adjoining it, demolished before I lived there in 1935, I have been told it was in the early 1900's. The last building at the end of Cape Street, on the left hand side was the Burnt House.

My grandfather used to take us all to Sandy Beach at Buildwas in his car, where we spent the day by the river, taking a picnic with us and paddling in the water, carefully watched by our parents, we could do a lot of outdoor things in the lovely sunny days we had when I was a child, sadly the weather is not so nice now, but on the other hand we do not have the very harsh winters we suffered then, how the seasons have changed over the years!

Frederick died in 1932, and his four sons Edwin, Jack, Fred and Will carried on the business for several years. By the 1940's the only business left was the garage on the High Street and the Scrap yard next door. Walter went to live in London and Ernest became a teacher, he was a Headmaster before he retired to Codsall.

The picture of the horses and carriages belonged to my mother, and the coachman on the right was her father Edwin, his brother Fred was on the left and the man in the centre was 'Flookey' Sargeant.

The picture below of the people in the horse and trap, was given to me and I was told it belonged to Oakleys. It was taken on the top of Barratts Hill, the building in the front was the old Cape of Good Hope, with some very old cottages adjoining it, demolished before I lived there in 1935, I have been told it was in the early 1900's. The last building at the end of Cape Street, on the left hand side was the Burnt House.

Horse and trap, belonging to Oakley's, outside the old Cape of Good Hope on the junction of Barratts Hill/Cape Street in the early 1900's

There were a lot of Oakleys in Broseley in the 1920's, my uncle told me that when he was at school there were sixty Oakley children in Broseley School at the one time. But like many other large families, over the years some have moved away, sadly many have passed away, and the women have married and changed their names, some never married and some had no children at all. It has soon reduced the numbers. My grandmother was Florence Doherty, and she married Edwin Oakley, they had 9 children. The family came from Co. Mayo in Ireland and went to Sheffield but I have no more information than that. They must have moved to Coalport, near Jackfield as that is where she lived when they met. Tragically she was killed in a bus accident in 1935.

We are also lucky to have a photograph of one of great granddads charabancs, crowded with people, it looks as if there are over thirty people packed into it.

The charabancs were called the 'Daisy' and 'Felix' and my mom's brother used to drive them. He told many stories of his life when he talked to me, they are in another part of this book where I spoke to several old people, and they told me of their lives when they were young, they were very interesting to listen to.

Charabanc belonging to Frederick Oakley in the early 1900's, named the Felix or Daisy

I have been lucky to find out so much about my ancestors, through research and help from my family and older relatives, many who have sadly passed on. The photographs I have got were in a shoebox at my dads, but when I asked if I could put them in an album for him and he said I could have them, I never realised the pleasure I was going to get learning of how, and where my family had existed in the past two hundred and seventy years.

As Frances Aston and James lived at The Mines in the 1800's, we now live at The Mines in the year 2003, not knowing I was so near to where my ancestors lived in the 1730's.

But even stranger is the fact that the house we actually bought 45 years ago, was where my grandfather's sister lived, and died, in the 1920's. She was Lizzie (Elizabeth) Beddow and she was married to William Owen, grandson of Frances and James, who lived just up the road from them. She was a sister to William Beddow who married Alice Corfield, who was a granddaughter to Frances and James. Lizzie had a sister Mary who came to The Mines to look after the seven children of her departed sister, with her own four children in the 1920's. She eventually married her late sisters husband William, and they had one daughter, making 11 children and two adults in all, in this cottage.

Other families have lived here since the 1930's when the Owen family moved out, but how strange that we should be here at The Mines today, where my ancestors were born and lived so many years ago.

A survey has been done on this property recently and we were told that it was built about 1550-1650, originally a one up and one down wattle and daub timber framed building. This was rebuilt and extended over the years by brick from about 1725.

OLD BROSELEY

It is very interesting to look back to how life was years ago, and it is with the help of John Randall's book, written in 1879, that I have been able to do this. I have not read another book that tells of how life was here in Broseley itself, so this is my primary source of information and I have used this in writing this part of my story because it is so different to our lives today.

According to John Randall's book on Broseley dated 1879, Broseley was part of the great Shirlott Forest that extended from Jackfield and the River Severn to Benthall, Barrow, Caughley, Sweney, Buildwas, Shineton, Coalmoor, Astley Abbotts and Erdington. In ancient records it was called Burwardsley, probably from the family of that name to whom it belonged or from its vicinity into the Borough of Wenlock.

Broseley, Benthall and Willey are on the south side of the River Severn and were part of the Forest of Shirlett, with open woodland where animals grazed. The deer parks created about the twelfth century became almost non-existent but deer can now be seen again at Willey Park, in the Benthall area and nearby Tickwood Hall, at Wyke.

View of Quarry Road, Broseley Wood

It tells of how Broseley came about in 1220, originally called Burwardsley, of the trades that came from the richness of the coal, iron, clay etc. found in the area and worked by wealthy industrialists, and the growth of the population. The town has a fascinating history, it was an early industrial town, hard to imagine in these modern times.

Life was very different in the early 17th-18th centuries, and crime was dealt with very harshly. There were manorial courts held by the Lords of Burwardsley for the cases of misdemeanors, disputes and nuisances. At a court session at Much Wenlock on 21st July 1653 a collier was charged with disorderly conduct in the Birchmeadow, Broseley, one with an assault at Benthall, and another was charged with stealing grass for his horse from a field at Wenlock.

Edward 1V granted a Charter of Incorporation, every person convicted of drawing or smiting with a weapon in a church or churchyard is to have one of his ears cut off, if he has no ears he should be marked and burned in the cheek with a hot iron, with the letter 'F' for fighter or fraymaker. A dog must not be permitted to roam within the sacred shade of the Forest where the Royal deer roamed without it first being 'expediated', that is without having the balls of the feet cut off, otherwise its owner was liable to heavy penalties, as the stags were carefully guarded Royal beasts, and could not be injured without risk of mutilation or death.

Hanging seems to have been an amusement invented for the elite, who hired windows or rooms the preceding nights, which they passed in feasting or card playing, at 8.00 next morning ladies and gents would take their seats at the window to watch the executions. Hangings were so frequent, at last the country got sick of them, and the judges recommended 12 months imprisonment.

Judge Jefferys who was not altogether unconnected with Shropshire had no such scruples, during what was called the 'Bloody Assizes' he hung on circuit estimated numbers at 320, 600 and 700. Old people have been heard to say seven men of Broseley and Barrow had gone on a poaching exhibition at Patshull with a horse and cart, the feet of the horse and the wheels of the cart were muffled, they were tried and convicted and hung one at a time, after adding sheep stealing to their other offences.

Duties were imposed on bricks, tiles, glass, salt and a thousand other things. There was an act of Charles 11 which encouraged the manufacture of wool, and an obligation to bury in wool whether they could afford it or not, seen from instructions signed by George Weld and Thomas Crompton in 1693. Other silly laws passed about this time were the prohibition of making starch from potatoes, and cultivation of potatoes in common fields.

Vagrants and beggars were to be strictly looked after, they swarmed through the country giving themselves up for pilfering, the women breeding children whom they brought up in the same idle way of living. According to one writer in 1677 there was 100,000 paupers in England. Harsh measures were required, the law of settlements was passed and once more the poor were reduced to bondage to the soil from which they had been emancipated a century or two before. The poor rate continued to increase and to press most heavily upon Parishes, and with a view to lessening the pressure, the system of farming the paupers at so much a head was introduced.

This was done at Broseley and Benthall and revolutions on a small scale now and then broke out among the paupers who would go in a body and smash the windows of the unfortunate contractor, under the impression that he was unduly harsh, from a desire to make money out of them. From minutes of a Parish meeting held in the Town Hall, Broseley in 1827, it was agreed to farm the poor of the Parish to Samuel Pugh for £850 for one year, and in 1829 for £1,000.

Each Parish, in most cases looked after/maintained its own poor, down to the introduction of the New Poor Law. One abnoxious law abolished by William 111 was the Smoke Penny Tax or Chimney Tax as it was sometimes called.

Interesting to see how the laws have changed over the years, they are now more humane, but still there are protests that conditions are not good enough.

A map in 1618 shows how the settlement had grown, particularly in the Broseley Wood, Calcutts and Salthouse areas along the river. By 1700 Broseley had grown very rapidly with about 2,000 inhabitants, and was described as a thriving country town. Between 1700/1800 the population reached its peak as it roughly doubled to 4,000, many of the fine buildings date from that time.

The River Severn in the 18th century was only the second in importance to the River Thames, carrying merchandise to and from Shrewsbury, Bristol and many other places.

As John Randall tells us in his book, there are no means of judging the numbers of men employed on the Severn about 1639, but the collieries of Broseley and Benthall were known to be in operation and some half a century later there were 55 owners and 87 barges on the Broseley side of the River Severn, besides about half that number on the Madeley Wood side, employed in carrying 100,000 tons of coal annually, besides great quantities of grain, hops, wood, cider and provisions, earthenwares, iron and iron manufactures.

Upon the navigable part of the river there were 400 vessels in 1756. There were several different kinds of barges and boats, the largest and most well known were the Severn Trows, some 60 feet long and 16/20 feet wide, each of which would require an average crew of 4 or more hands, the cost of these boats was about £300 when new.

Group of boys in front of Kings Head pub, King Street, Broseley Wood, early 1900's

Trow boat on River Severn

Men who were employed to haul the boats up river, were called bow haulers, and described by John Randall as a distinctive class of men 'recognizable anywhere with their broad backs, and legs which swelled at the calves like skittle pins'. They worked in gangs along the riverbank hauling the boats, there were no towpaths and they had a very hard life. The River Severn was at that time looked to as an important nursery for seamen.

Many mining and manufacturing operations were carried on in Broseley, and it grew from a very small to a very big community when it was discovered there was a market for the coal, ironstone and clay found there.

By about 1580 a Gloucester man named James Clifford owned most of the Manor of Broseley. When he realized that the area was so rich in minerals, and with the importance of the closeness to the River Severn and its barges for transporting these goods, he brought in miners from Staffordshire and Wales, to dig for the coal, tunneling in from the Severn Gorge. He persuaded these men to come by telling them they could build houses on Broseley's Common, in Broseley Wood, just north of the village of Broseley.
This was very unpopular with the existing inhabitants, as in the Middle Ages they cut the trees for wood and grazed their animals on this common land. The cottages were literally built anywhere, and in later years the streets and roads were laid in between the houses, resulting in the small winding lanes and 'jitties' we now have in Broseley, and explaining why there is no regular pattern of streets.
In 1607/10 there were riots between the inhabitants of Broseley and these miners, described as "the scum and dregs of many counties, thieves, horrible swearers and drunkards". There were troubles about this time, one group of miners was employed to pull up other miner's rails, as different parties of industrialists competed for

the work in the area, these were some of the earliest wooden railways, and reports have been found of early railway lines in the area, and on the Birchmeadow.

By 1840 the mineral reserves were running out, particularly the ironstone and coal where the big money was made, so the wealthiest people began to drift away. The clay was used for brick and tile works and the clay pipes for which Broseley has been famous since the 1500's.

Broseley was critical to the whole industrial issue of the area because of the importance of its coal mining, and old interesting mining remains have been found going back to the 16/17th centuries, and probably earlier in the woods in Benthall, Broseley and Broseley Wood. Original coalpits and spoil from these medieval style mines still survive in these woods, most of them quite unspoilt by the passing of time.

Children in front of the Duke of Cumberland pub and shops, King Street, Broseley Wood about 1900

View of the old Free Bridge

BROSELEY – THE TOWN

The Town (Information from various directories etc. at Shirehall records office, Kelly's, Robsons, Lewis's Topographical etc, and from John Randall's Book of Broseley,)

Broseley is a town with a fascinating history, hard to image in these modern times. The story of its birth and growth over the years is well worth reading. According to John Randall's book (1879), it originated as part of a forest, the Royal Chase of Shirlott. In about the year 1200 a deed was granted to the Abbey and convent at Buildwas, by Philip De Burwardsley, allowing them to quarry stone for the Abbey and the right of way from their quarries to the River Severn, where they took the stone down the river on barges to Buildwas. This may have been to repair or add to the the Abbey, as it is said to have been founded in about 1135 AD in the reign of Henry 1.

There was no road to the river then, only the one made by the monks. This quarry was on a hill, near to a spot where a pub called the Seven Stars and several cottages were built in later years in Broseley Wood, it was very appropriately called Quarry Road for as long ago as I can remember. (Deeds relating to this building at Fearney Bank are dated as far back as 1822 but there is a mention of a John Cranage and his son John dated 6 March 1753 and also as occupied by James Rowley -Shoemaker and Thomas Such - Chimney sweep).

Broseley was a market town and Parish in the Union of Madeley, the franchise of Wenlock, and Southern division of the County of Salop. It was 4 miles east from Wenlock, 14 miles south-east from Shrewsbury and 144 north-west from London, on the road from Worcester to Shrewsbury. Its jurisdiction extended over the parishes of Broseley, Benthall, Posenhall, Madeley, Barrow, Linley, Willey, Little Wenlock and Dawley.

The Town was described in 1811 as irregularly but pleasantly built on an eminence rising from the Western Bank of the River Severn, from a distance of nearly 2 miles. It consisted mainly of one long street, from which a few smaller streets branched off towards the different collieries, brick works and other places of work, these streets were really only dirt roads at this time. It was neither paved nor lit, and the inhabitants were very scantily provided with water, which they carried in winter from a well called the Down Well situated at the top of the Haycop, about one and a half miles eastward from the town, and in summer from brooks still at a distance of a mile and a half.

As were most towns at that time, it was very self sufficient, the trades consisted mainly of mining, but this declined later as the mines became exhausted. There were numerous coal pits, many named in this book, also iron foundries and furnaces, fine earthenware, tobacco pipes, bricks and tiles works. Firebricks were made for building the furnaces and were of great repute, they were sent to various parts of the kingdom by barges and trows on the River Severn.

Broseley became important with the discovery of coal and ironstone, and as the mines and works were opened so the population increased, in 1811 there were 4,850 inhabitants.

The houses were built of brick and were of a mean appearance, intermixed with some of a more respectable character, and larger handsome buildings built by the wealthier people of the town.

In 1750 John Barratt Esq of Broseley, bequeathed £110 for charitable purposes and a Mr Richard Evans, a legacy of £100. Together with smaller sums amounting to £380, an investment was made in purchasing land on which the Town Hall and other houses were erected. After deducting the expense of keeping these in repair, the rents of the houses and the standings in the Market place were distributed among the poor in Broseley.

The Town Hall was built in 1777 in the High street in the centre of the town, originally called Cole Pitt Hill. It was a large brick building supported on pillars and arches, the basement formed a spacious market place. On the first floor was a room where the courts and public meetings were held, also used as an assembly room, and two smaller rooms used for Sunday School.

There was a small prison attached to it for confining criminals and debtors before their committal by the Borough magistrates.

It consisted of 3 rooms, the larger room holding 150 persons and it was restored in 1837 at a cost of £600. The Town Hall was said to have once contained a beautiful carved oak chair dated 1626.

Market days were held on a Wednesday but were not very well attended after 1851. Before that they were held at Whitehall on Church Street.

Courts for the Manor were held there in April and October annually, four constables being appointed in the October session. A court of requests for the recovery of debts under forty shillings was generally held every alternate Wednesday. Petty sessions were held every six weeks.

Broseley High Street, Lion Hotel and shops, early periods (both photos)

The National School was held in the spacious 61' x 21' room over the Market hall with about 195 scholars attending. The Victoria Institute and Assembly Hall were formerly the Gospel rooms built in 1837, used in 1902 to provide social amusement, billiards, concerts and non-sectarian purposes. There was a News Room and library in the High Street in 1853, containing 1,000 volumes.

From 1811 the fairs in Broseley have been held every last Tuesday of April and October annually, the children having a half holiday from school to attend, they were pleasure fairs with a considerable number of pigs being sold.

On an old 1840 map of Broseley there is shown the site of an old workhouse in Mill Lane and a workhouse garden by the Foresters Arms, a Glass House Yard in Cockshutt Lane and a Mill/Malt House in Mill Field at Harris's Green.

Transport in 1835 was provided by coaches to Cheltenham by 'The Old Worcester' from Shrewsbury via Tontine and Red Lion Broseley, about 8.30am every Monday, Wednesday and Friday morning and goes through Worcester. To Shrewsbury 'The Emerald' from Birmingham via The White Hart.

To Shrewsbury 'The Old Worcester' from Cheltenham calls at the Red Lion Broseley every Tuesday, Thursday and Saturday afternoon at 4.30pm.

The Postmaster in 1828 was Isiah Guest, the Post arrives from Wenlock in Broseley every morning at half past three, and returns the same evening.
From Shifnal to Broseley every morning at half past four.
In 1840 the Postmaster was J J Guest, letters arrive every morning at 8.00, and are despatched every evening at a quarter before six.
In 1851 the Postmaster was Jeremiah Ashwoods, letters arrive at 8.00am and are despatched 5.35pm.

Charities were recorded from 1851 as:
John Barratt Esq bequeathed the sum of £200 to the poor of Broseley,
Frances Morgan left £50, the interest divided among 12 poor widows on Christmas Day annually,
Richard Evans of Rowton left £100 to be laid out in lands, the profit distributed on Christmas and Easter Days in equal shares among the poor widows of the Parish the minister and his heirs think fit.
Esther Hollyman left £20, to be added to the poor's stock in 1730.

Broseley Town Hall and High Street

William Lewis in 1740 granted a yearly rent charge of 20 shillings from 2 acres of land and a building near Broseley Church, with a penalty of 6 shillings for every day the payment should be in arrears, this to be distributed among 20 poor widows.

Andrew Langley of the Woodhouse left 12 shillings yearly to be paid out by the church ministers and wardens on St Andrews Day yearly.

Mary Cotton who died in 1838 bequeathed £300 of consolidated trusts to the ministers and wardens of the Parish at that time, to receive and divide the interest among 40 widows on 29th December yearly.Fanny Pritchard left £100 in trust to the same parties to be invested in government securities and the interest to be divided among 10 poor widows on St Thomas's Day.

Group at the top of Barratts Hill, from cross roads - 1908

Photograph of Broseley Square with the Monument and railings about 1900

Industries

Broseley was an extensive mining district with an abundance of coal, clay and ironstone, the numerous mines provided work for many of the inhabitants here and attracted miners as the works proceeded. The plentiful supplies of coal and the easy transport by river seem to be the reasons for the mining here in the 1600's.

It was here, in Broseley, that the industries began to flourish and grow, barge builders, ironworks/foundries, pits, potteries, brick and tile works and the clay pipe works. The industries provided the barges with work, carrying their products to many places and ports, and because of all this the population increased, and further trade was brought in by the shops and other amenities needed for the community to survive.

The white coarse clay at Broseley was used for the porcelain works in the area. The surface clay was used for making inferior bricks and tiles, and the deeper clay for firebricks and pottery. Clay has been used for making bricks and pottery etc. for hundreds of years and many local brickworks were found on the banks of the River Severn, through the search for clay and coal in the area, the pits have caused the surfaces to collapse when they were worked out.

Advertisements from the 1800's show the names of some of the brick and tile works in the area, 'The Dunge Brick & Tile Works, George & Francis Davis, Est. 1811, Superior Broseley Pressed Roofing Tiles, Plain & Ornamental, Flooring & Fire Clay Goods, Malt Kiln Tiles, Common & Sewerage Drain Pipes &c. John Doughty - 1862, Manufacturer of Best Broseley Pressed Roofing Tiles, Crest, Hips & Gutters, Flooring Squares, Fire Bricks &c. Josiah Wase & Co. Holywell Tile Works 1885. Prestage & Broseley Tileries Co. - Madeley Wood Co. Broseley Roofing Tiles, Hopley & Duncan -Madeley, Broseley Roofing Tiles, George Legge & Son, Woodlands & Madeley Wood, Broseley Tile Works, Broseley Tileries Co. Limited, 1885, Bricks and tiles. C R Jones & Co Ltd and the Milburgh Tileries 1926, just to mention a few.

There were several Iron Foundries in Broseley and Benthall in the 16/17th centuries, where sophisticated parts for bridges, engines and domestic utensils like frying pans etc were made. John Onions and John Guest were both Broseley Iron Masters of note, but the most famous was John Wilkinson.

John Wilkinson (1728-1808) was called 'the father of the English iron trade', he was the greatest ironmaster of his time and had works through his career at Bersham, in Denbighshire, Bradley near Bilston, Snedshill, Hollinswood and New Hadley, as well as Willey in Shropshire.

The Lawns, was the home of John Wilkinson in 1763

The Dog – Church Street

John Wilkinson bought a house in Church Street, Broseley in 1763, called The Lawns (built in 1727), and made most of his iron inventions in Shropshire (the house was later lived in by John Rose, the china manufacturer).

There was a blast furnace at Willey owned by John Weld in about 1620, refitted at that time to working order, but after a 21 year lease ran out the furnace remained unused for 3 years. It was again refit, and worked in conjunction with a new furnace built in 1757 by the New Willey Company of which John Wilkinson was a partner, until 1774. He later became the sole lessee of the New Willey Iron Works, said to have closed about 1804. He first used charcoal and leather bellows, worked by a water wheel, horses and a man, before steam engines were installed, which continued into the nineteenth century.
He met James Watt and Matthew Boulton of Birmingham and cast an iron cylinder for their steam engines, as well as other parts in iron. An engine made by Watts and Boulton was ordered by Wilkinson to operate the bellows of the blast furnace of his iron works at Willey, and was erected ready for use in 1776, Watts and Boulton became famous throughout the Midland Counties.

He cast cannon for guns, iron pulpits, the first coal cutting machines and the first iron boat called "The Trial" which was launched successfully 17th July 1787 on the River Severn. This idea was laughed at by the barge owners when first talked of, but it was so light and moved so easily on the water, many more barges and canal boats were built.

Wilkinson cast the pipes and ironwork cylinders for Paris Water Works and the first steam engine in France. He also made his own copper tokens, and just a few silver ones in 1780/1795, with three designs, a likeness to himself on one side of each coin and on the reverse side of the three coins were a sailing vessel - a forge, large hammer and a man - and a man, a hammer and an anvil. He made his own iron coffin, and an iron mausoleum was erected over the great iron masters grave when he died aged 80 in 1808. He was buried at Bradley where he died, a very wealthy man.

The first meeting to discuss the building of a bridge across the River Severn, to connect the Broseley and Madeley banks of the river, was said to have been held at Hurstlea house, Queen Street in Broseley, the views of Abraham Darby were supported by John Wilkinson who proposed the use of iron, his favourite metal. He was called 'iron mad' but as he was a large shareholder and he insisted, his suggestion was adopted. The bridge was designed by Thomas Farnolls Pritchard, a Shrewsbury architect, and cast at Coalbrookdale by Abraham Darby 111. This was the first Iron Bridge built in 1779 and has since become world famous, with visitors coming from all over the world to see it, still standing proudly over the Severn.

John Onions was another Broseley ironmaster, who lived at Whitehall, in Church Street. He designed the railings of the bridge over the River Severn at Coalport, by the Woodbridge pub, it has a design of overlapping O's, the initial of the John Onions iron master. His foundry was at Foundry Lane by the Dog or Talbot pub. In about 1810 they also built an iron boat, called the 'Victory', for the Severn trade, and designed what was believed to have been the first iron vessel for the River Thames at their Brierly Works.

He was a member of the Baptist Chapel, but in 1801 there were disagreements between the members and a break away took place. John Guest, iron master and George Crompton, draper of Broseley bore the cost of a new chapel built at Birchmeadow in 1803. John Guest and John Onions and their families were buried at this chapel where their tombs had beautiful cast iron rails around them in the grounds at the front of the Chapel.

There were other foundries in Broseley and Benthall, the Benthall Ironworks at Coach Road (now Bridge Road) was worked at one time by the Hill family, it was worked by a water wheel and pumping engine, and called the Benthall Smelter by the locals, it was working in the 1770's and it is said to have been making steam engines by about the 1780's.

These ironworks relied on water mills to work them, and according to a copy of an early map, there were three mills on the Bridge Bank, the first one was situated in the garden of a property just opposite the old Pitchyard pub, which may have been called Mill House. The second one was just down the bank not far away, on the same side of the road, and the third one was the near the bottom of the bank, called the big Wheel. The ruins of this mill still stand there, but the wheel was taken away during the Second World War, taken by my grandfather who dealt with scrap iron. Many things made of iron were scrapped during the war year's, railings and many other ornamental things were re-used for the war effort.

Benthall Ironworks mid 1770's, later the site of Maws Tile Works

There were ginny rails across the road, which ran between the Benthall Works on either side of the bank. It was said to have been a bumpy ride to passengers who stayed in the coach on the journey down. Many got out and walked.

It produced pig iron for castings and made cast iron goods at the foundry where it has been quoted they employed about 700 men. It seems to have closed in the early 1800's.

Another Broseley furnace was at the Coneybury, called the Bottom Coal furnace, operating in about 1788, it was owned by Banks and Onions. It was opposite the Toll Cottage on Ironbridge Road (then called New Road), just below the cemetery, and was working in the 1820's. Onion's also worked the Guest furnace, built in 1806 on the Coalport Road.

Maw's Tile Company was situated on Bridge Road, Benthall, just up the bank from the River Severn. It was previously the site of the Benthall Ironworks Foundry pictured and described above.

Maws works Jackfield

The company was formed in 1850 by George and Arthur Maw, two brothers who moved here from the Worcester Porcelain Company they ran in 1852. Clay from the Broseley/ Benthall area was transported there by river for their works. As the clay here was of a very high quality, the coal was cheap for firing the kilns, the area was rich and plentiful in minerals at the time and the river was very close by for transporting their goods, they decided to move to the premises at Benthall.

With the success of the tile business, the Benthall premises, which were situated on both sides of the road, became too small and it was eventually moved to a site at Jackfield and opened in 1883. It became the largest decorative tile business in the world, keeping the name Maw & Co. Benthall Works over the work's entrance gates.

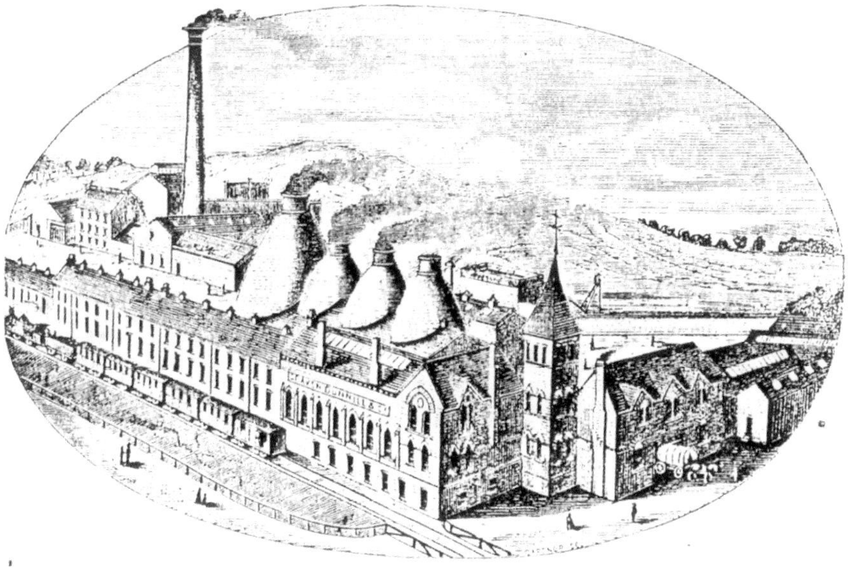

Craven Dunnills Jackfield

Their tiles were used in churches, commercial and public buildings throughout Britain and the British Empire, floor tiles and later glazed tiles for fireplaces, walls and washstands. The early tiles were red and buff clay, but progressed later to as many as six colours, and many different designs as shown in their catalogues. As the skills and techniques improved the wall tiles were decorated by hand-painting, transfer-printing and stencilling with many amazing colours.

George and Arthur Maw lived at Benthall Hall for a time, where George collected and grew many crocus plants, some still seen there today. He got his inspiration from medieval abbeys and travelled as far away as the Middle East, Venice and Rome. Maw's won many awards for their tiles in London 1862, Paris 1867, Philadelphia 1876, Adelaide 1887 and Chicago 1893. Some of their tiles can be seen in Benthall Hall, the Tontine and Valley Hotels in Ironbridge, and Maw's and Craven Dunnill's tiles can be seen in Jackfield Church.

Maws continued until the late 1960's but after many changes became part of the Johnson-Richards Tiles of Stoke, in January 1970 the Works were closed and moved to Stoke-on-Trent.

Craven Dunnills were also famous for their encaustic and decorative tiles, made at Jackfield in the 1870's, the company was formed in 1871.

In 1867 it was owned by Hawes and Denny, encaustic tile makers, and later by Hargreaves and Craven but it was very run down, and in 1875 it was rebuilt and opened as the new Jackfield Works, by the firm Craven Dunnill & Co. their work being similar to that of their neighbours, Maws. The tiles made were of very good quality and durability, and the clay used may have come from the site itself. Their tiles were of medieval patterns and designs used in many churches and cathedrals, most of them bore the trademark of a tile works with a smoking bottle kiln on the back of the tile.

Garden party at the home of Mr Howells – now Cumberland Hotel

Coalport Works

Despite being a very successful firm through the first half of the 20th century, Craven Dunnill closed in 1952. It later became a foundry. Wilfred Howells was the last owner of Craven Dunnills and lived in the large house in Queen Street, Broseley, which later became the Cumberland Hotel in 1948, when the Duke of Cumberland pub in King Street closed.

They both had national and international fame for their products, but by the 1900's changes in fashions and designs and with other competition, the industry began to struggle, the situation was made worse with the start of World War 1 (1914-1918) and the depression which followed. The kitchen and bathroom tiles, fireplace and hearth tiles later produced there, employed many of the local people from around the Jackfield, Broseley and Madeley districts, as they had done for many years in the past.

CLAY PIPE INDUSTRY

(Information from Clay Tobacco Pipes Shire Album 37 by Eric G Ayto). The craft of clay pipe making began in England after the introduction of tobacco in 1558, to satisfy the demand of people to take up smoking.

The variety of the style and sizes of the clay pipes was due to fashion, different skills and the availability of tobacco at that time. The earliest reference was 1573 by William Harrison, describing the spoon like shape as probably derived from the Indian pipe, which was used for medicinal and religious purposes and ceremonies.

The shape changed in 1580, making a better container for the tobacco, the base of the bowl was flat enabling the pipe to stand upright on the table, and the stem was 4 - 6 inches long.

In 1640 the inside diameter of the bowl had to be 3/8 of an inch and no change in the length of the stem. After this date the bowl became much larger and the stem longer, about 10 - 14 inches, and this basic shape remained the same for the next 60 years.

A milled or plain ring at the top of the bowl was common for this period, and except for the occasional makers mark, the majority of 17th century pipes were otherwise plain. Towards the end of the century the inside diameter of the bowl was 1/2 an inch. Most stems were straight, but some curved up or downwards, probably from distortion during firing.

A few elaborately decorated pipes were made during the first half of the century, some English and some Dutch designs. The designs were either stamped or incised by hand, on both bowl and stem, or moulded in relief.

Just after 1700 some important changes in quality took place. Pipes were made more accurately, more brittle and smoother, suggesting a steady improvement in the skills of the craft, firing techniques and mould making. The top of the bowl was trimmed level with the stem instead of sloping at a downward angle to the front of the bowl. This particular change, as well as a more upright bowl than before may have been a new method of manufacture.

Early 18th century pipes favoured a flat bottom spur, and some, no spur at all, these were popular in North America from 1720 - 1820 and are believed to have been exported by Bristol pipe makers. During the mid 18th century, extra long pipes became fashionable with the gentry, they were called 'Aldermen', but later became 'Straws', the stems about 18 - 24 inches long, the first pipes to have a specific name at the time of their use.

By 1750 pipes were being made with emblems, designs of pub names and regiments. The Aldermen Straws and short plain pipes were the most popular well into the 19th century. Some pipe stems had a small corded mark, so far from the bowl that when held between the fingers at this spot, the pipe was balanced.

After 1850 the very long pipe was introduced they were about 36 inches long. Later in the century these pipes were called Church Wardens but were not very practical. In the second half of the century the production of decorated pipes increased, and in Victorian times were used as an advertising medium, events of the time, slogans, names of public houses, sporting activities, animals, fish, etc. the length of the stem and size of the bowl varied according to the design. The stem at this time had a vulcanite mouthpiece. The sizes of the pipes were churchwardens 24", smaller churchwardens of 22", other sizes are 20", 16", 12 - 10 - 6" all very popular in their day.

Most fancy pipes had the design on the side of the bowl, but some bowls were shaped to represent the subject itself. Some of the subjects used on these pipes were peoples heads or faces, and very artistic designs like the eagles claw, the bowl resting in the claw representing an eagles egg, the bunch of grapes, fish, acorn, a hand holding a tankard, the royal family, R A.O.B. and footballers, etc. The working man in the 19th century preferred the ordinary short clay, which was very cheap, and often given away with a pint of beer by the local publican, the stems of pipes were often broken off to suit the needs of the individual. The ends of the broken stems were treated to prevent the lips sticking to the porous clay, broken off pipe ends were dipped in tea or beer, or bound with thread to overcome this problem.

A Charter of Incorporation to Pipe makers was granted in 1619 by King James 1, to protect the interests of pipe makers, they carefully guarding the secrets of their trade. By 1650 there were at least 1,000 pipe makers in London alone, many in other towns, Bristol, Chester, Gateshead, York and Hull, including Broseley, where the Southorn Family had their factory.

It has been written that pipes came about with the introduction of tobacco at the time of Sir Walter Raleigh, but early pipes found, point to their being used for medicinal purposes to smoke herbs and plants like coltsfoot and maybe dock leaves.

One of the first pipe makers in Broseley/Benthall was Richard Legg (according to John Randall the names of Legge and Southorn occur together in 1558) and some of his work dates back to 1575, the Southorn family have been recorded as sited at the Pitchyard Benthall and at Legges Hill Broseley Wood, later moving to the Crown Pipe Works in 1923.

(How Broseley Pipes were made - reprinted from the Shrewsbury Chronicle Friday August 12th 1932) (Also some information from Victoria County History, The Archaeology Newsletter Vol 5., Tobacco Pipes of Broseley, Shropshire by D R Atkinson, and some information is taken from John Randall's book),

Clay pipes have been made in Broseley for over 3 centuries, it was an ideal place for making clay pipes, as it had its own clay, coal for the kilns and the River Severn for transporting their ware. Broseley clay was of a rough gritty texture and in about 1700 a smoother, whiter clay was brought in from other parts of the country, Dorset, Cornwall and Devon, on barges up the River, and later from the Ironbridge/Broseley railway station, in the 1800's. This was then brought up the very steep bank to Benthall, from Ironbridge in horse drawn vehicles, stopping at the Pittsyard or Pitchyard pub for a breather, where, I have been told, the horses were given a bucket of water each and the drivers had a pint and some bread and cheese. From the Pitchyard it was taken over 'The Brook', round by the 'Cross Keys' pub to Southorns works on Legges Hill, the clay was then put into what was called a midden or mixen.

The clay had to be dried, then soaked to a be made easy to work with, then passed through a 'pug mill' several times, it was rolled by hand into the various lengths required and each length was threaded with a steel wire to form the vent, it was then pressed into the mould of the pipe design required. An iron stopper was inserted to form the bowl. These were then left to partly dry out, any marks or rough edges were removed and the trade or 'Made in England' stamp were pressed onto the pipe. The shorter varieties were dried out, then placed in round saggars or earthenware firing pots, but the long pipes were sprayed with water until thoroughly moist, the curve of the long pipe was obtained by having a curved bottom in the saggars, the pipes were embedded in china clay dust. The saggars were put in piles inside the kilns, the doorway bricked up and it was ready for firing. The most burned in one kiln in the early pipe works was 20-24 gross but towards the end of the pipe making 500 gross or more of small pipes, or 200 gross of long pipes were burnt at once. Great care was taken with this process, it took about 16 hours to be done, very slowly at first and then the heat increased gradually. It took about 2 tons of coal to fire one kiln, the kilns were then drawn, the pipe mouthpieces tipped, and the pipes were ready for selling. The short pipes were packed in various quantities in cardboard boxes, made on the works, the churchwardens were packed in one dozens in strawboard cases. The people who worked at making these pipes were very skilled craftsmen (Reprinted from the Shrewsbury Chronicle Friday 12 August 1932).

There is a photograph of Alice Corfield and Beatrice Corfield, her aunt, who was a sister to my grandmother, she, and my husband's mother both worked at Southorns Pipes in the early 1900's, he recalled their earnings were 4d for putting the wire up every 13 dozen pipes made.

In Broseley there were many clay pipe making families, carrying out their work moulding and burning their clays in work shops and kilns next to their cottages, these cottage crafts became a thriving industry, and their pipes have been found all over the world.

Some of the names and dates of manufacturers are as follows:

1590 John Jones, 1600, John James, 1608 William Legg, Morris Decon 1608, Thomas Evans 1615, Richard James 1620, John Hartshorne 1620, Morris Shaw 1630, Thomas Hughes 1641, Thomas Clarke 1647, Thomas Roden 1681, Oliver Price 1685, Richard Legg 1687 + 96, Edward Decon 1692, William Darbey 1700, Jane Overton 1700, Thomas Ward 1700, Thomas Legg 1703, George Smith 1709, John Partridge 1718, Samuel Decon 1729, William Wilsone 1733, Samuel Legg and Thomas Legg 1750, and some families not so well known are Harper, Dry, Hart, Overley, Williams, Peck, Powell, Tonkiss, Upton and others, some of these family names still live on from all those years ago.

Noah Roden I (1767-1827). Noah Roden II (1800-1855) was at the New Inn, Benthall in 1828-42, and built the new pipeworks next to the New Inn. It was taken over by Edwin Southorn (1820-1876) about 1858 and renamed The Broseley Pipe Works, employing between 30/40 people from 1861 up to 1871. It was reopened in 1876 by Hopkins & Co and called the Raleigh Pipe Works but went bankrupt in 1881 and was taken over by William Southorn.

Others in Benthall in 1829 were John Bradley, John Gethin, and Richard Shaw, and in 1840-68 Richard Tonkiss of Barratts Hill. Richard Bradley, and Joseph Southorn of Broseley Wood in 1861, employing 3 males and 4 females.

In a reprinted leaflet from the 'Shrewsbury Chronicle' 12/8/1932 we are told that Noah Roden's business (he brought about the perfection of the long pipes and died about 1829) was taken over by William Southorn in 1823, who improved on the quality of the pipes, winning a medal at the Great Exhibition in 1851, and an honourable mention for its products. Twenty years later in 1871 at the International Exhibition in London Southorns gained a certificate of merit.

William Southorns father had been a pipe maker, and his brother Edwin had his pipe works at Benthall until he died in 1876, when William carried on both works until his death in 1891. He was succeeded by his son William, who continued to manufacture pipes until his death in 1910. The two businesses were amalgamated in 1902.

The book on the re-opening of the Pipeworks gives the history of the Southorn family as follows:

William Southorn (1792-1853), Broseley Wood in the early 1820's, He founded his own company in 1823, and his factory on Legges Hill in 1838 at Broseley Wood where he employed 36 people by 1851.

William Southorn (1827-1894) at Legges Hill works 1853, took over his brother Edwin's New Inn Works in 1881. He renamed his Legges Hill factory Broseley Pipe Works. Employing 28 people in 1861, (16 girls/6 men/6 boys.)

William Edwin Southorn (1850-1910) was in partnership with his father at the Legges Hill works, until he died in 1910. In 1930 Henry Starr Southorn, (1887-1957) the youngest son took over the Legges Hill works, by 1935 the business moved to Rowland Smitheman's Crown Pipeworks in King Street, in 1957 production finished when Henry (known as Harry) died.

Southorns Pipe Works

In 1881, according to the book on the re-opening of the Pipe works, Rowland Smitheman began to make clay pipes, and called the cottages he had converted in King Street the Crown Pipe Works, where the famous Southorns Pipe Works still stands today. It also says that the oldest part of the works was probably erected about in the 1700's and added to at the end of the century, it may have been a cotton factory in Broseley about 1792. Other cottages were added about 1840, and later turned into workshops. The pipe works were abandoned in 1960, and when they were re-opened many years later it was like finding something where time had stood still, that had been sealed and left exactly as it was the day the last workers walked out after the days work, and everything was left ready for work the next day, it must have been a fascinating experience opening it.

Pipes have been made in Broseley since Elizabethan times. They were so famous they were known as 'a Broseley', they have been found in many countries, as far away as America, Africa and New Zealand. According to a Broseley Parish Register dated 1572, Richard Legge had a daughter baptised in 1575, ten years before Sir Walter Raleigh introduced tobacco to this country.

One of our oldest residents, whose father worked at Southorns, Legges Hill factory, told me when they went on outings to Worcester, they called at a pub on the way there, and all these men were sitting round the fire smoking wood pipes, they got talking about clay pipes, and we said "we'll bring you some clay pipes the next time we come", and we did. Each year we went afterwards, they used to be waiting for us. We took them a box a piece, they used to put their wooden pipes away, and smoked the clay pipes when we went in.

There have been many old pipe bowls with the stamps or marks of the old names, going back as far as 1688, dug up in a garden in Benthall, easy to identify with their own marks, which show the name and date of the pipe maker, but not known where the kilns were that these pipe makers used, difficult to know as there are so many different names on the pipes found in this one area, it may have a been a tip, where any pipe maker tipped his rejects etc. It has been suggested that the stamp marks dated on these very old pipes, commemorates some family or public event, but there does not appear to be confirmation of this in any old records.

Works photo of Southorns Pipes Workers, Legges Hill, early 1900's
the character bottom row, first right was named as Johnny Morgan from Simpsons Lane.

There have been many old pipe bowls with the stamps or marks of the old names, going back as far as 1688, dug up in a garden in Benthall, easy to identify with their own marks, which show the name and date of the pipe maker, but not known where the kilns were that these pipe makers used, difficult to know as there are so many different names on the pipes found in this one area, it may have a been a tip, where any pipe maker tipped his rejects etc. It has been suggested that the stamp marks dated on these very old pipes, commemorates some family or public event, but there does not appear to be confirmation of this in any old records.

There was an old pottery in Benthall, where Broseley pipes were manufactured many years ago by Edwin Southorn according to some of the Directories at the Shrewsbury Records Office, this building is still standing and was owned at one time by the Jews in the 1930's, where they manufactured pottery, teapots and jugs etc. and it is known that the words 'Salopian Pottery' were painted on the front of the building, in the early 1950's. At that time it was a lorry and tool hire firm, belonging to Ken Bryan and later became a paint shop. At the present time, it is a private residence.

Around the 1930's the pipes were used by children as bubble pipes, and were found in sherbert bags, and as targets at shooting ranges in fairgrounds. By 1914 the clay pipe manufacturing had virtually come to an end, leaving a few established makers to meet the small but continuing demand. There has always been a demand for clay pipes from the Masonic and other societies for the after dinner smoke. The Royal Order of Buffaloes still uses them for initiation ceremonies.

China Works

The first Caughley China Works were said to have been established at Caughley on the estate of Squire Edward Browne, set in fields and woodlands which led down to the River Severn and using the clays and coals on the estate. Pottery may have been made here many years before this. In about 1754, after the death of Squire Browne, the Works were run by his nephew Ambrose Gallimore, who had made china in the locality.

Mr Gallimore's daughter married Thomas Turner, a man connected with the manufacture of porcelain, with experience gained as an engraver, from the Worcester China Works, before he came to Caughley 1772.

Thomas Turner, born 1749, took over the China Works from Mr Gallimore and enlarged the works. He changed the manufacture from earthenware to china where it gained great importance for the delicate ware produced and the beauty of the designs and transfers painted on the china by local artists.

He introduced the famous 'Willow Pattern' and 'Broseley Blue Dragon' patterns in 1780. This was the year he went to France to gain more knowledge about the manufacture of porcelain, and he brought skilled workmen and artists back with him where they worked with many of the fine artists in England. About this time, John Rose who had worked an apprenticeship with Turner, left to set up his own small business at Jackfield.

Caughley China Works as drawn by Roger Edmundson of Shrewsbury

About 1798 when Turner retired, the Caughley Works were sold to John Rose, who was established at Coalport by this time. Rose was so successful that Caughley began to lose much of its trade, Rose however still used the Caughley works for producing ware for about fifteen years. John Rose now had the best workers from Caughley and Jackfield working for him, many of them lived in Broseley, crossing the river each morning and evening by ferry. It is said that on 23rd October 1799, after a long day at work and with very stormy weather, the ferry capsized and twenty eight of the workers were drowned, including many of the best Coalport artists.

Caughley was finally closed about 1814, the men and materials were taken to the Coalport site and Caughley ceased to trade, the buildings were destroyed about 1821. John Rose, who died in 1841, became famous for the fine porcelain china he produced, where the modelling, painting, and perfection of workmanship were unsurpassed.

Coalport China was exhibited at the Great Exhibition in 1851 and at the first World Fair in Chicago. At the Great French Exhibition in 1855 Coalport gained yet another gold medal.

POTTERIES

There were several potteries in the Broseley/Benthall area in the 18th and 19th centuries. One of these was the pottery on the site of the old pipe works that belonged to the Roden family and then Edwin Southorn, next door to the Pitchyard pub.

They seem to have made 'yellow slip ware' there, in the 17th/18th century, some remains of this type of earthenware have been dug up in our garden that is nearby, and we have been told they date back to the 1750's. There is a piece of information written by Miles Taylor in his book, about a jug at the Boat Inn at Jackfield, he was shown a newspaper report which read that it was a yellow earthenware harvest jug, made at Pitchyard Pottery by John Harrington or Hartshorne, he was a local potter in the 18th century, the initials JH were on the jug, and the date –65, probably 1765. Many of the local people were employed there, and the ware was undecorated pottery, in colours of brown, green, pink and cream. Teapots, mugs, jugs, vases, steins, and basins were just some of the products made here. Jones and Bathurst had an Earthenware Manufactory at Easthope in 1840, and not far away was the Benthall Pottery Company in 1868, another earthenware pottery situated by the Haybrook pottery.

There was a pottery at Benthall called the Haybrook pottery, or the 'Muguss' by the locals. A pottery was established at Haybrook in about 1742 by John Thursfield, he also had a pottery on the opposite side, the Benthall Pottery Company. They made very decorated ware at Haybrook, vases, jugs and bowls. Teapots, mugs, and steins were many of the items made here by the local people. The site closed in the 1950's, the last owner was Mr Allen. The site on the other side of the road became Benthall Pipe Works where they made land drains.

But in 1920 there is a record of buildings and premises formerly used as tobacco pipe manufactory at Pitts Yard, in the Parish of Benthall, from Lord Forester to Abraham Woolfson, John F Rowe and Harold Geo. Cleveland. In 1922 Abraham Woolfson a Jewish businessman, made decorated earthenware there until the war, it was called Salop Pottery Co. Ltd. I came to live here in 1956 and remember seeing the words Salopian Pottery painted on the front of the building. He apparently went bankrupt, I do know he gave my grandfather some basins, for a payment on a bill he owed, but when he went to sell them on they were 'seconds'. One thing I remember about the Jewish family was the daughter, who is alleged to have bathed at the local Spout. The tale told is how the men would walk to work down Spout Lane, just to see her.

I remember going with my mother to the building opposite the New Inn, where she did some work painting dolls faces, just the flat front of a face, during the 1940's.

COAL AND CLAY (MINING)

(From Archaeological Newsletter Vol.5 (Mar + April 1955) Adrian Oswald/R E James, Also Lewis's Topographical Dicting of England 1811, Shropshire Gazeteer Gregory 1824 SLS, The Salop Directory 1828, Tibman & Co Shrewsbury, Robsons 1840.) A Catalogue of Mines by I J Brown

By 1851 Broseley was an extensive mining district where coal, ironstone and clay were obtained, the numerous mines attracting miners as the works proceeded, and increasing the population at the same time. The trade consisted mostly of mining operations but when the mines became exhausted, soon rapidly declined. Plentiful supplies of coal and easy transport by river seem to be the reasons for the mining taking place here in the 1600,s. The coal was transported down the Severn in trows and barges, to Worcester and Gloucester, carrying loads as heavy as 40-60 tons

((John Randall) The clay at Broseley was a coarse white clay, formed naturally and differing in quality, firmness and colour, the surface clay was used for making inferior bricks and tiles, and the deeper clay for firebricks and pottery. Red clay gets its colour from iron and alumina, fire clay is usually free of iron, china clay or kaolin contains felspar. Clay is one of natures materials, used abundantly for making bricks, pottery etc since prehistoric times, many of these local brickworks were found on the banks of the River Severn, and the areas honeycombed with pits through the search for clay and coal.)

In 'A Catalogue of Mines' by I J Brown there were coal pits in Broseley about 1891 at:

Ash Coppice	Bells Rough	Broad Meadow	BroseleyWood
Coneybury	Deersleap	Pottery Pit	Trial Pit
Wallers	Willey Park in 1863.		

There were others pits at:

Benthall Coal Pit 1943	Benthall Level 1945	Birchmeadow
Bottom Coal 1921	Caughley	Foxholes
Haycop	Silver Hill 1910	

Cockshott/Cockshutt), Double Pits
Dunge Colliery Nos.1,2,6,7 1907

Coal and fireclay were found at:

Benthall Potteries and Bennets Bros 1923/4,
Benthall, Willey and Posenhall No's: 1,2,3,4,5,6,7,8,9 pits,
Benthall Lane 1925/42,
Broseley Wood No.1 & 2 1891/1916,
Fish House 1900,
Ladywood 1903/1921
Tuckies Shaft 1922,
Turners Yard 1950's,

Red tile or brick clay was found at:

Alder Meadow 1940
Broseley Hill 1891,
Broseley Wood,
Broseley Wood Green 1916,
Guests Deep Pit 1941,
Doughties 1902,
Dunge Colliery No.3 & 4 1905,
Exleys 1908,
Gitchfield 1950,
Green Pit,
Holly Grove Jackfield 1905,
Jubilee 1910,
Knowle 1914,
Ladywood 1939,
New Pit 1910,
Rock 1902,
Stable Hill 1891,
Stocking 1905,
Woodlands Green 1914,
Works & Calcutts 1908,
Wynd Road 1913.

Ironstone was found at Barnetts Leasow.

Other pits with little information of them are Cold Oak, Dark Lane, Dingle, Hemans Field Pit, Inetts, Langfords, Milburgh & Wallace Shafts, Red Lane, Rudgewood, Slang Pit, Three Stiles, Tynning, Vigar Drift, White Brick Kiln, White Level, and Yew Tree Calcutts.

Well of Inflammable Gas

Ref: 1824 Shropshire Gazetter, Gregory
In 1711 a remarkable burning spring was found at Broseley, said to have been in the area of the junctions of Spout Lane and Cobwell Road. (Called the Iron Plate by the local people.) The report below is taken from an account of this by the Rev Mason Woodwarden, a professor at Cambridge: There was a 4-5ft deep well, about 6-7ft wide, with a smaller hole of similar depth, dug into the clay. A cylindrical earthenware vessel of about 4-5 inches diameter at the mouth, and having the bottom taken off was placed in the bottom of the well, with the sides well fixed in and the clay rammed close around it. Within the pot was a thick brown water, continually forced up with a violent motion, like that of boiling water, with a hollow rumbling noise, rising and falling by fits of 4-6 inches, there did not appear to be any vapour rising, though some may have been visible if the sun had not shone so brightly.

Putting a candle down on the end of a stick, at a distance of a quarter of a yard, it took fire, darting and flashing in a very violent manner, about half a yard high, like spirits in a lamp, but more agitated.

It was said to have boiled a tea kettle in about 9 minutes, and had been left to burn for 48 hours without subsiding. It was distinguished by putting a wet mop on it for some considerable time, otherwise it would not go out. Sulphurous smoke rose for about a minute when the mop was removed, yet the water was cold to the touch.

The most probable cause of this inflammable property is the mixture of the water with petroleum, which is one of the most inflammable substances in nature, and will burn on a water surface. In 1755 the well disappeared completely after the sinking of a coal-pit in its neighbourhood.

POPULATION

According to various records showing the population of Broseley over the years, it is surprising to find that there were nearly as many people in Broseley in 1801 as there is today. The following figures show this:

1801 - 4832
1811 – 4850
1824 – 4814 1019 houses
1828 – 4814 1010 houses
1831 – 4299
1841 – 4829
1851 – 4738
1861 – 4724
1871 – 4639
1881 – 4458
1917 – 2774 Ecclesiastical Parish, 3663 Civil
1926 – 211 Ecclesiastical, 3037 Civil
1934 – 2211 Ecclesiastical, 3216 Civil
1996 – 5,500

The reduction in the population figures was due to the depression of trade, when people moved away to find work elsewhere. They were attracted here in the early 1700-1800's, by the discovery of the richness of the minerals in the area and came from Wales and Staffordshire to make their homes here.

WATER SUPPLY FOR BROSELEY 1863/4 PRITCHARD MEMORIAL.

(According to some letters dated about 1862 written to newspapers/correspondence at the Shrewsbury Records Office).

According to correspondence from Frederick H Hartshorne to George Maw Esq of Benthall Hall and various newspapers letters discussing the water problem in Broseley, there seems to have been some grievance about a solution to the problem of water supply, which came from Mr Hartshorne. The following information from these letters is of great interest, describing how hard life was at the time, in the 1860's.

Before 1861 there was a deplorable deficiency of water in Broseley causing great suffering to the poor people. The scarcity of water since the exhaustion of the reservoir (5 quarts a day, not gallons) was so inadequate, poor people paid 4d per week for water and many were compelled to leave the well without water, any water they had was carried great distances, in all weathers. Private families and brewers paid large amounts of money weekly for the carriage of water.

The only water the Broseley people had was the Down Well (by the Haycop) and the Delph, this being only a pool filled with rain water and sewerage, near the centre of the town but described as filthy and foul smelling, with people being afraid to use it as it was too thick at times to ladle into a bucket.

The Down Well was about 600 yards from the main street, but when the weather was dry it was so hard to supply the people waiting to fill their buckets from the spring, often there was fighting as some spent all day and nights waiting for water for their families. One extract says that a person waiting at the well at 6 o'clock in the evening for a bucket of water, left at 3 o'clock the following morning. Another that the rain water from the Wesleyan School Room was sold for £7 per year.

During the winter when there were severe frosts and the water was even frozen on the Severn, poor people stood at the well for water for days and nights in the ice and snow with no shelter. One account mentions a poor woman who accidentally spilled a pan of water on the floor, for which she had just waited five hours and paid 3d, she had two children sick with scarlet fever who later died from the disease. She used water sparingly from weekend to weekend, finally using it to clean the floors.

The Delph was filled up in 1861 and the poor people from the higher parts of the town near Cape Street had to carry their water from a quarter to half a mile away.

It seems that Frederick Hartshorne discovered a water supply on his own property, he provided a pump with a good supply of water at his own cost, after much damage and trouble to himself.

At a public meeting in June 1861, where all present were witnesses, George Pritchard guaranteed Mr Hartshorne £10 per year without limitation for a supply of water for the public, which he offered to do on those terms. Persons present said they would have not hesitated to accept it themselves if the cost had been £10,000. Mr Hartshorne fulfilled his undertaking and his expenditure was made, Mr Pritchard later withdrew his guarantee privately to limit it to his lifetime. In an unusually dry year this supply of water proved to be sufficient for the whole town so that the Down Well was never emptied, no other source of water for any purpose being availale at that time.

A public meeting was called to propose a memorial to Mr Pritchard. One suggestion by the public was a Memorial Window in Broseley Church and a Memorial Fountain in the centre of the town, 'to supply the poor of the place with water' which seemed right. A good supply of water had been craved for at least a century, and to persons ignorant of the underlying intrigue, gave deep satisfaction. Mr George Pritchards last intended gift to the town was this useful supply of water, an appropriate memorial to his name and position.

After several discussions a stained glass window in the South side of Broseley Church was proposed and for defraying the expense of a fountain by which a supply of water may be obtained £500 raised by subscription. But it eventually led to the erection of a Memorial Church at Jackfield. A circular was issued for a meeting at the Town Hall, Bridgnorth on 3rd February 1862. Mr John Pritchard MP resolved not to continue his brother's concern in this matter and the committee determined they would neither pay the stipulated £10 per annum, nor reimburse Mr Hartshorne's outlay in finding water in Broseley.

At least honesty demanded that he should have been left in possession of the water, for he could then have obtained an ample return for his expenditure. Probably no scarcity would have been known had the committee acted less unfairly and retained the whole instead of only part of Mr Hartshorne's supply, as it seems that the supply was traced, intercepted and cut into before it reached Mr Hartshorne's property.

The Rev Cobbold avowed that to pay Mr Hartshorne's outlay was a debt of honour.

Mr Hartshornes property was Alison House, Church Street.

All Saints Church Broseley

PRITCHARD MEMORIAL

The Pritchard Memorial was erected in 1862, in memory of George Pritchard, a gentleman and native of the town, and late High Sherriff of the County, he was a prime mover for an improved water supply to the town.

After twelve months of arguments and debates, to decide what should commemorate his name, it was finally agreed to have a memorial in Broseley Square and a Church at Jackfield to replace the Red Church.

The memorial at Broseley was designed by Robert Griffiths of Bridgnorth, it was a handsome fountain of Grinshall stone built in the High Street in 1862, in the early decorated style, it was of an octagonal shape with four moulded arches, over each are ornamental gables with a scroll bearing an appropiate inscription over each arch. The roof which was of carved stone, terminated with an ornamental weather vane, rose from moulded eaves cornice decorated with ball flowers.

It was erected over a well, which was bricked over due to a strong taste of iron in the water, making it unusable. Because of this the iron drinking cups attached to the fountain with chains and the drinking bowls for the dogs, now relied on the rain water to serve their purpose.

When the new St. Mary's Church was built at Jackfield in 1863, as part of the memorial to George Pritchard, the old St Mary's, or Red Church was left to crumble and decay. It was built by Francis Turner Blythe in memorial to one of the female members of the family in 1759, the founder died in 1770 and a marble tablet was put in the church to his memory. It contained seating for 272 people in tall oak pews. It was a neat, red brick building with a square embattled tower crowned with pinnacles. The East windows contained beautiful coloured glass leaded with beautiful blue colour predominating. There was one bell inscribed with the name of Blythe.

The old church, taken down in 1961 because it was by now unsafe, gave rise to many weird ghostly tales of apparitions said to have been seen by local people, probably due to the mass burial of the unfortunate victims of the dreadful cholera disease when so many people died, this was about 1832, the last epidemic being recorded as 1875.

Pritchard Memorial, Broseley Square

BROSELEY LADY FORESTER HOSPITAL

According to records at Shrewsbury Records Office, there were letters about a water supply on the proposed site for the hospital in 1896, and a meeting was held at the Town Hall to discuss a report on the site and its valuation.

There was a draft agreement for the sale and purchase of six houses and a smithy garden as the site in 1900, and in 1901 a declaration as to lands at Broseley to be bought by Forester Charity trustees as the site of the cottage hospital, the area was called Main House or Miners Meadow on a Broseley Parish map dated 1840, near to the church.

The hospital was established in 1907, in Church Street, and was bequeathed to the people of Broseley by the Forester family, opened according to the only date I have seen, on 8th April 1907, supported over the years by locally raised public funds. It was for Broseley, Ironbridge, Madeley and Jackfield people, and used for convalescence by Wolverhampton patients, who loved the country feel here.

It contained 24 beds, plus special wards for patients under radium treatment. Wenlock Municipal Borough Small Pox Hospital was erected in 1903 costing £800, it had eight patients.

I have heard it said my mothers Aunt Poll was one of the first patients in Broseley Hospital in 1907, and that her father delivered the sand for building the hospital wall and the house the Miss Potts's had built on the opposite side of the road.

Entrance gates to Broseley Lady Forester Hospital, about 1950's

The local doctors referred their patients there and went to the hospital to treat them, and many babies of the area were born in the maternity ward there.

There was a Matron, nursing staff, kitchen staff/cleaners and gardeners, the produce grown in the gardens was used to feed the patients.

It was considered a very adequate asset to the community, dealing with accidents and dressing wounds etc. Doctors and surgeons came to the hospital from Shrewsbury and Wolverhampton to see and treat patients, clinics were held there too. There were huts in the grounds for the patients to sit in and enjoy the sunshine.

Broseley Lady Forester Hospital

The doctors in the town in the 1930/40's were Dr Fox Davies at Fifield, Barratts Hill and Dr Boon at Whitehall. Following them were Dr Sherlock Hoy at Fifield House, Barratts Hill and Dr Rupert Whitney at a surgery by Lloyds Bank in the High Street, later at a new surgery at Hockley Road in the 40/50/60's. The receptionists that I remember were Miss Turnbull, then Sheila Rowe for Dr Hoy and Sarita Watkins then Jean Williams for Dr Whitney.

We had two district nurses then that I remember, Nurse Maul and Nurse Gutsell, I know they were the local midwives in 1944, but they were here before then, and between them delivered many babies at home during their time, as well as attending to other sick patients at their homes. They delivered my twins at home in 1959, near the end of their careers, so had worked here for many years.

From the 1930's we attended Dr Hoy's surgery as he was our family doctor, I remember him as a nice, kindly man, he would chuckle with the children when he came on home visits. My mother used to say 'hide the newspaper' when he was coming on a home visit, as he would sit down and browse through it while he was there. Some used to offer him his favourite tipple of whiskey, but I wouldn't like to say if he accepted it. He was still at Fifield house in the 1970's, when Dr Bhageerutty came to practice at this surgery with him about 1975.

Old photo of Broseley Hospital and staff

Dr Whitney was the other doctor and between them they looked after the people of our town. The population has not varied much over the years, there are now approximately 5,500 people and it has not changed very much.

We didn't have to book appointments then, the surgery was held in a building on the side of Dr Hoy's house. If you were not well you just went to the surgery and waited your turn. The receptionist got your card out as you booked in, and took it to the doctor when your turn came. Morning and evening surgeries and house visits were the norm then and any problems the doctor could not deal with, the patient was sent on to a specialist.

In 1985 there was a threat by the Area Health Authority to close our cottage hospital, and at a public meeting called by the League of Friends of our hospital, held at the Victoria Hall on December 16 1985 a Hospital Action Group was set up, consisting of every society and public and political body in Broseley. A long drawn out fight took place but the hospital was closed in April 1989. In 1989 the trustees signed a 99 year lease, and in 1992 two housing associations started work on redevelopment of the site grounds. There are now several houses built where the hospital gardens used to be.
There is no local hospital to see you now, it is a Day Care Centre serving a different but needy part of the community, only in use because there was a very strong fight by the people to open it again after it was closed in 1989.

There was, and still is, a lot of fund raising and work done by the League of Friends and many others who are dedicated and work really hard to raise funds for our hospital, including a hospital shop worked by volunteers, to keep this hospital open.

The Day Care Centre open day was Sunday 15th October 1995, and they had the first patients the following week.

BARROW

Almshouses in Barrow were built by John Slaney a citizen and merchant of London, in his lifetime. He erected an almshouse at Barrow for 6 poor men and women, who must not be under the age of three score year and ten, past labouring, lame and unable to work, and needing means to live.

Barrow School

A school house for the free teaching of 20 children, and 6 acres of land to be laid out for gardens and orchards, to improve their lives. In his last will dated August 17th 1631, he gave, for the yearly maintenance of these, for ever, the following allowances, he gave weekly to the six (only) of the poor people in the almshouse 16d. Every second year he provided a gown, and hose and shoes, also one load of coal for their provision. He also paid for burials of these poor people, among many other things. Of the schoolhouse, he gave one wain load of coals yearly for the provision of fire for the master of the schoolhouse, and one for the scholars to burn in the schoolhouse in winter, where they should be taught. All repairs should be done through his appointed kinsman. He gave £10 per year towards the maintenance of the schoolmaster, for teaching 20 poor scholars.

It appears an exchange was effected in 1816 by Mr Forester, Lord of the Manor of Willey, and the John Slaney almshouses were taken down, being in need of repair, and a new one was built upon other land situated near the Parish Church of Barrow. This new almshouse was more commodious and comfortable than the old one and each house had a garden attached.

Barrow Church

CHURCHES

BROSELEY ALL SAINTS CHURCH, CHURCH STREET.

According to John Randall the exact date of Broseley Church is unknown, but about the twelfth century the Lords of Burwarsdley had a church erected, presumably the first. There is a presentation to the Chapel by the Prior and Convent of Wenlock on nomination of Lady of the Manor in 1322.

There is also a record in Shrewsbury Archives that mentions the earliest date of a register as 1570-1750 and a licence for a burial ground in 1595, burials before this date were at Much Wenlock, the Manor of Broseley stood within the bounds of the Church of St Milburgh there. The chapel at Broseley in 1291 was founded as a subject to the Mother Church of Wenlock, the oldest gravestone in the church dates at 1628, in 1201 the Church or Chapel of Burwardsley was valued at £6.13s.4d (John Randall).

There are records of 'sale of kneelings' in 1645 and 'surrender of seats' in 1618 and 1696, and a mention in a document at the Shrewsbury Archives states that in 1706 the church was in ruins, there appears to have been a new gallery in 1794/5. Plans showing the erection of the new church are dated around 1845.

Broseley Church

The present church was built on the same site as the one demolished in 1844, this was built of brick with the exception of the tower which was built of free stone, with sittings for 782 people. Some of the original character was preserved in the interior in the octagonal pillars and the pointed arches which supported the roof. In 1880 the churchyard was added.

The incumbent in 1840-1859 was the Honourable Reverend Orlando Watkin Weld Forrester M. he was followed in 1859-1873 by the Reverend R H Cobbold. In 1873 Reverend G F Lamb M.A. was rector for 36 years, and in 1909 the Reverend A C Howell B.A was rector until 1922. He was followed by the Reverend W A Warner M.C and in 1926, the Reverend Charles Strathnam Jackson M.A became rector of Broseley church for many years, he was still here in the 1940's.

The present church, All Saints, (on the site of St Leonards) was rebuilt in 1845 at a cost of £9,000, raised by voluntary contributions, and in consequence of a grant of £400 from the Incorporated Society, 694 of the sittings are free, and unappropriated forever. There was a sumptuous feast, enjoyed by all when the church was completed.

The foundations of a previous church were found on this site, dated from 1785 –1844, but the earliest records show that a church has existed in Broseley from very early times, probably from the pre Norman times. There seem to have been at least three other churches on this site, it has been said the one previous to the 1785 church was built of wood and burnt down in a fire.

The new church was dedicated to All Saints, with seating for 1200 people, neatly fitted with oak sitting and the roof was of grained timbers. The fine large East window is of great beauty, with its size and richness of colour, there is also a West window of stained glass, and a stained glass window of fine colours was erected in the North wall by the children of William and Elizabeth Thursfield in 1852 in memory of their parents.

A freestone structure consisting of nave chancel and side aisles, it had a square tower with 6 bells originally, increased to 8 in 1945, and a clock with three dials, the nave was separated from the side aisles by five pointed arches on each side, over the side aisles and at the west end were galleries, upon the latter was placed an organ.

There have been several alterations carried out within the church over the years.

The organ was moved in the early 1970's when the galleries had to be removed due to dry rot. Following the removal of the gallery the Chancel was re ordered a few years later and the choir stalls were removed. New choir stalls were erected and other improvements were carried out at a cost of £250 in memory of the late Miss Julia J Nicholas in 1890. The graveyard seems to have been added in 1880.

Broseley Church early 1900's

In 1929 there was a memorial Chapel on the North side to those who fell in the great 1914/18 war, and choir vestry on the South side, the Reverend at this time was Charles S Jackson, M.A. .

All Saints was famous for its church choir, which was considered one of the finest in the Diocese, outside the Cathedral. There were an average of 45 voices in this choir, with a very high standard of choral singing, they performed in many festivals and services through the years. The choir vestry was replaced by the present Lady Chapel in 1982, created in memory of Gerald Oakley (Reader from 1947– 81).

Church procession through the town

BAPTIST CHAPEL, CHAPEL LANE

The Baptist Chapel in Chapel Lane, Harris's Green was built in 1741, according to a leaflet to celebrate the 250th Anniversary that took place in 1991, it is the oldest place of worship in the town, and among the oldest in the country.

It was erected by Isaac Wyke a Broseley surgeon, who died age 79 in 1755 and he left the property he had purchased to the chapel, according to his will. Some of this property was purchased from Benjamin Legge (the Elder), one of the early manufacturers of the famous Broseley clay smoking pipes.

The Baptist Chapel attracted many middle class people and had a large number of trustees, the original trust deed of 1755 expressly states that when the trustees by death or otherwise are reduced to five in number the survivors are to appoint 14 others to act besides themselves. This may reflect the early persecution of Dissenters - the more trustees, the greater the protection at law in times of trial, especially as some of the trustees lived miles away, some of these included George Dukesell of Coalbrookdale, Mercer - a dealer in textile fabrics, Jeremiah Barker of Broseley, Jeremiah Jordan of Ludlow – farmer and George Brooks of Broseley, grocer.

It seems some of the property was sold over the past couple of centuries, but the chapel, ministers house, garden and pigsty, a cowshed, meadow and Corporation stock are still in the ownership of the trustees, though the house has not been occupied by a minister for many years. The field and cowshed were acquired by Deed of Gift in 1854 by descendant of Isaac Wyke and contains the interesting gift of 'all mines and seams of coal

Baptist Chapel built 1741

lying under the messuage and premises and land adjoining (the afore mentioned meadow)', most of the mining rights in the area belonged to the powerful landowners. This deed still stands.

In 1801 there were disagreements between members on points of doctrine, and on the 27th December 1801 a break away took place, the declaration was signed by 39 dissenting members. The Reverend in 1861 was Edward Jones.

The Old Baptist Chapel and schoolroom, by 1870 had fallen into a bad state of repair and was not really safe for services or Sunday school. Since the congregation was by this time very small, and poor, the trustees had no option but to appeal for public help, and a bazaar was held in the Town Hall in September 1871 to help clear off the debts. According to school records of that time, it was held on 19th September 1871. There was between £60 and £70 raised from this bazaar, and the Chapel re-opened for services on 10th September 1871 (D Mason leaflet).

Some of the events at the chapel in the 1900's were

Prize Distribution 21st January 1905, (an annual event) the recipients being Nora, Hilda and Lucy Tonkiss, Dorothy and Florrie Gough, Florrie Hall, Sarah and Ethel Beaman, Edith Chapman, May Boden, Elizabeth Beddoes, Maggie and Sarah George, Bessie, Nora and Edith Thomas, William Roden, John Everall, Harold Gough, William Chapman, Alfred and Thomas Beaman, Charles Jones, Fred and Charles Beddow, Jack Beaman.

February 18th 1905 Reopening of the chapel and school after it had been completely renovated.

September 23rd 1905 Anniversary services, hymns sung by the choir, Mr Richard Tonkiss at the harmonium.

In January 1910 Mr Sidney Gilpin replaced Mr Richard Tonkiss as organist.

April 29th 1911 The First wedding at the chapel took place, the first since it was built 170 years ago – between Mr Sidney Gilpin and Miss Eleanor Maud Atkins, the bride looked exceeding pretty in a blue dress with hat to match.

November 3rd 1911 A Harvest Festival, the church nicely decorated by willing workers.

August 3rd 1912 Mr H Jennison, secretary/organist of the church, leaving for America.

January 3rd 1914 The Sunday School children had their Annual Christmas Treat on Friday last, when about 60 sat down to an excellent tea. The prizes to the elder scholars consisted of wearing apparel, made and given by Mrs Pinner, Mrs Hall, Mrs Ball, Mrs Fletcher and others. The 'Round O' prizes of two bibles and two hymn books were given to Thomas Everall and Florrie Hall by Mrs Harry Evans. A Christmas tree, well laden with toys was a source of great delight to the children. A selection on the gramophone was given by Mr De Valle. Each child left for home with a mince pie and an apple.

April 21st 1919 Home coming entertainment for the local soldiers who had returned from the fronts, in the Great War. 60 soldiers enjoyed the spread.

July 5th 1919 Sunday School Anniversary, the large congregation enjoyed the singing of the children.

August 3rd 1929 Local success. Mr John Harrison, Baker and Confectioner of 1 High Street, Broseley, was awarded two special prizes for Hovis bread in the Hovis National Competitions held at Macclesfield on 17th July.

August 15th 1931 Sunday School Summer Treat on 5th, upwards of 80 scholars, friends and congregation met on a field kindly lent by Mrs H Onions, there were various games and sports, including netball, cricket and children's races for prizes. Other amusements were swings, Aunt Sally and the Bran tub. After tea in the schoolroom, they returned to the field for further games and little Louie Devall presented a silver mounted walking stick to Mr Thomas Denstone in appreciation of his services in conducting the singing at special services from time to time. After leaving the schoolroom later, each child received a bag of sweets.

August 6th 1932 On Wednesday about 40 children went to Church Stretton in motor coaches, where they had a good time climbing the hills. Each child had an ice-cream and a stick of rock. When they returned to Broseley at 4.15 they had tea. After tea a good time was spent with games and racing in a field in the Deer Leap, lent by George and Bert Onions of Barratts Hill Farm. Mr Correll of Mill House kindly lent his pony for pony rides for the children.

The old Sunday School room had been built in 1741 as a vestry to the Chapel, but in 1941 it was found to be too small for those using it and an appeal fund was set up with Mr Henry Evans as chairman, Mr Walter Oakley as secretary and Mr Frank Watling as treasurer, with a view to erecting a larger building for use as both a Sunday School and a place to hold functions. This was built just after the last war (1939/45) and has been used by the Chapel and the town since.

One of the annual events held by the four Non-Conformist churches Sunday Schools in Broseley was the 'Anniversaries' and they were very popular with the children, the girls were dressed in their best white smocked dresses and white ankle socks and shoes in the years after the war, and looked forward to being on the Anniversary, and to the outings that the churches took the children on to various places, they also held Sunday School Treats which meant half holiday from school.

A prize label to a Mrs Denstone dated 18th November 1895 was awarded by the 'Pleasant Monday Evening Class' and a ticket to a 'Tea Party' admission one shilling on Easter Monday 1860, showing some of the things that went on at that time.

The Baptist Chapel held its bi-centenary in September 1941 and its 250th anniversary in 1991, and is still used by Broseley people today. Most of this information has been taken from the The Old Baptist Chapel leaflet by Dennis Mason produced for the church's centenary, and documents loaned to me by Henry Pritchard.

BIRCHMEADOW CHAPEL Birchmeadow Road

In 1801 there were disagreements between members of the Baptist Church, on points of doctrine, on the 27th December a break way took place by 39 dissenting members. These members and others left the old chapel and shortly afterwards, in 1803 a new Chapel was built at the top of Birchmeadow, expense being borne by John Guest, iron master and George Crompton, draper, both of Broseley.

It was opened for worship to the people on the 31st August 1803 by Mr John Sharpe of Bristol, records show that in 1917 there were seatings for 300 in this chapel. In the graveyard were the tombs of John Guest and John Onions, and their families, both Broseley ironmasters of note, these tombs had beautiful cast iron rails around them and were in the grounds at the front of the chapel. There are records of baptisms, marriages and deaths for this chapel. The font is still in the main room, under the floorboards.

The Chapel built at Birchmeadow in 1803

The Coalport Bridge was cast by the Onions family at their foundry in Foundry Lane, the pattern design of the rails are all 'O's for Onions. They also built the first Iron boat to sail on the Thames.

This Chapel flourished during the 19th and earlier part of the 20th century, but in time it declined and was closed to public worship a few years before the last war.

The building became a centre for the Home Guards during the last war, later becoming the 'Elite' cinema, and then a private nightclub, The Bladen Club, licensed to sell alcohol. Many popular stars performed here including Kathy Kirby, in the early fifties.

In 1981 it was taken over by members of the local football teams and re-named the Athletic Club. Events held here then were very varied, discos, horse race nights, roller blading, variety shows, ladies nights, gentlemens nights, rummage sales, bingo, fancy dress, parties, presentation nights for the football clubs after their seasons had finished, also used by the BROADS, the local drama group – (their pantomimes were always so popular after Xmas, and still are), Xmas parties for the children, darts and domino teams.

Most of these events were used by - and for - the football teams to raise funds to help finance the cost of running these teams, a costly concern with the washing of the football strip, insurance, cost of pitch, referees and linesmen fees etc. What would the religious people have had to say if they had been around today, to see such a change in the use of their building.

It was purchased by Broseley Parish Council in September 1995, for use of a Community Centre, still to run as licensed premises. It was named the New Town Hall briefly, but there were some objections to this name and it was later re-named Birchmeadow Centre. It is still running today but there does need to be a lot of money spent on it to make it a place that people feel is appropriate for a nice time out in a decent environment, the council are still trying hard to get improvements done there, but it is a struggle to get the money to do this. The Town Hall was ideal for holding social events, and has been sorely missed.

Broseley High Street – outside the Lion Hotel

Broseley Memorial Green from back of the Delph

Old view of Church Street

BROSELEY METHODIST CHURCH, DUKE STREET

The old Methodist Chapel, demolished about 1965

The old Methodist Church as we remember it was built in 1796 and was enlarged in 1802. It has been altered at various times since then. It has a very interesting history being the first Wesleyan Methodist Church to be erected in the district. It was a large square shaped building, the white faced front facing towards Broseley High Street, with iron gates and railings around the low boundary wall.

John Wesley visited Broseley on two occasions, once in July 1774 and again in April 1780, when he held an open air service in Duke Street. This started the desire to build a church in Broseley to be called Wesleyan. In about the mid-nineteen hundreds the Primitive Methodist Church became obsolete, and the Wesleyans and Primitives joined together and were now known as the Methodist Church.

It has been used for Children's Anniversaries, Music Festivals, Rallies, the United Brotherhood etc over the years, together with the other churches in the town it has stood as a monument where people could worship and participate in some way in the service this church has to offer.

The Anniversaries were very popular with the children as described in the Baptist Church, they loved to sing together and dress in their best clothes, usually all in white, may be because it was in the Spring time. The Methodists were close members and could be seen on Sundays after their evening church service going for walks around Broseley together. They also had various outings and trips organised within the church, by the 'Crusaders Club' visiting many different places with other clubs. Mr Thomas, and Mrs Thomas of Mill Lane who died about 1993 did a tremendous amount of work for the church in their time, and there are lots of photographs taken on these outings and of the many things they participated in.

Crusaders group photo

Crusaders Scarborough 1950's

Another couple who deserve a mention for all the hours they have spent doing things for the church, are Les and Joyce Pugh. They have spent many hours running the Crusaders Club, especially after Mrs Thomas passed on, helping to keep Broseley children entertained and involved with all sorts of activities, as well as helping to keep the grounds around the church in good order and work for the church itself.
Over the years, despite continual care and renovation, materials perished and structures decayed and it became apparent that the building was beyond repair, the decision to abolish it was made after experts agreed that renovation work was out of the question.

The last service in the old Church took place on November 8th 1964. From then on services were held in the old schoolroom until the new Church was built and opened on 23rd October 1971.

THE CONGREGATIONAL CHAPEL (DUKE STREET) 1837 - 1950'S

The Congregational Chapel was built in 1837 (Kelly's Directories) with sittings for 250 people, it was bought from the Quakers who had been using it since then, by local Congregationals in February 1848. The original Quaker room was used as a schoolroom, the foundations visible in the burial ground are those of the chapel.

When Abraham Darby 1 came to Coalbrookdale in 1708 there were no members of the Society of Friends in the area on the North side of the Severn, but there was a meeting house at Broseley on the South side, built 1692, which he and his family attended, he was buried at the Quaker graveyard at Broseley.

This church was still being used in 1956 as my grandmother was buried there in April of that year but it was later demolished, there are papers at the Records Office referring to the closure about 1961/7. Most of the people who used the chapel then went to the old Baptist Chapel and some to the other churches.

There are photographs of chapel outings in the mid 1900's. There do not seem to be many records relating to this chapel in existence.

Jubilee Celebrations 1953 - Residents of Bridgnorth Road, Broseley

THE CATHOLIC CHURCH OF SAINT WINIFRIDE Barber St

Little was known of an early Catholic Church in Broseley, although the Catholic faith had been practised there, for many years. The present Church was built in 1979 according to a Commemorative Brochure produced in September 1989 to commemorate its 10th anniversary. Some of the information in the leaflet is as follows and mentions an earlier church.

Sale of Property - February 5th 1870, Broseley.
On Monday evening last 'Barbers Row' - A row of buildings of a very old type, almost in ruins – was auctioned by a Mr Enoch Leadbetter, wretched in appearance as in fact - as is the present building. The sale caused keen competition, and was purchased by Mr William Allen of Benthall Pottery.

Rumour has it that the property so purchased is for the purpose of erecting upon the site of these hovels, a chapel, for the use of the Roman Catholics. As far as can be ascertained this was the first attempt to establish a Roman Catholic Church in Broseley.

The report goes back 100 years to 1888 on the opening of a Roman Catholic Church: For several years the Roman Catholics of Broseley have been without a church, and have used the one at Madeley 2 miles away, but the growth of this religion has led to a permament place of worship being built, thanks to the effort of Father Bowen of Madeley and other friends.

The building, an iron one, was erected near the Town Hall probably Barber Street to accomodate 150 people. A small vestry adjoined it and a porch was built later. The cost amounted to £150 and the work was done by a Mr Marrian of Madeley.

The evening service at Madeley was discontinued and held at Broseley, at which there would be no morning service. A charge of one shilling each for admittance was made, and a collection was made at each service, there was a large attendance throughout the day. The services were fully choral and the organ was presided by Miss Martin of Bridgnorth. At 9 O'clock low mass was conducted by the Bishop, and at eleven, High Mass by Father Bowen.

There does not seem to be much information after this but Broseley Scout group was formed in 1912 and used the Catholic Church as their first headquarters.

Encased in corrugated iron, the chapel was of an iron frame structure and was dismantled, about 1915, by Oakley's Timber Hauliers and Contractors, a Catholic family, and conveyed to Ironbridge Railway Station then taken by rail to Birkenhead, probably for munitions.

The custodian was Mr Ben Fletcher who related this event. There was also an archway with a gas lamp top that was lit by the lamplighter, Mr Jim Colley, the archway remained for many years, and I remember it when I was a child.

My mother, and her sisters Betty Jones and Norah Jones, (my aunts), remember walking to Mass in Madeley during the 1930's, through Corbetts Dingle, over the Memorial bridge at Coalport and up the steep hill past what is now Blists Hill Museum, they also remember carrying mops and buckets to Madeley to clean the church. Christmas parties were held in the presbytery at Madeley for all the Catholic children of the area and they also have happy memories of outings to the seaside during the summer.

Broseley Catholics went to Madeley church by bus (owned by Parr's at this time) when I was a child in the early 1940's. The local priest realizing the difficulty of getting to Sunday Mass arranged the use of the Town Hall for Sunday mornings.

The total congregation at this time was 28. The things needed for Mass were transported down and back every Sunday morning, by John Kavanagh, (he was the local gas man/fitter) and he often had to sweep up the debris from the Saturday night dance before Mass could begin. Sadly the Town Hall was demolished in the early sixties. Our son was christened there in 1957.

The next site to be used for Mass was a private schoolroom at Fifield House belonging to Mrs Hoy, the doctor's wife, on Barratts Hill, confessions however were held in a private sitting room. I have been told this was at Rooneys house.

In 1960, the present site in Barbers Row was soon to be re-discovered to be the property of the Catholic Church although no church building had been present for many years, a semi permanent building, an old army hut was obtained from RAF Cosford by Greg Rooney, and aided by several men from the parish the site was cleared and the hut re-erected as a church. £17 was paid for all the benches.

The new Catholic Church built 1979/80

The present building is a tribute to the Catholic people of Broseley who persevered through many difficult situations to ensure the survival of the Catholic faith and tradition in Broseley today. The evacuees from Liverpool who came to Broseley during the war and who made their homes here were mostly Catholics and remained staunch members of the church.

When we were children, every Sunday afternoon we went to Sunday School at an old lady's called Mrs Ford at her home, in Carvers Road - next door to Hockley Hall. She taught the Catechism to Broseley children for many years. Sunday mornings we had to go to Madeley Catholic Church, by Parr's bus.

The new church was built in about 1979/80.

RED CHURCH OR ST MARY'S JACKFIELD

A chapel dedicated to St Mary was built in Jackfield/Broseley in 1759 by Mr Francis Turner Blythe, it was situated on a hill overlooking Jackfield, a part of the parish some distance from the church. Called the Red Church by the locals.

It was red a brick building with a neat interior and a square embattled tower crowned with pinnacles, it had one bell and a nave and chancel. On the South side there was a tablet to the memory of Alexander Brodie Esq. ironmaster of Calcutts who died 5th June 1830. Another neat tablet remembered the founder of the church F T Blythe who died 22nd September 1770 aged 61, also a tablet to Thomas Carter Philips who died in 1783. It was referred to as the Chapel of Ease in 1851. The Rev R H Cobbold was at the church at this time.

There are many stories to be told about the Red Church as it has always been said it was haunted by a lady in grey, many people over the years have been at the church at midnight, waiting for the ghost to appear.

The story of the ghost haunting the Red Church is that Lady Mary Blyth wanted a church for the Jackfield people, but she died before it was done. Lady Mary had wanted the church built facing east to west – overlooking the river, but as she died before the church was built, and she was buried at Broseley Church, the building of the church was started with it facing the other way towards Broseley Church, over the fields, to where she was buried. She also requested that she be reburied at the new Church when it was built.

The story told is that each morning when the workmen went to work, the work they had done the previous day was scattered about the place. So two workmen stayed there at night to watch for the culprit. As Broseley church chimed midnight, the form of a lady appeared, she scattered the day's work about – then vanished.

The following night the builder himself watched and saw the apparition, a lady in grey. The parson and a party of other people visited the site at midnight, and the 'lady' told them she would not be content until the church was built as she had wished, facing east to west, and she was reburied there. This request was agreed to by the parson's party and the 'lady' vanished.

The Red Church 1870

The church was built facing the right way, finished, consecrated and opened two years later. Lady Blyth's body was re-interred at the Red Church and the spectre was never seen again.

Several years after the church was built there was a cholera epidemic in the area, said to have been brought up the river on the barges from Bristol. The cholera victims were buried at the Red Church, but it has been said that cholera deaths were not buried on consecrated ground, and that the burials were in a field near to the church, called the 'Cholera piece'.

There was a spring, or well in a field by the church, and the locals, who were very superstitious and afraid of the cholera, thought that if they anointed themselves with brandy, then washed or drank at the well, they would recover the cholera – which many did.

There is a tale of a man with the cholera, who after drinking the brandy was found in a drunken stupor and taken for dead. The funeral was taking place, in the new ground near the church, when a groaning sound was heard coming from the coffin, when it was opened the man sat up wanted to know where he was – the cholera had left him.

These were the tales told of the Red Church when I was young, whether there is any truth in them, I do not know.

The Red Church was deemed unsafe due to under mining for minerals, and fell to ruin. A new church, St Marys, was built at Jackfield in 1863, as a memorial to George Pritchard, the late High Sheriff of Shropshire. He was born and died in Broseley.

The Red Church was demolished in 1961.

THE MISSION CHURCH - BROSELEY WOOD

The Mission Rooms were used by the Primitive Methodists in 1851, and by the Church Mission in 1929. It is known that concerts were held there at some time, too. There are reports of this Mission being used as a school in the late 1800's. I have been told that this was used in the 1950's as a Youth Club, and boxing was done there too at this time. This property is now a private house.

The Mission Rooms or Chapel, Sycamore Road, Broseley Wood

BENTHALL CHURCH

The Mission Chapel, Sycamore Road, Broseley Wood – probably early 1900's

Benthall Church is a very old building, in the grounds of Benthall Hall, it has been written that it may have been a private chapel to the Hall, dedicated to a Welsh missionary St Brice, the original chapel may have dated back to the 11th century. A church existed here before 1221, and Benthall became a separate parish at the time Elizabeth 1 reigned.

The church was damaged during the Civil War and rebuilt about 1667, it was then re-dedicated to St Bartholomew. A porch and extension at the west wing were added about 1893. All that remains of the old church is a Saxon font and some 13th century decorated floor tiles. The pulpit is Jacobean with three carved panels.

There is a sundial in the south wall, added in the late 1800's and restored in 1962. Below it is a lions head, the mouth forms an entrance to a beehive in the church gallery, often used by bees. The church is still used today.

Many of the old Benthall families have been buried in Benthall churchyard, some of their headstones now lean against the boundary walls as in many cemetery's today. There are not many graves left there now, the churchyard is grassed over and cut to keep it tidy and there is a new burial ground just across from the old one where the people today now bury their loved ones.

BENTHALL HALL

The early history of the village of Benthall is recorded in the Domesday Book as a part of Wenlock. Before the time of Edward the Confessor it belonged to the Priory of Wenlock. The first documented member of the family was Anfrid de Benetala, (d.after 1128) who was probably Lord of the Manor, they are said to have been here before the Norman Conquest.

Although there must have been a house here earlier as family records date from about 1100, the first recorded reference to a house dates from 1250 when Philip de Benthall (d.c.1281) gave Buildwas Abbey some land between Benthall and Buildwas, with the right to carry coal and stone over his land in Benthall Edge. The earliest part of the existing house dates from about 1500 to 1520, but this is not visible and the main building seen by visitors dates from 1585.

At the time of the Civil War, in 1643, Lawrence Benthall owned the estate and he was a supporter of King Charles 1, Benthall was one of the Kings garrisons, but in 1645 the Royalist stronghold at Shrewsbury fell to Parliamentary control and Benthall was taken over by them. Benthall and Broseley were very important coalfields at this time, producing 30,000 tons of coal a year, and the Parliamentary leaders prevented the coal being taken by the River Severn to the royalists at Bridgnorth and Worcester and beyond.

The importance of the position of Benthall Hall was known by the Kings army, and an attack was made on the Hall by the royalist forces of Bridgnorth, Ludlow and Worcester in the same year, to try to recover it. However several of the attackers were killed after a hard battle, and they were forced to withdraw.

Lawrence and Katherine's son Cassius (1623-46) was taken prisoner at the fall of Shrewsbury, and after making his escape he was promoted to colonel at the age of twenty three. He was killed in 1646 when the King's last field army was destroyed at Stow-on–the-Wold. In 1651, after being defeated at Worcester, King Charles 1 went as a fugitive to Boscobel House, where he intended to escape to Wales. On reaching Madeley, he found all the river crossings guarded by enemy soldiers, and he returned to Boscobel, where it was said, he was hidden in an oak tree. It seems that the King and his friends may have been trying to get to Benthall Hall, just across the river on the opposite bank to Madeley Court.

The medieval village of Benthall was just to the north of the Hall, it was razed to the ground in 1645 during the Civil War when Benthall, after falling to the Parliamentary forces, was besieged by the Royalists. The only surviving buildings of the original Benthall village are the timber-framed barns at Benthall Farm, near to the Hall, now farmed by private tenants.

The Hall was the home of the Benthall family from the 16th century, until 1843 when it was sold, and was bought back into ownership of the Benthalls about 1934. In the 1940's open cast coal mining took place in a field by the chestnut trees, this was refilled and landscaped and the fields are now pastures for cattle with new trees planted, recreating the country setting for a lovely country house. The avenue of chestnut trees, set in the fields in front of the Hall was the original entrance to the Hall, this was changed in the 18th century, the way in now is still called 'the avenue' but is a road which turns off from the Broseley/Much Wenlock Road to the Hall and church.

Benthall Hall

It lies in an impressive setting, less than a mile from the Severn Gorge, high above the River Severn, in woodlands that slope downwards into the valley below. Coal, fireclay and limestone have been mined in the Benthall area for over 700 years, the profits from mining minerals and farming helped to keep the house in good repair. Limestone was quarried at Pattens Rock in Benthall Edge until 1934 and is a land mark in that area today, the remains of the old pits and quarries can still be seen in the woods, despite the trees and bushes which grow rampantly everywhere hiding these relics from the past. The walk through Benthall Edge has been used and enjoyed by many people over many years.

The appearance of the Hall was well designed when built and is much the same today as was at the end of the 16th century, with the charm of the five gables, the two five faced two storey bay windows, the parapets and the four 16th century chimneystacks, built of moulded brick, a lovely old house in a fine setting. The entrance porch seems to have been added after the wall behind it was built, as it contains a hiding place that may have been built after 1583 to shelter Catholic priests fleeing persecution. The inside of the house has wonderful decorated plaster ceilings and wood panelling, paintings and porcelain.

The house was sold to the 2nd Lord Forester of Willey Hall in 1844, and until 1930 was occupied by various tenants, the most notable in 1860 being George Maw, a distinguished botanist and tile manufacturer, whose tile works – with his brother Arthur – were on Benthall Bank, but later moved to premises at Jackfield. The gardens created by George Maw, grew many alpine plants and bulbs, with a large variety of crocus species, still flowering in the gardens there today. The dovecote seems to have been built, in the rose garden, by Robert Bateman who lived at the Hall from 1890 to 1906, they also laid out the terraces and rockeries.

In 1934 the property came up for sale again and may have been shipped off to America, but it was bought by Mary Clementina Benthall, granddaughter of Edward Benthall. He was a judge in Bengal in 1843, and had tried to buy the property then, but he was outbid by Lord Forester while he was in India. She and her husband James Floyer Dale (who was Edwards grandson) changed their name from Dale to Benthall, and she had the added interest of being descended through her mother's family, from John Penderel one of the five brothers who had saved Charles 1 at Boscobel.

James Floyer Benthall died in 1942 and in 1958 Clementina was going to leave the estate to her cousin Sir Paul Benthall, another grandson to Edward. Sir Paul persuaded her to leave it to the National Trust, it was repaired in about 1960, by members of the Benthall family, the National Trust and the Historic Buildings Council. Mary Clementina died in 1960 and Sir Paul and Lady Benthall became the first tenants of the National Trust from 1962 to 1985. James and Jill Benthall became tenants in 1985, and finding the gardens in need of attention planted clematis, shrubs and roses to create colour in the summer season and an herbaceous border in the walled kitchen garden. Richard and Stella Benthall who now live at the Hall, continue to look after the grounds and gardens today. The house is open to the public twice a week from April through to September each year as a National Trust building and is well worth a visit.

SCHOOLS

Broseley National Schools (Boys, Girls and Infants) was built in 1854.
Broseley Wood School at Legges Hill opened 12 Feb 1892.
Benthall school opened 28 October 1872 at the Floyer Hall.

On 7th February 1845 there was a draft conveyance between Francis Blithe Harries/ Wm.Egerton Jefferies to the Rector and Church Wardens for a piece of land for the site of the erection of a school in Broseley, to improve the facilities for teaching the children here. The National School foundation was laid in 1854 and the school was built the following year, at a cost of £1600 - attendances 300.

Previous to the new school being built, the school was held in a spacious room 61x21 feet, over the Market Hall, the average attendance was the 195 , the new school was enlarged in 1876 to take in 550 children. The school at Broseley Wood took in 110 children. Children had to pay to attend school in those days, the children not attending were chased up by the Attendance Officer.
Before this time the schools in the town were privately run, some of the names as follows:

1829-42 William Childs Academy and Day School
1829-42 Mrs Onions (Ladies day and Boarding)
1835 William Thomas
1835 Misses Wyke (Ladies boarding)
1840 Mary Ann Ball
1851 Miss Helen Bayliss(Ladies Boarding)Church St
1861 Sarah Jones, Harris's Green
1871 Greenhalg (Ladies Boarding) Church St
1885 Miss Dawson(Boarding and Day School)Alison House Church St. successor to Miss Hobday.

The way of life before my time was fascinating, looking back over old school books it is very interesting to compare the way children were taught in 1863, the children who started school were named, and many of these families still live in the area one hundred and forty years on, ages were given too.

Children seem to have been admitted and withdrawn, then re-admitted at any time, some of the names at the time were William Barratt, John Southorn, John Sherwood, R Tonkiss, J H Nock, G Farmer, G Overend, Dudley, Green, Hughes, Pearce, Woollan, Fellows, Rowe, Wilde, Wilkes, Jones, Harsthorne, Gough, Broadhurst, Tench, Goodall, Gittens, Bradeley, Shaw, Dodd, Chaddock, Oswell, Leadbetter, Clarke, Foster, Cleobury, Kelsey, Griffiths, Headley, Taylor, Corfield, Pountney, Sargeant, Simmonds, Onions, Bagnall, Evans, Bowen, Boden, Whale, Clinton, Hassall, Price, Hayes, Golding, Lane, Bullock, Edwards, Venn, Hurdley, Owen, Davis, Meredith, Adams, Garbett, Ashton, Bulan, Smallman, Stokes, Brown, Wall, Posting, Chadwick, Wood, Golling, Baxter, Acton, Cox, Bennett, Bromley, Aston, Fletcher, Goodall, Andrews, Church, James, Russell, Plant, Wilkinson, Ward, Lloyd, Barker, Harris, Smith, Thompson, Beaman, Miles, McCoy, Wright, Oakes, Reynolds, Hickman, Brazier, Cartwright, Thomas, Oakley, Langford, Hubbard, Rhodes, Norry, Nicklin, Bagley, Gallier, Weekes, Mantle, McGowan, McCormick, Steventon, Roberts, Pinner, Senior, Smith, Benbow, Bright, Legge, Allen, Cross, Roden, Wiggins.

Holidays were given for various reasons, other than the usual annual holidays like Easter and Xmas etc. Sunday School and School treats were popular and the Broseley and Benthall Wakes. The Fair and Circus, Sports days and Flower Shows were usually half-day holidays. More unusual events were 'Day of Humiliation for the Cattle Plague' – 'Bazaar in the Town Hall' – 'Wild Beast Show' – 'Wombells Show' – 'Clown Cricketers' – 'Magic Lantern Show' – Royal and local dignitaries weddings – and funerals, Elections, Church events, School concerts, 'Fur and Feather Show' – Lecture 'Band of Mercy League' – Harvest Festivals, Broseley Athletic Sports days, Fetes, Jubilee Rejoicings, and Queens birthday to mention some special events. Also the Market Hall Club walked the town. Elections were held in the schools.

Looking at the Medical problems in the nineteenth century, Scarlet Fever was one of the nastier illnesses, with Whooping Cough and Measles being prevalent through the whole of the Registers. Mumps and Chickenpox were also around and much time was lost through coughs and colds, sore throats and sickness. Ringworm and Scabies were quite common too. An Elizabeth Evans of the 3rd class died from Scarlet Fever in 1877 and Alice and John Hurdley were sent home as their sister had the fever, the room was sprinkled with Candys Fluid and all children with sore throats were sent home. The school was closed when there were epidemics.

The school had regular visitors at that time, the School Attendance Officer, the Church Rectors, Mr & Mrs Bathurst, The Misses Potts, Thorne and Davey, Mr and Mrs Pritchard just to mention a few and of course the School Nurse.

The weather was interesting to read about –

27/1/1866 snow 2 foot thick	23/12/1874 14" snow fell
5/6/1885 weather very hot	7/7/1886 weather very hot indeed

Other days mentioned 'very wet all day' – 'severe weather' – 'cold, snowy weather'. The winters seemed to have been much colder and the summers much warmer then compared to our changing seasons and climate in year 2000. The school was closed in extreme weather conditions.

The lessons done by the children then were Scripture, Arithmetic, History, Reading, Writing, Numbers, Needlework, Knitting, Alphabet, Object Lessons, Gallery Lessons and Moral Quality. The classes were examined regularly and if unsatisfactory, more attention was given to the subject needing it, to bring it back up to the required satisfactory standard. Carols and Hymns were taught too, some being 'There is a Green Hill Far Away' and 'There's a Friend for Little Jesus'. The Teachers for the Infants Department consisted of Head Mistress (which seemed to change quite often), Pupil Teachers and Monitors. In 1865 the Mistress was Elizabeth Willoughby, Pupil Teachers were Martha Philips, Mary Wase and Mary Hepple.

Some of the events which took place are of interest, punishments for telling lies, stealing, throwing stones, coming to school late, being unruly in the street, using bad words, playing truant, breaking windows and one boy cutting another boy with a penknife. There were many children caned for these offences.

Some of the absenteeism was due to sickness, but many of the parents could not afford to pay the school fees, on 31/8/1863 handbills were given to the children of intended admission fee rise to 2.386 (would this be 2d)?

Schooling was paid for some children by the Board of Guardians.

A new school opened at Benthall, at Floyer Hall on 28/10/1872, some Benthall residents named as M T E and J Cartwright and R Shaw left their school to attend there.

4 children died, two in 1875, one of inflammation and one burnt to death. In 1877 one died from Scarlet Fever, one accidentally shot by his brother.

The children had a treat each Christmas presented by Mr and Mrs J Pritchard of a bun and some prizes of books.

There was an exhibition of curiosities and articles of Chinese manufacture, girls were taught to knit, boys to sew and the children had to pay for any slates broken as they used slates to do their lessons on.

The annual School Treat must have been quite a special day as a lot of thought and preparation seems to have been put into it. The children met at 1.30, walked through the town headed by a band of music, then on to the church – except the little ones – where after a short service they returned to school where a good tea was provided, all seemed to enjoy it thoroughly. They then went to the Dunge Field and amused themselves with various games till 7.30pm. The field was kindly lent by E Potts Esq. and they each had a toy and a bountiful supply of sweets and gingerbread to take home.

What a vast difference in the education so many years ago to the way schools operate in the 21st century. The schools in Broseley today have a computer room, a nice playground, go swimming – on buses to swimming pools outside our town, and quite a wide variety of choice with lessons. Most of the children wear school uniforms, and the central heating is a vast improvement on the old smoky fires and stoves used many years ago.

Broseley School built in the 1850's, now our Health Centre

Old photograph of Broseley School

We now have a junior school at Dark Lane, opened 31st October 1967 and the John Wilkinson School at Coalport Road, opened in September 1977. We also have a school at Barrow. After the age of eleven Broseley children go to William Brookes School at Much Wenlock, I have been told there are about eight buses of our children who go to Wenlock each school day. Some choose to go to the Abraham Darby School at Madeley and some to the Endowed School at Bridgnorth. Because of the situation of no senior school here, leisure facilities in Broseley are very sparce.

Broseley C of E School, Dark Lane year 2000

John Wilkinson School, Coalport Road year 2000

Pattern Boys - Never absent, never late 1898

Model Girls 1897 - Never absent, Never late

Pattern Boys 1897 - Never absent, never late

Broesley School Group about 1925

Broseley School Group about 1929

Broseley School Group about 1944

Broseley School class about 1970

Legges Hill School Broseley Wood

Floyer Hall, was once Benthall School

BIRCHMEADOW PLAYING FIELDS

Since 1980 most of the Broseley children have gone to senior schools at Madeley, Bridgnorth or Much Wenlock, about eight buses (free) go to Much Wenlock daily on school day's, I believe transport to the other schools has to be paid for by the parents. A strange occurrence, considering we have a population of approximately 5, 500 people in Broseley, Benthall and Barrow, while Much Wenlock have just over half this figure. This has resulted in a Leisure Centre being built at Much Wenlock where the school is, leaving the larger populated Broseley with no recreational facilities, other than the Birchmeadow Playing Fields, which caters for football (8 teams a season) and has a small Play Area for the smaller children. There is a play area in Park View, originally put there by the residents, but has now been up graded by the Town Council.

There were new changing rooms built on the Birchmeadow in 1990, after the roof was ripped off the old ones by a severe storm, injuring two people. Negotiations had been going on for about eight years with Bridgnorth District Council, who own the Playing Fields, for new changing facilities when this incident happened. £9,000 was spent on renovating the children's Play Area to a decent standard in 1993, by the Birchmeadow Committee of Management, plus a new piece of playground equipment costing £15,000 bought with grants and money from the Birchmeadow Committee, District and Parish Councils, in 1995.

The Birchmeadow Playing Field from Cockshutt Lane

Opening of the new Changing Rooms June 1990, above people who had given donations, football representatives and District and Town Councillors and BMPF Committee.

There have been moves made to try to get more leisure facilities in this area in the future, but so far they have not been successful.

There have been different stories about the history of the Birchmeadow Playing Fields told over the years, but according to documents relating to this land it was left by Mrs Bathurst to her nephew Thorn-Pudsey in 1924, who then sold it to the Trustees of Broseley Victoria Institute for £500, approximately 9.724 acres, for the use and benefit of the Institute and members. The Trustees were J A Downes, G Potts, D L Prestage and R A Instone, and the Cockshott Mound, 3.659 acres, was purchased by these same trustees and N Fox-Edwards, from Weld-Foresters Willey Estate Company on 16/12/1927 for the sum of £35.

In 1937 the surviving trustees J A Downes and G Potts, donated the Playing Field to the Mayor, Aldermen and Burgesses of the Borough of Wenlock, a resolution was passed by the Committee and majority of the members of the Victoria Institute that all land pass to the Borough, subject to the covenants, conditions and stipulations restrictive to the user, shall be held by the Borough for the sole purpose of a free Public Recreation ground and Playing Field for the inhabitants of the Broseley Ward, forever. When the Borough of Wenlock was dissolved, the ownership was conveyed on 1/4/1966 to Broseley Parish Council.

On the 18/6/1968 part of the Cockshutt Mound was transferred to Salop County Council for road widening at Cockshutt Lane. On the 27/2/1975 Broseley Parish Council sold the Playing Fields to Bridgnorth District Council, approximately 13 acres for the sum of £2,000, the purchaser to observe the covenant and conditions as above. The Birchmeadow Playing Fields now belong to Bridgnorth District Council. According to a report in the Bridgnorth Journal of 20/11/1992 of which I have a copy, it was said at a Broseley Parish meeting in September 1992 that no money changed hands at this transaction, but £2,000 worth of work was done on the field.

A lot of voluntary work has been done for the playing field over the years, by the football teams and people interested in the football pitches. There are no netball or tennis facilities for girls, or cricket teams on the playing field. We do have a very good private tennis and cricket club, both recently renovated with lottery money. There have been many efforts made to increase the usage of this fine field over the years, but it always goes back to the old cliché, money. It would be nice to see it used for fun days, fund raising and local events, by local organizations, but sadly, the insurance costs for public liability seem to put people off pursuing the venture.

THE VICTORIA HALL

The Victoria Hall was built in 1837 and was once known as the Gospel rooms.

Billiards were played in the hall by the men of the town. It had 3 or 4 big tables in it, card tables where the men played crib, and seats all around for the people to watch the games of billiards. There was a committee and the membership cost four shillings a year. It was closed for sometime after the war.

The Victoria Hall

Members of the Victoria Hall Recreation Room Club at the buildings official opening in 1904.
Kindly donated to enhance the book by the Ironbridge Gorge Museum.

In March 1971 the Victoria Hall was conveyed by Trust Deed to the Rural District Council of Bridgnorth, to be held upon trust for the use of the people of the Parish of Broseley, and the neighbourhood, for recreation and leisure time occupation, meetings, lectures and classes with the object of improving the conditions of life for the said inhabitants as the committee think fit, the Council being the Custodian Trustees of the Charity. The first Trust Deed was dated 9/11/1904, in March 1971, with the approval of the Charity Commissioner's, the Victoria Hall was sold to the Bridgnorth Rural District Council for the sum of £2,350.

The Victoria Hall now has its own licensed premises and is used for badminton, indoor bowls, social functions, weddings and parties etc. Over the years a lot of voluntary work has been done by Broseley residents to raise money for the improvements done to this building, as well as the voluntary services.

BROADS

BROADS is the name of a Broseley drama group, they celebrated 21 years together in the year 2001.

According to the programme of this year's pantomime called Cinderella, the first panto was Aladdin performed at Dark Lane School Broseley by the P.T.A starring the Head Master the late Philip Spearman as Wishee Washee.

The Director was Mike Kaiser who after the success of Aladdin, encompassed the talents of other Broseley groups - The Amethysts Players, Victoria Players and the John Wilkinson PTA to broaden the 'acting net'. One year later BROADS was officially begun and they performed Cinderella at the Athletic Club in 1980.

This club is now renamed the Birchmeadow Centre since it was purchased by the Town Council in about 1994. In the early 90's their base was the Cricket Club for five or six years.

This club has been, and still is, very popular with the local people, especially the annual pantomimes. One reason is that the actors are well known to Broseley people, especially early on with Sheila Picken, Ida Tookey, Ken and Norma Holloway, Joan and Mike Banks, Brian Haycock, Margaret Owen, Sandra Jones, a great team with Mike and Di Kaiser, Cherry and Alan Jones, Ann and Chris Whall, Debbie Pritchard, Lucy Hudson, Frank Williams, Cynthia Tench, Sheena Selkirk and many more who have come and gone over the years, too many to mention but who have given pleasure and enjoyment to so many people. They encourage children to join in with these shows too.

A lot of work and cost is involved putting the plays etc on stage, making costumes, scenery and props amongst many things. Time and dedication by many people writing, directing, lighting, music, make up – the work is endless. But these people are very dedicated and have won many awards over the past years for their efforts.

It is such a shame that Broseley has not got a better building for the Broads to stage their shows, and indeed to encourage other people to do things in our town, there is a desperate need for a decent community/leisure Hall or Centre here.

They have won many accolades including the All England Theatre Festival in 1997. They have won numerous best director and best actor awards at the Shropshire Drama festival and the Wellington Theatre Festival for the adult and youth sections, a record to be proud of.

The pantomime in 2003 was Aladdin, very well attended, as usual.

Broads pantomime Aladdin 2002

FOOTBALL IN BROSELEY BOYS SCHOOL
22 SEPT 1923 TO 26 JUNE 1937

FOREWORD:
It seems that Charles Ashby, Headmaster was very keen on football and made sure that the school team took part in as many competitions as possible, but after Mr Wilkinson became Headmaster in Aug 1933 the interest in football declined. In fact although the Broseley Hospital Cup was run in 1936 - 1938 and 1939 and the school team must have taken part in it, the school has no record of any game.

Sat 22nd September 1923
A Friendly football game between Madeley C/E School and Broseley C/E School at Madeley and an attempt made to inaugurate a school league. A win for Madeley 6-5.

Thurs 16th October 1924
The Headmaster, Mr Ashby, wrote to Messrs Shaw, Wignall and Wragg, Headmasters at Madeley C/E Boys, Madeley Wesleyan and Ironbridge C/E Schools respectively concerning the formation of a schools football league.

Thurs 3th Feb 1925
Registers closed at 1.30pm in order that the school football team could leave early in the afternoon to play Jackfield in the 1st Round of the Shropshire County Shield competition. Result a draw 1-1.

Wed 4th Feb 1925
Registers closed at the same time as yesterday. The school football team played Madeley Wood on the Birchmeadow at 3.30pm in the 1st Round for the Mid Shropshire Cup and won 1-0.

Thurs 26th Feb 1925
The replay football match between Jackfield and Broseley took place this afternoon. Mr Brooks was the referee. Jackfield won.

Mon 2nd March 1925
Jackfield who defeated Broseley in the 1st Round for the County Shield lost to Madeley C/E today 3-0.

Fri 13th March 1925
Registers close at 1.30pm. 1st football team left school at 3.35pm in order to play a friendly match with Madeley Wood at Hill Top, Ironbridge.

Wed 18th March 1925
The 1st Round football match on the Birchmeadow for the Madeley Tradesmens Shield between Ironbridge and Broseley ended in a win for Broseley 6-0. Kick off 4.15

Fri 27th March 1925
Friendly football match on the Birchmeadow between Broseley and C.B.Dale. Result C.B.Dale 2 Broseley 1. Kick off 4.30pm

Mon 30th March 1925
Friendly football match on neutral ground (Mr Ball's field) between Broseley and Madeley Wood. Result draw 2-2. Kick off 4.15pm.

Sat 2nd May 1925
The Broseley boys having made a draw with Shifnal boys during the Easter holidays in the Semi-Final of the Tradesmens Shield, the replay took place today at 2.30pm on the Birchmeadow when Broseley won 3-1. Over 30/- was taken by the sale of tickets, 17/- being given by the Headmaster to the Shifnal Sportsmaster to pay travelling expenses.

Mon 18th May 1925
The Final for the Madeley Tradesmens Shield between Broseley and Madeley C/E took place at Madeley at 6.30pm, and resulted in a win for Madeley.

Wed 16th September 1925
The first match of the season took place on the school field this evening between a School 11 and an Old Boys 11. The kick off was at 6.30, the result was a win for the Old Boys 6-5.

Wed 7th October 1925
Broseley played their 2nd match of the Boro of Wenlock schools football league this afternoon on the Knowle when their opponents were Madeley Wesleyan. Kick off 4.20pm. Referee Mr A B Wignall. Result Broseley 14 Madeley Wesleyan 0

Mon 12th October
Registers closed at 1.30pm so that the school football team could play Madeley Wood a friendly match on the Knowle. Kick off 3.40pm. Result a draw.

Fri 30th October 1925
Broseley played their 3rd league match this afternoon against Jackfield at Jackfield. Kick off 3.30pm. Result Broseley 5 Jackfield 1.

Wed 4th November 1925
Broseley played their 4th league match on the Knowle this afternoon, their opponents were Shifnal. Result Broseley 8 Shifnal 1.

Wed 18th Nov 1925
Broseley played their 5th league match v C.B.Dale Secondary School. Kick off 3.30pm on the Regatta Field. Result C.B.Dale 4 Broseley 2.

Sat 21st Nov 1925
The Boro of Wenlock Elementary Schools Football team played Kings Norton on the Madeley Town ground in the 1st Round (Preliminary) for the English Schoolboys Shield. Kick off 2.30pm. 4 Broseley boys were in the Boro team viz Harold Oakley (left back), Percy Weston (left half), Alfred Watson (centre half) and Ernest Humphries (outside left), the result of the match was 3-2 in favour of Kings Norton. The Boro team was severely handicapped in so far that the centre forward chosen could not play, thus necessitating a last minute change in the forward line.

Fri 12th March 1926
The football match between Ironbridge and Broseley arranged for this evening was postponed by a message from Mr Wragg. This league fixture should have been played last December.

Tues 16th March 1926
6th league match at the Birchmeadow Broseley v Ironbridge ended in a draw 3-3.

Tues 23rd March 1926
7th league match at Madeley Wesleyan. Result Broseley 8 Madeley Wesleyan 0.

Wed 21st April 1926
The return match with Shifnal in the Boro of Wenlock league was played at Shifnal this evening. The result Shifnal 3 Broseley 1.

Wed 5th May 1926
The return match with Madeley Wood was played at Castle Green this evening. The result was Broseley 3 Madeley Wood 0.

Sat 8th May 1926
Broseley played Chelmarsh at Bridgnorth in the 1st Round of the Windsor Clive Cup. The result was a win for Broseley 11-0.

Tues 18th May 1926
Broseley played Highley (last seasons finalists) on the Old Track Bridgnorth in the semi-final for the Windsor Clive Cup. Kick off 7.00pm. Result Broseley3 Highley2.

Sat 22nd May 1926
Broseley played St Leonards on the Old Track Bridgnorth in the final of the Windsor Clive Cup. Broseley won 5-0. A great reception was given the winners when they arrived in Broseley at about 9.45pm.

Wed 29th September 1926
In the first football match of the season between a team of Old Boys - The West End Wanderers and a team of school boys, the latter won 4-0, the match took place at the Birchmeadow at 6.15pm.

Wednesday 20th October
The schools first match this season in the Boro of Wenlock football league took place on the Regatta Field against C.B.Dale High School. The kick off was at 3.30pm . The result was a win for Broseley 4-1. Mr R A Instone kindly loaned his motor lorry for the conveyance of the school team to C.B.Dale.

Sat 23rd October 1926
Two old boys teams have joined the recently constituted Madeley and District Junior Football League. The Broseley teams are to be known as the Broseley Victoria Rovers and the Broseley Victoria Cubs. The first to play in Division 1 and the second in Division 11 of the league. The league is the first, or one of the first of its kind in the country. It is intended to provide football facilities for youths of 14 and upwards and has the support of 5 or 6 local Headmasters as the executive committee. The Broseley schoolmaster is a member of the executive and is the Chairman of the Junior and Senior Football Committee responsible for the Broseley teams playing in the leagues.
The first match took place today.

Fri 12th November 1926
League match at Madeley. Kick off 3.05pm. Result Madeley Wesleyan 1 Broseley 1.

Tues 16th November 1926
League match on the Birchmeadow, kick off 3.40pm. Result Broseley 14 Ironbridge 0.

Fri 19th November 1926
League match at Madeley, Ben Cartwright inside right for Broseley injured in the first minute of the game. He was conveyed to Broseley Hospital and detained there. Kick off 3.40pm. Result Madeley C/E 6 Broseley 0.

Thurs 25th November 1926
League match at Birchmeadow, kick off 3.30pm. Result Broseley 9 Jackfield 1. Mr Brooks the Headmaster deputised a Mr Cross, a workman from Jackfield to act as referee. The Broseley Headmaster reminded Mr Brooks that this was in direct contradiction to what the Headteachers had decided at the commencement of the present football season.

Thurs 9th December 1926
League match at Birchmeadow, kick off 3.35pm. Result Broseley 4 Madeley Wood 2.

Thurs 10th February 1927
League match on Birchmeadow, kick off 3.30pm. Return match with Madeley Wesleyan School. Result Broseley 13 Madeley Wesleyan 3.

Thurs 24th March 1927
League match return fixture with Ironbridge on the Regatta Field. Result Broseley 5 Ironbridge 1.

Wed 30th March 1927
League match return fixture with Madeley C/E the league leaders, on the Birchmeadow. Result Draw - Broseley 4 Madeley 4.

Sat 7th May 1927
Windsor Clive Cup 1st Round, played at Bridgnorth this evening Broseley defeated Bridgnorth Blue Coats 8-0.

Sat 14th May 1927
Windsor Clive Cup Semi-Final played at Bridgnorth this evening, Broseley drew with Highley 2-2.

Thurs 22nd September 1927
A fixture list of the Broseley matches in the Boro of Wenlock football league for the season 1927/28 received today.

Fri 23rd September 1927
1st league match v Madeley Wood at Hill Top. Result Madeley Wood 3 Broseley 0.

Mon 26th September 1927
2nd league match, another away fixture on the Regatta Field. Result Broseley 10 Ironbridge 1. Mr Jack Roberts was kind enough to drive the Broseley team to and from the Regatta Field in his lorry.

Mon 3rd October 1927
Afternoon session commenced at 1.20pm instead of 1.30pm in order to allow the scholars 10-15 minutes grace at the end of the session to see the football match between Jackfield and Broseley. Mr Perkins assistant master at Jackfield was the referee. Result Broseley 5 Jackfield 1.

Fri 7th October 1927
League match at Madeley. Kick off 3.30pm. Result Broseley 5 Madeley Wesleyan 1.

Fri 14th October 1927
League match on the Birchmeadow between Broseley and C.B.Dale. Result C.B.Dale 2 Broseley 1.
The C.B.Dale school being without a permanent Headteacher, Mr Jenkins Assistant master has the arranging of the matches. He sent the C.B.Dale team in charge of Mr Charles Shaw, student teacher, who refereed the match. After the match the Headmaster of Broseley wrote a letter to the Chairman of the league protesting about a boy named Duckett who he had found, left school and who had finished work early in order to play with the C.B.Dale team. He was suspicious of one or two other players but did not mention these suspicions in his letter of protest as he could not support them with facts.

Sat 22nd October 1927
A letter from the Hon Sec Boro of Wenlock Schools football Association stating that "The protest brought forward by you was duly considered at a meeting of the council last evening and it was decided that your match with C.B.Dale should not count and that it be replayed. Enclosed please find your PO for 5/-. It was also unanimously agreed that as from this date rules 4 and 6 must be strictly adhered to.

Fri 4th November 1927
Afternoon session began at 1.15pm to allow boys to attend a league match on the Birchmeadow between C.B.Dale and Broseley. Result Broseley 3 C.B.Dale 0.

Wed 16th November 1927
League match at Madeley. Kick off 3.35pm. Result Broseley 2 Madeley C/E 1.

Fri 25th November 1927
League match on the Birchmeadow. Result Broseley 9 Ironbridge 0.

Mon 5th December 1927
League match at Jackfield. Result Jackfield 2 Broseley 9. Field muddy & light bad.

Fri 16th March 1928
Registers closed at 1.30pm in order to allow boys time to get to Hill Top for a league match between Broseley and C.B.Dale. The field was ankle deep in mud, which made against good football. Result Broseley 5 C.B.Dale 1.

Thurs 22nd March 1928
The Headmaster visited the Headmasters of Madeley Wesleyan and Madeley C/E schools about 7.00pm to ask them to arrange for the return football matches to be played before Easter, Broseley have 3 fixtures outstanding viz Madeley C/E, Madeley Wood and Madeley Wesleyan. All these are home matches and are fixed for the 17th/24th and 31st of March respectively. As Broseley school has incurred rather heavy expenditure in visiting each of these schools, the Headmaster feels that he cannot be a party to carrying on the league next season unless a determined attempt is made to fulfil this seasons obligations.

Tues 27th March 1928
A letter received from Mr Evans, Headmaster of Madeley Wood school saying that he cannot play the return match with Broseley this week.

Wed 25th April 1928
Registers closed at 1.30pm to allow scholars to see part of the football match between Broseley and Madeley Wood. Though the Headmaster has made every effort to have this return match played as arranged in the league fixture list, namely on or before 24th March last. Madeley Wood could not find it convenient to play till today. The game took place on the Birchmeadow and resulted in a win for Broseley 3 goals to 2 (see 22nd March 1928).

Thurs 26th April 1928
Madeley Wesleyan school football team came up to Broseley, unexpectedly, at 3.30pm. Though Class1 was gardening at the time, the school team changed and went down to the Birchmeadow. The result of the match was a win for Broseley 14-1.

Mon 7th May 1928
Last league match Broseley 1 - Madeley C/E 2.
In the Local Football League this season Broseley School have played 12 matches, won 10, lost 2. Scored 66 goals against 15 and made 20 points.

BROSELEY LEAGUE RECORD 1927/28

P	W	D	L	F	A	PTS
12	10	0	2	66	15	20

1.	Madeley Wood	3	Broseley	0
2.	Ironbridge	1	Broseley	10
3.	Broseley	5	Jackfield	1
4.	Madeley Wesleyan	1	Broseley	5
5.	Broseley	3	C B Dale	0
6.	Madeley C/E	1	Broseley	2
7.	Broseley	9	Ironbridge	0
8.	Jackfield	2	Broseley	9
9.	C B Dale	1	Broseley	5
10.	Broseley	3	Madeley Wood	2
11.	Broseley	14	Madeley Wesleyan	1
12.	Broseley	1	Madeley C/E	2

Broseley tied with Madeley C/E for League.
After losing their first game they won 11 consecutive matches before losing the last and deciding game against Madeley C/E school.

Thurs 10th May 1928
1st Round Bridgnorth Infirmary Schoolboys Cup at the Old Track Bridgnorth, Thursday night. Result Broseley 3 Bridgnorth St Marys 2.

Mon 14th May 1928
A letter received from Mr Rogers, the Secretary of the Bridgnorth Infirmary Cup Competition asking that Broseleys next match be ante-dated from Thursday 17th May to Tuesday 15th May.

Tues 15th May 1928
2nd Round Bridgnorth Infirmary Cup at Bridgnorth. Kick off 7.00pm. Result Broseley 1 Highley 0.

Sat 19th May 1928
Bridgnorth Infirmary Cup Final on the Old Track, Bridgnorth. Kick off 7.00pm.
Result Broseley 2 Wenlock 0.
Cups and Medals presented by Mr Woolley, solicitor, Bridgnorth. Great reception of winners at Broseley about 9.30pm.

Thurs 12th July 1928
A photographic enlargement of last seasons football team, framed and hung in school. Besides tying with Madeley C/E on points at the head of the Boro of Wenlock Schools Football League, this team won the Bridgnorth Infirmary Cup and in doing so created a record by carrying off the Cup twice in three years. William Bright the schools left back was in the team that won the cup two years ago and is thus the proud possessor of 2 medals.

Fri 21st September 1928
Committee meeting of the Boro of Wenlock Schools Football Association at the Labour Exchange, Ironbridge at 7.00pm. It was decided to continue the Association for the season 1928-29, but not to run a League as in previous seasons, friendly matches to be arranged mutually between the various schools in the Association.

Thurs 27th September 1928
A football match at Madeley this evening between two teams (Greens and Whites) chosen from seven schools forming the Boro Association, the object of the match is to select an eleven to compete against other Associations in the Wrekin Area, and ultimately to choose a team to compete in the English Schoolboys Shield. 6 Broseley players figured in the test teams tonight, 2 or 3 of whom were later chosen for the Boro eleven. The old difficulties of expenses, Broseley contingent was the only one that was compelled to drive to the match owing to the distance and to the comparatively early time of the kick off.

Mon 1st December 1928
Another 'test' Football match at Madeley this evening, 3 Broseley boys chosen to play in the eleven to meet Dawley District eleven later in the week, namely E Austin (goal), J Cleobury (inside left) and C Hill (inside or outside right).

Thurs 4th October 1928
Another 'test' football match at Madeley this evening, the rival teams being drawn from the Boro of Wenlock and Dawley areas respectively, from the teams an eleven was chosen to play an eleven from the Wellington, Oakengates and the St Georges area.
2 Broseley boys were elected.

Thurs 1st November 1928
1st football match of the season for the school team, the venue was Castle Green and the opponents Madeley Wood School. The result was a win for Broseley by 3-2.
As the Broseley Girls were playing a Netball match with the same school the team travelled in the same conveyance, the Headteacher thus saving a few shillings in travelling expenses.

Thurs 8th November 1928
Football match on the Birchmeadow between Ironbridge and Broseley schools 1st and 2nd teams. Kick off 3.40pm. Results Broseley 1st's 5 goals - Ironbridge 1st's 1 goal, Broseley 2nd's 7 goals - Ironbridge 2nd's 1 goal.

Thurs 29 November 1928
3rd football match of the season, Broseley entertained Jackfield on the Birchmeadow, kick off 3.30pm. Result Broseley 4 Jackfield 0.

Mon 25th March 1929
4th match of the season at Jackfield, owing to rain the teams only played 20 minutes in the second half, the score was 6-2 in favour of Broseley.

Monday 22nd April 1929
A football match on the Birchmeadow between Old Boys and Present Boys, kick off 6.50pm. Result Old Boys 7 - Present Boys 4.

Wed 8th May 1929
Football match on Birchmeadow at 7.00pm between Present Boys (the school team) and Church Choir (nearly all Old Boys). Result 4-3 in favour of Present Boys.

Tues 14th May 1929
In the Semi-Final for the Bridgnorth Infirmary Cup at Bridgnorth tonight, Broseley defeated Bridgnorth St Leonards 4-1.

Sat 18th May 1929
In the Final for the Bridgnorth Infirmary Cup tonight, the holders Broseley were defeated by Jackfield 1-0.

Wed 19th February 1930
Football match at Castle Green, Broseley 3 - Ironbridge 0

Fri 21st February 1930
Football match on Birchmeadow Broseley 3 - Madeley Wesleyan 1.

Fri 28th February 1930
Friendly match at Jackfield, Broseley 3- Jackfield 3.

Tues 8th April 1930
In the 1st Round for the Shropshire Football County Shield at Jackfield this afternoon, Broseley beat Jackfield 5-2. Owing to rain and the bad state of field, the junior teams of the schools did not play their match for the 1st Round of the Wrekin Junior Shield Competition.

Sat 10th May 1930
In the 1st Round of the Bridgnorth Infirmary Cup, Bewdley defeated Broseley by 3-2, a penalty goal deciding the issue. Match played on Bridgnorth Grammar School ground at 7.00pm.

Thurs 4th December 1930
3rd match of the season, Mr Alan Jones of Madeley conveyed about 24 boys and girls to Madeley and back for 8/-. Result Broseley 2- Madeley Wesleyan 1. Mr Smith, Headmaster of Madeley acted as referee.

Wed 8th April 1931
The Rector and Headmaster took a football team to Bewdley to play the school team there, the result was a draw 2-2. With the exception of 2 players the Broseley team was the school team.

Thurs 23rd April 1931
In an unfinished football match at Hill Top, Madeley Wood School scored 3 goals to 2 scored by Broseley. The match, a friendly, was spoilt by rain.

Thurs 30th April 1931
In the 1st Round for the Bridgnorth Infirmary Cup tonight, Broseley made a draw with Bridgnorth St Leonards 0-0.

Tues 5th May 1931
In the replayed match between Broseley and Bridgnorth St Leonards tonight, Broseley won 3-1.

Sat 9th May 1931
In the Semi-Final for the Bridgnorth Infirmary Cup on the Bridgnorth playing field tonight, Bewdley beat Broseley by 1 goal to 0. The winning goal was a penalty kick awarded in the first five minutes of the game.

Fri 6th May 1932
The school football team entered for the Bridgnorth Infirmary Cup. They had to play Jackfield in the 1st Round. The result of the match was Broseley 4 Jackfield 0. In the Semi-Final Broseley had to play Bewdley. Result Bewdley 4 Broseley 0.

Thurs 22nd May 1934
School closed at 3.40pm to enable boys to see football match v Bridgnorth.

Tues 29th May 1934
The school football team, playing in the Semi-Final of the Broseley Hospital Schools Challenge Cup, won 7-0 v Wenlock C/E school.

Sat 9th June 1934
The Boys football team played on Saturday evening in the final of the Broseley Hospital Cup. They were victorious over the Madeley C/E team 4-0. Broseley therefore held the cup for the first year.

Wed 28th November 1934
Mr S R Brookes took 12 boys to Bridgnorth to play football v the Grammar School.

Tues 14th May 1935
The school football team entered the final of the Broseley Hospital Cup beating Shifnal 8-0.

Thurs 10th June 1937
The school football team won the 1st Round of the Broseley Schools Cup last night, beating Bridgnorth St Leonards by 4-1.

Wed 16th June 1937
The School football team drew with Wenlock 1-1, in the Semi-Final of the Hospital Cup.

Thurs 17th June 1937
The school football team entered the final of the Hospital Cup by beating Wenlock 3-1.

Sat 26th June 1937
The school team lost to the Madeley Senior school in the Final of the Hospital Cup 10-0.

This has been put together by my husband Leslie Griffiths, and may be of interest to some of the football fans here in our town, with thanks for doing this for my book.

PUBLIC HOUSES, INNS, TAVERNS & BEER HOUSES

Albion, High Street
1840 John Smithyman, 1851 Miles Thomas, 1861/71 John Bentley, 1885 Robert Lowe, 1891 Ezra Millward, 1916 Miss E Millward, 1917 Julian Millward, 1926/29 Miss J Millward, 1941 Gilbert Harrison. Still trading as a public house in 1996

The Albion

Angel, High Street
Dr Edwards (1818-78).
Still standing as a house in 1996

The Angel

Ash Tree - Jackfield
1829/35/40 John Williams, 1851 John Yates, 1871 J Nicholls,

Barley Mow, Duke Street
Mr Preen, closed before 1879

The Bell
22 Quarry Road, Broseley Wood
Still standing as a house in 1996

The Bell

Birchmeadow Centre, Birchmeadow Road
Broseley Parish Council 1996

Birchmeadow Centre – was The Bladen Club and The Athletic Club

Black Swan, Lloyds Head
1835 William Oakes, 1851/61 Charles Parker. Still trading in 1996

Blue Ball, 55 King Street
Mr J Wilkes (1818-78) Mr Davies.

The Blue Ball

Boat Inn, Jackfield 1840

Brittania Inn, Bower Yard
1859/75 Mrs M Gother, Benthall.

Brittania Inn, The Werps
Susan Oswell, ceased trading before 1879

Bulls Head, site unknown
1829/35/42 Samuel Preen

Butchers Bar, High Street
Opened 29th July 1994 Clive Maiden/Nigel Venn

The Butchers Bar

Burnt House, (A record of a fire there on June 8th 1883). Still standing in 1996

The Burnt House

Cape of Good Hope, corner Cape Street
1829/35/40 John Turton, 1851 Arthur Fawkes, 1871 Thomas Lane, 1885 Thomas Harley, 1891 Valentine Roberts, 1917/26 Harry Russell, demolished about 1960's.

The Cape of God Hope

Castle Rag, Mill Lane now demolished

Coalport Inn, Swinbach
1829/35 Samuel Price, 1871 W C Harris, 1891 Thomas Morris.

Cricket Club, Broseley

Broseley Cricket Club and Pavilion

Cross Keys, 32 Simpsons Lane 1866, Still standing as a house in 1996

The Cross Keys

Crown, High Street (new) later renamed the Ironmaster
1829/35/40 Samuel Matthews, 1851/61 Elizabeth Yates, 1871 Richard Matthews (maltster), 1885/91 John Powis, 1916/17 Miss Florence Powis, 1926 George Frederick Wall, 1929/34/41 Arthur Frank Drumgole.
In 1996 Ye Olde Taverne

Crown and Anchor, site unknown
1829/35 Mary Higgins, 1840 William Palin, John Pool 1879, ceased trading 1879

Cumberland Hotel, Queen Street
Joe Bryan was there in 1956, Ivor Southorn 1976 to present time.
License transferred from the Duke of Cumberland in 1948. Was the private residence of Mr Howells.

The Cumberland Hotel

Delph Tavern, The Delph R Dixon 1818-78, Mr Burton 1879, ceased to trade.

Dog or Talbot, Church Street
1829/35 John Geary, Dog, 1840 William Edwards, 1851 Susannah Amplett, 1861/71 Benjamin Humphries Talbot, 1885 William Meredith, 1891 Thomas Meredith. Now demolished.

The Dog, or Talbot

Duke of Cumberland, King/Duke Street junction
1840/51/61 Thomas Davies, 1863 Mrs F Davis, 1868/71/85 John Shaw, 1891 William Brazier, 1929 George Millward, 1934 Fred Dillow, 1941 Ernest Bird. Demolished in 1950's. Licence transferred to Cumberland Hotel in 1948, this was the private residence of 'Howells', family Queen Street.

The old Duke of Cumberland, junction King/Duke Street, on left behind children

Duke of Wellington, The Werps, Tuckies Field.1851-61
1835 Robert Jones, 1835 J Leadbetter, E Cranage.

Duke William, site unknown
1835 Eileen Cooke

Duke of York, Hockley Road or Bank
1840 Richard Ward, 1851 William Watkins, 1861 John Leadbetter, 1868/71 Ann Miles, 1885 John Oakley, 1891 Richard Evans, 1929 Mrs Annie Moore, 1934 Richard George Lewis, 1941 Francis Benbow. Still trading in 1996

The Duke of York

Dustpan, site unknown

Elephant or Elephant & Castle, High Street
1829/35/42 John Bradley, 1840/51 Edward Lister, 1861 Philip Birbeck (China Painter), 1868/71 Thomas Jones, 1885 Fred Turner, 1891 Charles Rigby, 1917 Mrs M Hill, 1926 Thomas Parker, 1929 William Birchall, 1934 William Percy Parr, 1941 George F Wall. Still standing as a house in 1996

The Elephant and Castle

Five Alls, site unknown

Foresters Arms, Lower Church Street, 1929 Avenue Road
1840 William Edwards, 1851 Ann Edwards, 1861 Elizabeth Edwards, 1861 J Cleeton, 1868/71 Richard Turner, 1885 Abraham Britton, 1891 Mrs Harriet Britton,
1926/29 Thomas Smith, 1934/41 Mrs Nellie Smith Telephone Ironbridge 19.
Still trading in 1996

The Foresters Arms

Fountain, Lloyds Head
Ceased trading before 1879.

Fox, Barber Street
1829/35/42 Richard Poole, 1840 John Davies, 1851/61 John Hayman,
1879 Mr Roberts - ceased to exist as a pub from this date.
Still standing as a house in 1996.

The Fox

George & Dragon, King Street
Mr Hiskett,

Globe, King Street/Legges Hill junction
1835, 1861/68 Sarah Lloyd. Still standing as a house 1996.

The Globe - on the right

The Green, Harris's Green
1819 Peter Smith.
Still standing as a house in 1996

Half Moon, Jackfield
George Richards 1835.
Still trading.

Hand & Tankard, Workhouse Road, changed to Woodhouse Rd 1980's
1840 John Jones, 1861 Alfred Nicholas, 1868/71 William Moore, 1885/91 John Matthews, 1861 James Aston.
Demolished 1960's.

The Hand and Tankard

Hangsters Gate, Willey

Harp

Hen & Chickens, High Street
H Rushton. 1879 William Colley, ceased to trade from 1879.
Another site suggested by locals was Queen Street, house at the bottom of the yard of Broseley Fires.

Hockley Inn, Hockley
1803 Mary/Benjamin Gough. Inscribed on a plaque on the wall 'Good Ale and Beer sold here' by Benjamin and Mary Gough. Still standing as a house in 1996

Hockley Inn

Hole in the Wall, Carvers Road
1829/35/42 George Wilkes, 1861 Ann Wylde, 1885 Noah Hill
Demolished

Kings Head, Kings Street
1829/35 William Bill, 1840 Ann Higgins, 1851/61/71 Hannah Rufus, 1885/91 James Daniel Smith, 1916 George Keay, 1926/34/41 Henry Starr Southorn. Ceased to trade 1990's.

The Kings Head

Lamb, 15 Duke Street.

The Last Inn, High Street
T Instone (1818-78.) Became a butchers shop, was then closed for many years, re-opened in 1994 as a Wine Bar, re-named Butchers Bar (see Butchers Bar)

Lion & Pheasant, Legges Hill Ceased to trade from 1879.

Lion, High Street, **Commercial Inn**
1828 Benjamin Law, 1840 John Dyer Doughty, 1851 Charles Rhodes, 1861 W Holmes, 1868/71 William Jones, 1885 John Instone, 1891 Emma Haughton, 1917 Thomas Instone, 1926/34 Archibald George Oswell, 1941 Mrs Edith Oswell, 1940/50's Clifford Hall.
Closed and empty in 1994-96. Reopened later, re-opened again in 2002.

Lion Hotel

Lord Hill, Duke Street/Cockshutt Lane junction
1829/35/42 Benjamin Cooke, 1861/71 Elizabeth Weekes, 1885/91 Stephen Hill, 1929/34 Mrs Elizabeth Marlow, 1941 Miss Ivy Marlow. (A Guest House in 1994.)

Lord Hill

Maypole, Woodlands Road/ Green
1829/35 Charles Jones, 1861 John Morris,

The Maypole

Napoleon, Woodlands Road
Closed in the 1940's

The Napoleon

Nelson Inn or Nelson Inn, Legges Hill
1829/35 M Jones, 1840 Richard Poole, 1861 Ann Southorn
Ceased to trade as a pub from 1879, still standing in 1996.

The Nelson

New Inn, Ladywood Jackfield
Ceased to exist as a pub during last 60 years to 1879.

New Inn, Benthall formerly Pitchyard
1829/35 Elizabeth Lloyd, 1835/40 Noah Roden, 1861 William Watkins, 1868 Thomas Roberts, 1871 John Morris,
Ceased to trade in 2001.

New Inn or the old Pitchyard

Old Crown, Church Street
1829/35/42 Richard Wyre, 1851 Joseph Cooke, 1861 John Reynolds
Still standing as a house in 1996

The Old Crown

Old Red Lion, Queen Street
1829/35 John Law, 1835 William Wilson, Mr Williams, T Griffiths (1878).
Ceased to trade from 1879.

Pheasant, Church Street, **Commercial Inn & Posting House**
1829/35/42 Samuel Pugh, 1840/51 Adam Jones surveyor, 1861 John Jones, 1868/71 Samuel Instone, 1885 Emma Haughton and son, 1891 Thomas Beard, 1916 Mrs Lloyd, 1917 Thomas Smith, 1929/34 Frances Kennedy, 1941 Alfred King.
Still standing 1996, and still a public house.

The Pheasant Hotel - on the left

Plough, Barber Street
W N Thompson 1835 Thomas Challinor 1840 William Davies
1851 Robert Everall butcher, Mr Smith. Ceased to trade from 1879. Still standing as a house in 1996

Potters Arms, Quarry Road

Prince of Wales, King Street
1861 T Smitheman. Still standing as a private house in 1996

The Prince of Wales

Red Barn, Barber Street
Mrs Williams. Ceased to trade from 1879.

Rose & Crown, Broseley Wood
Mr Collins, ceased to trade from 1879.
Was the old Post Office

The Rose and Crown

Royal Oak, Jackfield
1829/35/40 Robert Richards Ceased to trade from 1879.

Royal Oak, Woodlands Broseley Wood Mr Bill, ceased to trade from 1879.

Seven Stars, Fearney Bank, King Street
1850 Samuel Danks, 1893 Benjamin Garbett, 1904 George Keay, 1916 Thomas R Hill. Still standing as a house in 1996. Referred to by John Randall in 1795.

The Seven Stars

Severn Trow
1835 Charles Lloyd, 1851 Robert Richards, 1861 H Lloyd

Social Club (Broseley)
Became a club in 1919 – limited membership for doctors, solicitors and gentry.

Broseley Social Club

Spotted Leopard, Benthall
1829/35/40 Thomas Jones, 1840 Robert Jones, 1868 Henry Cartwright

The Bell, 22 Quarry Road Still standing as a house in 1996

The Ship Inn, Werps
1835 Martha Jones, John Jones, ceased to trade from 1879.

The Star, Fearney Bank. - See Seven Stars

Star Inn, King Street
1838 J Jones (May be as above)

Station also known as **The Blue House** , Ladywood - **Sycamore** Brosesley Wood
1861 F W B Poole

Summerhouse, (bottom of Balls Lane)
1851/61 Edward Brown, Blacksmith. Still standing as a house in 1996

Sun Inn, Tuckies Ceased to trade from 1879.

Sycamore Broseley Wood
J Evans (1818-78)

The Rock
Thomas Jones, ceased to trade from 1879.

Three Horseshoes, High Street
1835 Sarah Lees, 1861 William Bourne Blacksmith

The Swan, Swan Street 1838 John Davies

Sycamore Tree, Broseley Wood Mr Dean, ceased to trade from 1879.

Tumbling Sailor, Coalford
1835 James Lloyd, 1840 John Walker,1851 William Cullis,1861/71 Thomas Cullis (or Collis)

Tuckies Inn
John Challenor, ceased to trade from 1879.

Turks Head
1835/40 Francis Griffiths

Unicorn, King Street
Later became Thomas's Paint shop

The Unicorn

Vaults, High Street
1926 Matthew William Grocott, 1934/41 Percy Ewart Hartshorne, Mrs Seddon, Nell George

Victoria, Lower Church Street was the **Old Crown.**
1868/71 Cyrus Edmund Onslow, Vetinerary Surgeon,
1885 Fennell Clement, 1891 George Gough. Still standing, a private house in 1996

Welps
1829/35/40 Richard Beards

White Swan, Hockley Road
1819 John Davies, ceased to trade from 1879.
Still standing as private house in 1996

The White Swan

Wheatsheaf
1829/35/40 George Lloyd

Woodbridge
1851 Thomas Holt, 1871 Thomas Roden

INTRODUCTION TO TRADES IN BROSELEY FROM 1828

It is very interesting to look back at how people lived in the past, one of the reasons I began to write this book.

During the research I did at the Shrewsbury Records Office, I spent a lot of time looking through the various directories available there, Kelly's, Robson's e.g and others, and was very surprised at the extent of the amenities in Broseley as far back as 1828.

I decided to use the information and put it in alphabetical and date order, the result is fascinating reading.

Broseley in the early 19th century was totally self-sufficient with over 200 different amenities and businesses trading here over the last 100/200 years.

In 1828 there were 16 butchers here, unbelievable in this day and age when we now have one, and a butchery department in the local SPAR market (the site of the old Town Hall).

The population in 1828 according to the census figures in the directories were 4,814, in the year 2000 it is approximately 5,500, so there are not many more people here now than 170 years ago.

This list covers medical, schools, farms, clubs, manufacturers, shops, private residents and of course the beer retailers and the public houses.

Beer retailers numbered 40 between 1840 and 1934, these were only licenced to sell beers and ales, not spirits. However the public houses and Inns were numerous then and there were as many as 89 named in various books and directories, in the year 2000 there are just 12 pubs and clubs left here to quench your thirst. It is hard to believe that so many have closed their doors over the years, if records had not been kept we would not have the information to compare life then and up to our present day.

The names of the pub landlords and the year's they were there make interesting reading, and the photographs of some of these pubs. Many of the old Broseley names are still here in the area.

TRADES – BROSELEY

Accountant
1851 Edwin Evans - High Street
1851 John Harvey - Cape/King Street
1871 John Pountney - High Street
1934 Andrew George Fenn - 29 High Street Telephone Ironbridge 40

Agent
1871 Edwin Prior - The Bank

Ale and Porter Merchant
1840 John Holmes Smith/Animal Painter
1861 William Evans - King Street
1871 William Evans - Queen Street
1871 Thomas Rushton - Barbers Row/Artist

Attendance Officer to the Union
1891 William Jones

Attorneys
1828 James Griffiths
1828/29/35/42 Pritchard and Sons
1851 John Westover - Duke Street - Attorneys Clerk

Auctioneer
1828/29/35/40/42/51 George Hartshorne - High Street
1851 Edwin Evans - High Street
1861/68/71 Enoch Leadbetter - High Street

Baker and Flour Dealer
1828 Peter Everall
1828 George Gwynne
1840 Ann Everall
1840/51 Thomas Everall - Cape Street/King Street
1840/51 Samuel Jones - Broseley Wood, 1861 Chapel Street
1851 Richard Boycott - Church Street
1851/61 Edwin Pountney - Church Street
1861 Henry Williams - Church Street
1868 Francis Hartshorne - Broseley Wood
1885 Jonas A Burnet - High Street
1885/91 Thomas Wm Cullis - Barbers Row
1885/91 Aquila Evans - High Street
1885 John Geo.Jay - King Street
1885/91/1916 Isaac Henry Onions - Upper Church Street
1885/91 Thomas Plimley - High Street
1885 Isaac Powell - King Street
1891 Joseph Abraham Burnet - High Street and King Street
1891 Charles Rowe - Church Street
1891/1916/26/41 William Kenyon - 38 King Street
1902 George William Aston - High Street
1916/17 John T Myatt - High Street
1916/17/26 John Rowe - High Street
1917 Mrs E C Onions - Upper Church Street
1926/29/34/41 John Davis - High Street
1926 Francis John Lyons - 53 Church Street
1929/34 John Harrison - 1 Cape Street or 1 High Street
1929/34/41 Thomas Wedge - 53 Church Street
1941 Joseph Reginald Towler - 1 High Street

Bankers
1828/29/35/42 J G & J Pritchard

Bankers and Solicitors
1840 Jno. G & J jnr Pritchard
1851 Pritchards Boycott & Nicholas - High Street
---- George Pritchard Esq - Church Street
---- Miss Pritchard - Church Street
---- John Pritchard - High Street
1861/71 Pritchard & Nicholas
1885 Pritchard Pritchard Gordon Potts & Shorting & Co - High Street
1916 Lloyds Bank Ltd. Manager J A Downes

Barber
1916 Richard Hudson - High Street

Barge Builder
1840 Francis Gother

Basket Maker
1828/35/40/42 James Gwynne
1851/68 George Gwynne - The Green
1851 Martha Gwynne - Barratt's Hill
1861/68/71 Enoch Gwynne - King St, Harris's Green
1861 Joseph Roderick
1868 John Duckett - Benthall

Beer Retailers (No wines and spirits)
1840 Susannah Amplett
1840 Joseph Colley
1840 William Collins
1840 John Davies
1840 William Dunch
1840 James Dunch
1840 Richard Hill
1840 Thomas Hiskett
1840 John Jones
1840 William Jones
1840 A Lloyd
1840 Henry Lloyd
1840/51 William Lloyd - Broseley Wood
1840 Mary Page
1840 Robert Richards
1840/51 Richard Weekes - Duke Street
1840 William Williams
1851 Jeremiah Bill
1851/61/68 William Bourne - High Street
1851 James Dean - Broseley Wood
1851 Ann Southorn - Broseley Wood
1861 James Cartwright - King Street
1861/68 John Hayman - Barbers Row
1861 William Bourne - High Street
1861 Thomas Smitheman - King Street
1868 George Gother - Benthall
1868 Thomas Roberts - Benthall
1868 Joseph Hill - King Street
1868 Emma Oakes - King Street
1885 Richard Bailey - King Street
1885/91 Samuel Danks - Broseley Wood
1885 William Davies - Quarry Road
1885 William Summerland - King Street
1891 Martha Hartshorne - Broseley Wood
1891 George Millward - King Street
1891 John Rowe - King Street
1917 John Charles Brown - Woodlands Road
1926 John Carrier - 19 Woodlands
1929 John Brown - 19 Woodlands Road
1934 Harold E Bowen - 19 Woodlands Road

Benthall Geometrical & Encaustic Mosiac Tile Works
1861 Maw & Company

Benthall Pottery Company
1868 Earthenware Manufacturers

Blacksmith
1828/29/35/42 Thomas Davies
1828/29/35/42 John Jones
1840 William Barker
1840/51 William Parsons - King Street
1840 Sarah Wilkinson
1840/68 Josiah Instone - Benthall
1851/61 William Bourne - High Street (1868 also Three Horseshoes Inn)
1851 John Wilkinson - Church Street
1861/71/85/91 Joseph Garbett - Lower Church Street
1868 John Morris - Broseley Wood
1868 Joseph Longmoor - Linley
1871 James Leadbetter - King Street
1871 Samuel Meredith - The Rock
1885/91 James Leadbetter - Upper Church Street
1891 James Fisher - Lower Church Street
1916/17 A Leadbetter - Lower Church Street
1916 James Poyner
1926 William Higgs - Church Street
1926/29/34/41 Thomas Meredith - Church Street

Board/Residence
1941 Mrs T Everall - 54 High Street

Bookseller
1840/61/85/91 Enoch Nevett

Boot & Shoemaker
1828/35/42 Edward Parsons
1829/35/40/42 William Williams
1835/29/42 John Booth
1835/40/61/68/71 Isaac Burnett - High Street
1840 James Burnett
1840/51 Richard Weekes
1840/51 Benjamin Wellings - Barbers Row
1851/61/68 John Weekes - Duke St 1851, Chapel St 1861/68
1851 John Beddoes - High Street
1851/61 Edward Hartshorne - High Street
1851/61/68/71 James Mason - High Street
1851/61 Thomas Molyneux - High Street
1851 Richard Watkin - Duke Street
1851/61 Thomas Weekes - King Street Broseley Wood
1861 Francis Glaze - Simpsons Lane
1861/71 J Leadbetter - Church Street
1861/68 George Roberts - Bridge Road? Benthall
1868 Thomas Hartshorne
1868 William Norry - Duke Street
1868 John Leadbetter - Church Street
1868/71/85/91 Nath. Hartshorne - High Street
1868/71/85/91 Thomas Howells - Barratts Hill 1868 then High Street
1871 Richard Chilton - King Street
1871/85 Patrick Thompson - Duke Street
1885/91 William Chilton - King Street
1885/91 William Wellings - Barber Row
1885/91 George Taylor - Duke Street
1885 Richard Wellings - The Delph
1891 Mary Ann Thompson (Mrs) - Barbers Row
1891 Fred Watkins - King Street
1916/17/26 Harry Harris - 52 High Street
1916/17 Edwin Howells - High Street
1916/17/26 Miss M Moor - High Street Boot Dealer
1916/17/29/34 William Thompson - Barber Street
1917 Charles Edward Jones - Quarry Road Boot Repairer
1926/29/34/41 Charles Cecil Davis - 25 Church St. Boot Repairer
1929/34 Sands Bros - 52 High Street
1941 Percy Sands - 52 High Street
1934/41 J Aston - 88 High Street Rapid Repair Service

Brazier and Tin Plate
1828 Widow Parker
1840/51 John Fenton - Barbers Row
1851 Thomas Hiskett - Barbers Row
1868 Thomas Child - Hockley

Brick and Tile Manufacturers
1828 Amphlett & Co
1828/35/40/42 Thos Davies
1829/35/42 John Burton (fire)
1829/35/42 James Davies (fire)
1829/35/42 Harrington & Greenwood
1829/35/42 Hezekiah Hartshorne
1829/35/42 Lumley & Co
1829/35/40/42/51 John Onions - Whitehall Church Street
1829/35/40/42 Richard Poole
1829/35/42 John & Thomas Roden
1835/61 Geo Davies - Dunge Works
1840 William Davies
1840 James Booth
1840 Theophulus Doughty
1840 Robert Evans
1840 William Cartwright
1840 Thomas Roden
1840 John & Edward Burton
1861 Edward Evans - Broseley Hall
1868/71 Penelope Jane Thorn Bros.

Brick & Tile Works Encaustic Tile Manf.
1868/71 Maw & Co - Benthall Works
1868/91 Geo & Francis Davies - Dunge Works
1871 George Warburton Lewis - High Street
1871/85 Francis & Geo Davies - Dunge Works
1885 Josiah Wase & Co - Holywell Tile Works
1926 C R Jones & Sons Ltd - Bros Roofing & Ridge Tileries
1926 Milburgh Tileries Tel: Ironbridge 10

Brick Layers
1828/29/35/42 Thomas Fowler
1828/35/42 Francis Legg
1828/35/42 William Legg
1828/35/42 Thomas Perkins
1828/35/42 George Pugh
1828/35/42 John Pugh
1828/35/42 William Pugh
1828/35/42 Charles Smith
1828/35/42 John Smith
1828/35/42 William Smith
1861 Richard Squires - High Street
1868 William Franks - Linley

Broseley Gas & Coke Company
1885/91 Sec/Manager John Pountney
1916/17 " " Rowland Smitheman
1926/29/34 " " William Edge - 6 Church Street

Broseley Hall
1851 Mrs Favell Lea Mortimer
writer of childrens books (Jessica's first prayer)

Broseley Cricket Club Broseley Wood
1941 Secretary R Davies - High Street

Broseley Hospital Tel: Ironbridge 15 in 1941
1917/26/29 John Goodison Boon Medical Officer
1917 Sec: T C Shingler - Coalbrookdale
1917 Matron C E Morris - Church Street
1926/29 Sec: Lt Col B Woodland
1926 Matron Miss F Condell
1929 Lady Forester Memorial Hospital
1934/41 Sec: Lt Col Samuel Pell Keyworth
1995 Oct 15 Opened as a Day Centre to public after being closed by Shropshire Health Authority 1989, opened for business 16/10/1995.

Broseley Lawn Tennis Club Duke Street
1891 Hon Sec/Treasurer Henry Rogers Botwood
1916/26/29 " " Raymond Nicklin
1917 " " G B Ledger
1929/34 " " Raymond Nicklin
1941 " " Walter Davis

Broseley Liberal & Labour Club
1917 Sec John Burns

Broseley Newsroom/Library Victoria Hall
1885/91 Secretary F H Martin
1885/91 Librarian B Lloyd
1916 Secretary T Jones

Broseley Roofing & Ridge Tiles
1917/26 W & P Jones

Broseley Sanitary Division
1891 Nathaniel Hartshorne - High Street

Broseley Social Club
1926/29 Secretary John Ritchings
1934 " Arthur Meredith
1941 " Thomas Goodall - High Street

Broseley Tileries Co Ltd
Geometrical & Encaustic Tile Manufacturers also manufacturers of the Bros Brick & Tile Works
1885 Story of a death there?
1891
1916/17 Manufacturers of bricks and tiles

Broseley Town Hall
1917 Caretaker Arthur Pountney
1926/29/34 " Mrs Elizabeth Evans
1941 " Mrs Nellie George

Builders
1851 George Hartshorne - High Street
1851 Richard Squires - Barratts Hill
1861 Rowland & Thomas Smitheman (Builders & Contractors & Steam Saw Mills)
1868/85/91 William Exley & Sons - The Rock Broseley
1871/85 Thomas Broadhurst - King Street
1871/85/91 Charles Hartshorne - High Street
1871/85/91 Rowland Smitheman - King Street (Builder Timber dealer & Contractor)
1885/91 Hiram Lloyd - Barbers Row
1885/91/1916/17 Charles T Smith - Upper Church Street
1891 Henry Broadhurst - Cape Street
1941 Benjamin Wood - Duke Street

Butchers
1828/35/42 Henry Booth - High Street
1828/35/42 Charles Cartwright - High Street
1828/35/40/68/71 George Cartwright - King Street
1828/35/40/51/61/71 James Cartwright - High Steet
1828/35/40/61/68 John Cartwright - Legges Hill
1828/35/42 Richard Colley
1828/35/42/91 John Corfield - High Street
1828/35/42 William Corfield
1828/35/42 Edward Crump
1828/35/40/51 William Crump - High Street
1828/35/42 Thomas Gough
1828/35/42 Thomas Holyoake
1828/35/42 George Knowles
1828/35/42 Thomas Pearce
1828/35/42 Charles Smith
1828/35/51 William Taylor - Queen Street
1840 William Cartwright
1840/51/61 Thomas Corfield - High Street then Church Street
1840/61 Robert Everall - Church Street
1840 Elizabeth Knowles
1840 Thomas Wootton
1851/61 Jeremiah Bill - Broseley Wood Woodlands Green
1851/68/71 Samuel Davies - Broseley Wood, Maltster/Farmer
1851 Robert Everall - Barbers Row
1851/68 Herbert Wootton Farmer - Duke Street then High Street
1861 Samuel Davis - King Street
1868 Thomas Lane - High Street
1868/71 John Davies - Broseley Wood
1868 Mary Corfield - Duke Street
1868 Humphrey Legge - Barratts Hill
1868 George Taylor
1871 Thomas Greatbach - High Street
1871 William Hill - Duke Street
1871 Humphrey Lake - Barratts Hill
1871 Adolphus Lloyd - Church Street
1885/1916 Samuel Thomas Instone - 69/70 High Street
Died 1917?/26/29/34/41 Executors
1885/1917 Henry James Rushton - High Street
1885 Jonas Burnet - High Street
1885 Davies & Hill - Barratts Hill
1891 Joseph Abraham Burnet - High Street and King Street
1891 George Haughton - High Street
1891/1916 Matthew Davis - King Street
1917/26/29 Mrs Matthew Davis - King Street
1926/29/34/41 Arthur John Cleobury - Barber Street
1926/29/34/41 Charles Frederick Instone - 37 High Street and in
1934 50 Church Street Telephone Ironbridge 83
1926/29/34/41 Thomas Henry Potham - 37 High Street
1934/41 Mrs Hayward Davis Telephone Ironbridge 131
1941 Richard Albert Jones - High Street

Cab Propietor
1902/16 Frederick Oakley - High Street

Cabinet Maker
1828 John Garbett
1828/35/51 George Hartshorne jnr - High Street
1840 Thomas Poole
1861 Charles Hartshorne - High Street

Capacity Tool Company
1917/26/29/34 Motor Car Accessories Manufacturers - King St
1941 Capacity Engineering Co. – King St. Telephone Ironbridge 54

Carpenter /Joiner
1840 John Davis
1840 Thomas Poole
1840 William Turley
1861 Thomas Cowley - Fox Lane
1861 Henry Rushton - Duke Street
1916/17 Benjamin Wood - Barratts Hill
1934 John Broadhurst - Queen Street Carpenter to Willey Estate

Carriers
1828/35/42 To London: Crowley Hicklin & Co from Ironbridge every Wednesday and Saturday
1828/35/42 London: John Jolly from George Hartshornes Broseley every Tuesday
1828/35/42 To Shrewsbury: Richard Parry from the Swan Inn Iron-bridge and from the Crown Broseley every Tuesday and Friday

1835 A horse Post despatches to Shifnal every morning quarter before 4.00am and arrives at 4.30pm for London
1885/91 George Davis - Duke Street
1885 R T Smith
1929 John Brown & Co - 19 Woodlands Road

Carting Contractors
1917 Samuel Thomas Instone

Charter Master
1885/91 Richard Aston - Workhouse Road
1885/91 Richard Jones - Broseley Wood

Cheesemonger
1828 J Easthope - Benthall

Chemist/Druggist
1829/35/42 Thomas O'Adams
1840 Joseph Merrigold
1840/51 Jesse Oakley - High Street
1868 George W Lewis - High Street
1868 J Stevens - High Street
1871 John Stevens - High Street
1885 Charles Kitching - High Street
1885/91 Thomas Norton - High Street
1916 John Jinks - High Street
1926 Thomas Freeman - 79 High Street
1929/34/41 Eric Hallett - 79/80 High Street

Chimney Sweep
1891 John Powell - King St./1916 39 Church St./1917 The Delph/ 1926/29 39 Church Street
1940's Mr Evans – Cape Street

China Dealer
1861/68 William Garbett - Duke Street
1868 John Hayman - Barbers Row
1868 Ellen Pugh - High Street
1871 Hannah Pugh
1917 William Parker - King Street

China Painter
1851 Thomas Pugh - High Street

Church Organist
1861 H Bathurst - Church Street

Clerk of the Peace for Borough of Wenlock and Registrar of the Madeley County Court
1871 George Potts - High Street
1885 Edward Bagnall Potts - High Street

Coaches
1828 To London: 'The Prince of Wales' every am, at 9.00am from the Lion
1828 To Worcester every day except Sunday
1828/35 From Birmingham to Shrewsbury 'The Emerald' every day 3.00pm called at the 'White Hart'
1829/35/42 To Cheltenham 'The Old Worcester' from Shrewsbury via Tontine via Red Lion Broseley about 8.30am every Mon Wed Friday goes through Worcester
1835 Return trips call at Red Lion every Tues Thurs and Saturday at 4.30pm, and 5.00pm at Tontine

Coal Dealer
1861/71 Benjamin Cow - Quarry Road
1885/91 William Love - King Street
1916 G Ball
1917/26/29 Arthur N Dixon - The Downs (Haycop?)
1934 Mrs Doris Whitehead - 57 Church St Telephone Ironbridge 126
1941 Percy W Parr - High Street Coal Merchant Tel:Ironbridge 107
1941 Edwin Oakley - 38 High Street

Coalmaster
1828 Evans & Son
1840 John Guest
1851 Thomas Birch - High Street
1851 William Holmes - Cape/King
1851 Hiram Hill - Barratts Hill
1861 Edward & Robert Evans - Broseley Hall
1861 James Aston -Windmill Lane
1861/68/71 Hill & Aston - Haycop
1861 George Langford - Fiery Fields
1861 John Raspass - Birch Row
1868 Evans & Gough
1868 George Evans & Son - Benthall
1868 Hill & Gethin - Benthall
1868 Hill & Venn - Bottom Coal
1871 Hill & Co
1871 James Aston - King Street

1871 Thomas Plimley - Barbers Row
1885/91 William Exley & Sons - The Rock

Coffee House
1885 William Edge - High Street

Collector of Taxes, Water Rates,and Assessor
United Parishes of Broseley, Barrow, Benthall, Linley, Posenhall & Willey
1917/26 Edward Oakes - 5 Barber Street
1929 Andrew George Fenn - 29 High Street

Colliery Propietor
1891 Samuel Meredith - Coneybury Pit

Commercial Traveller
1891 Thomas Rushton - Cape Street

Confectioner
1851 Susan Evans - Barbers Row
1851 Thomas Evans - High Street
1868 Robert James
1868/71 Edward Pountney - Church Street
1868/85/91 Francis Hartshorne - Broseley Wood
1885 Thomas William Cullis - Barbers Row
1885 Isaac Henry Onions Upper - Church Street
1885/91 Charles Rowe - Church Street
1891/1916 William Kenyon - King Street
1891 Maria Carter (Mrs) - High Street
1891 Thomas William Cullis - Barbers Row
1916/17 Miss Myf Carter - High Street
1916 John T Myatt - High Street
1916 John Rowe - High Street
1916 John Woollam - Upper Church Street
1917 Mrs Louisa Smith - High Street
1926 Miss Lizzie Hamlett - 1 King Street
1926/34 Frank Harold Lowe - The Square
1926/29/34/41 Mrs Clara Powell - 24 High Street
1926 William Toone - 75/76 High Street
1929 Mrs Dorothy Loach - 75/76 High Street
1929 Rt Owen - 1 King Street
1934 Mrs Edith Morris - 66 High Street
1934 Mrs Edith Neary - 89 High Street
1941 Mrs Ellen Loach - 75/76 High Street
1941 Miss Olga C Brooks - 89 High Street

Cooper
1828/35/42 Richard Jones

Co-operative Society - High Street
1916 and 1926

Corn Miller
1828/35/42 Jeremiah Ashwood
1829/35/42 William Morgan - Benthall
1828/35/42 William Knock
1934 R A Instone & Son Corn Merchant - The Square/15 Church Street Tel: Iron: 68

Coroner Borough of Wenlock
1851 William Glover Bartlam
1885 Edward Glover Bartlam
1885 Taylor

Corset Maker
1934 Mrs Ada Walker - 51 Church Street

Cow Keeper
1885/91 Joseph Langford - Lower Church Street

Cycle & Motor Agent
1916 James Davies - King Street
1929 William N Thompson - Barber Street
1902 Owen Bate - High Street

Dairy
1941 Miss Edith Matthews - 19 Barratts Hill
1941 Fred Mear - Coalport

Decorator
1916 Alfred Edgerton - Taylor High Street

Dentist
1934/41 W Bernard Wood - 23 High Street Attend on Thursdays
1934 Chris Clifford Meese - Part-time
1934/41 N G Lees - 51 Church Street Part-time

Draper & Mercers
1828 Thomas Roberts
1851 The Misses Baker - High Street
1851 Mrs Maria Evans - High Street
1851 John Harvey - Cape/King Street
1851/61 William Perrin - High Street
1861/71 Moses Smith - King Street
1885 John Bucknall Dickens - High Street and at Oakengates

1885 Miss Mary Ann Fletcher - Upper Street
1885 Ernest H Ledger - High Street
1891 Edward Kenneth Thompson tailor, clothier, boot maker etc
1916 Ledger & Ledger - High Street
1917 James Davies - King Street
1926/29 William N Thompson - Barber Street tailor, clothier, outfitter, bootmaker, cycle dealer & house furnisher
1934 James Davies - 49 High Street Tel: Ironbridge 6
1941 George Fred.Roberts - High Street

Dress Maker
1851 Helen Pugh - High Street
1861 Hannah Hartshorne - High Street
1885/91 Miss Elizabeth Cartwright - King Street
1885/91 Mrs Louisa Rowe Lower - Church Street
1916/17 Miss Lottie Margaretta Burnet - Cape Street
1916 Mrs C Cleobury - Chapel Road
1916 Hough - Upper High Street
1916 Mrs C Lloyd - High Street
1916 Mrs R Thomas - King Street
1917 Miss Ethel Jane Taylor - Barratts Hill

Earthenware Dealer
1871 William Garbett - Duke Street
1885 John Hartshorne - High Street
1891 Francis Hartshorne - Broseley Wood
1916 Thomas Denstone - King Street

Earthenware Manufacturer
1840 Easthope, Jones & Bathurst

Engineer
1916 William Roberts

Excise Office
1829/35/42 Thomas Roberts

Fancy Goods Dealer
1926 Mrs Lily Scott - 45 King Street

Farm Bailiff
1885 Benjamin Thomas - Dunge Farm to Dowager Lady Forester

Fancy Needlework
1891 Miss Agnes White

Farmers
1851 Henry Booth - High Street
1851 John Davies - High Street
1861/68/85 James Burnet - Woodhouse Farm
1861 Edward Clayton - Rowton Farm
1861/68/71 William Felton - Swinbach
1861/71 Edwin Rawlings - Swinbach
1861/68 Thomas Watson - Benthall
1868/71 George Clayton - Rowton Farm
1868/71 William Jones - Dunge Farm (and contractor)
1868/71 Bromley Jones - Hauleys Hatch
1868 Stephens - Linley
1868 Edward Gough - Willey
1868 Samuel Davies - King Street
1868 Stephen Davis - Willey
1868 Thomas Gwyllian - The Hems Linley
1868 George Howells - Posenhall
1868 John Humpries - Woodlands
1868 Miss Owen - Linley
1868 Thomas Pitt - Posenhall
1868 Edmund Raby - Willey
1868 Richard Shaw - Benthall
1868 Moses Smith - Willey
1871 Thomas Morris - Coneybury
1885 William Samuel Burnet - Upper Ridding
1885 Thomas Morris - Swinbach
1885/91 John Hurdley - Coneybury (and haulier)
1885/91 Thomas Watson - Barratts Hill
1891 Abraham Burnet - Woodhouse
1891/1916/29/41 George Corfield - The Dunge
1916 S A Powell - The Dean
1916/17 William Roberts - Coneybury
1916/17 Arthur Smith - Folley Farm
1916/17 W H Weaver - Rowton Farm
1917/26/34 William Exley & Sons - Woodhouse Farm
1917/26/34 John T Mear - Upper Ridding Farm
1917 Richard Price - Swinbach
1917 Alfred Orice - Lower Ridding Farm
1917/29/34/41 Joseph Thomas - The Dunge
1926/29/34 Alfred Downes - Swinbach Farm
1926/29/34/41 Albert Henry Norgrove - Rowton Farm
1926/29/34 Alfred Roberts - Lower Ridding Farm 1941 Egbert Roberts

1926 William Roberts - Coneybury
1929/34/41 Percy Roberts - Coneybury
1926 Mrs Mary Watling - Folly Farm
1929/34/41 F & R Watling - Folly Farm
1929/34 Alfred Downes - Swinbach
1941 Robert Watling - Swinbach

Fire Bricks
1828/35 John Burton
1828/35 James Davies

Fire Offices
1828/35/42 Abraham Wyke (Globe Insuranse)
1829/35/42 Stephen Jones (Salop Insurance)
1851/68 John Harvey - Cape/King Street
(Birmingham/Lancashire Fire Office)
Medical/Clerical/General Life Office
1868 J Stevens - High Street (Atlas - Fire)
1868 J H Cowley - High Street (Commercial Union)
1868 Enoch Leadbetter - High Street (Crown-Life, Shrops/N Wales-fire)
1868 Richard Rushton - High Street (Liverpool, London & Globe)
1868 William P Shaw - High Street (Salop - fire)
1868 John Humpries - High Street (Sun - fire)
1868 G W Lewis - High Street (Whittington - Life)

Fishmonger
1861 Thomas Jones - The Delph

Fried Fish Dealer
1934 Mrs Gladys Blake - 1 King Street

Furniture Dealer
1885/91 James Clarke
1917/34 James Davies (see also Motor Dealer)

Furrier
1861 Thomas Bennett - King Street

Garage
1929 F J & E Oakley - High Street Tel: Iron 23, Telegraph Oak-Bros

Gardener
1868 Thomas Harvey - Church Street
1891 Joseph Smallwood (To J A Exley Esq.The Rock)

General Dealer
1916 James Mason - High Street
1929 William N Thompson - Barber Street

Glass Dealer
1851/71 John Hayman - Duke/Barber Street
1871 Hannah Pugh

Greengrocer
1885 William Pugh - King Street
1916 G Ball
1916 James Jones - Church Street
1926/29 Thomas Lloyd - King Street
1941 James W Hurdley - 57 Church Street

Grocer/Tea Dealer
1828/35/42 Richard Evans
1829/35/42 Thomas O'Adams
1828 John Guest
1828 William Jones
1829/35/42 William Bell
1829/35/42 Hezekiah Hartshorne
1829/35/42 Stephen Jones
1840/68 Abraham Burnet
1840/51/61/71 John Harvey - Cape/King Street
1840/51/61/71 John Humphries - High Street (Wine & Spirit Dealer)
1868 John Humphries Tallow Chandler
1840 John Instone
1840 Thomas Oakley
1840/51 Samuel Pountney - High Street
1840 Thomas Speake
1840/61 Mary Weaver - King Street
1840 Thomas Wootton
1840 Abraham Barnet
1851 Thomas Beddow - Broseley Wood
1851 James Cowley - High Street
1851 Thomas Everall - Cape/King Street
1851 Hiram Hill - Barratts Hill
1851/61/71/85 Samuel Instone - Upper Church Street
1851/61/71/85 John Mason - Broseley Wood
1851 Jesse Oakley - High Street
1851/61/71 Richard Rushton - High Street
1861 John Evans - Simpson Lane
1861/71/85 Richard Instone - Lower Church Street
1861 George Warburton Lewis - High Street
1868 John Henry Cowley - High Street

1871 Abraham J Burnet - Church Street Provision Dealer
1871 Samuel Leigh Nevett - Sibby's Lane
1885 William Davies - Quarry Road
1885 Mrs Sophia Bradshaw - Upper Church Street
1885 John Burnet & Son - High Street
1885 William Davies - High Street & Fox Lane
1885/91 William Croudace - Broseley Wood
1885/91 Aquila Evans - High Street
1885 Thomas Perkins & Co - High Street
1885 William Henry Rushton - High Street
1891/1916 Edwin Davies - High Street and Fox Lane
1891 Mark Jones - High Street
1891 Mrs Mary Eliza Powell - King Street
1891 Stephen Hill - High Street
1891/1916 Edward Robert Instone - Lower Church Street
1891/1916 Richard Alfred Instone - Upper Church Street
1902 William Arlidge - High Street
1926/34 R A Instone - The Square/15 Church St (Hop Merch) Tel: Iron68
1916 Andrew M Williams - High Street
1916/26/34 Stephen Jones - 73 High Street
1916/17 Richard Henry Massie - High Street
1916 Mrs P Strephan - King Street
1916/17 John Woollam - Upper Church Street
1917/26 E Davis - 81 High Street
1917/26/34/41 Ezra Millward - 57 High Street
1917/26/34 Mrs Eliz.Jane Stephan - 32 King Street
1929 Walter Davis - 82 High Street
1941 J Wood & Son - 73 High Street

Haberdasher
1891/1916/17 Mrs Ann Bagley - Upper Church Street
1926/29 Mrs Jessie Beatrice Shaw - High Street
1934/41 The Misses Annie & Mabel Taylor - 86/87 High Street

Hairdresser
1840/51/61/71 Edward Glover - High Street
1885/91 William Henry Evans - High Street
1885 Thomas Shaw - Quarry Road
1917/26/34 Richard Hudson - 61 High Street
1926/34/41 George Harrison - 6 High Street (Georgie Potter)
1934 Marie - 87 High Street
1941 Albert William Rowbrey - 61 High Street

Hatter
1828/35/42 John Onions
1840/51 Henry Mason - Broseley Wood
1851 William Perrin - High Street

Haulier
1861/71 Thomas Morris - Coneybury Farm
1885/91 John Hurdley - Coneybury Farm
1916 Samuel Danks - King Street
1916 Frederick Oakley - High Street

Higgler
1861 Ann Williams - High Street

Hop & Seed Merchant
1828/35/42 Charles Guest
1828/35/42 John Lister & Son
1851 John Burnet - High Street
1851 Humphrey Charlton - High Street
1851 John Humphrey - High Street
1885 John C W Lister - High Street
1916/17 Richard Alfred Instone - Upper Church Street

Horse Dealer
1917 Herbert J Danks - Barber Street

Hosier/Haberdasher
1840/51 Henry Burnett - High Street
1861/68 Mary Ann Burnett - High Street
1851 Moses Smith - Broseley Wood
1851 John Salmon - Queen Street
1861 Mary Ann Thomas & Son - High Street
1871 Josiah & Mary Ann Thomas - High Street

House & Estate Agent
1851 Edwin Evans - High Street

House Furnisher
1929 William N Thompson - Barber Street

Inland Revenue
1851 Thomas Trupp - Barratts Hill
1885 Henry Pudney - King Street
1891 Charles Goodwin - Mill House

Inns
1828/35 Benjamin Law - Lion

Inspector of Nuisances & School Attendance Officer
William Simms

Insurance See Fire Offices
1840/51 Edwin Evans - High Street (Agent to Sun Alliance Co)
1851 Enoch Leadbetter (Agent to Crown Life Ass Office)
1851 William Shaw - Church St. Agent to Legal/General Life Assurance/Salop Fire Office
1917 Henry R Botwood - The Ferney Church Street
1917/29 Arthur N Dixon - The Down, Haycop
1926/34/41 Walter Williams - 22 Quarry Rd, From 1929 -19 King St
1934/41 William Denstone - 16 Barratts Hill
1934 John Wilkes - 46 Church Street

Ironbridge & District Gas Co Ltd
1941 - 36 Church Street

Iron & Coalmasters
1828/35/42 John Onions

Ironfounders
1828/35/42 Stephen Hill - Benthall
1840/51 John Onions - Whitehall Church Street
1840 Stephen & Hiram Hill - Benthall
1868 Senior & Standering - New Road

Ironmongers
1828/35/42 Richard Davies
1840/51 James Cowley - High Street
1851 Moses & Richard Peters - Duke Street
1871 John Henry Cowley - Fox Lane
1868/71/85/91 Richard Peters - Barbers Row
1868 John Henry Cowley - High Street
1885/91 Edwin Davies - High Street & Fox Lane
1916/26 Edwin Davies - High Street
1934/41 Walter Davies - 84 High Street Tel: Iron 96

Ironstone Pits 1871 Foster & Co

Job Master & Haulier
1901 Frederick Oakley - High Street

Joiners & Carpenters (Builders later)
1828/35/42 Joseph Cox
1828/35/42 John Davies
1828/35/42 William Turley
1851 Benjamin Hill - Barbers Row
1851 Henry Rushton - Church Street
1861 Humphrey Lloyd - High Street
1868 George Gother - Benthall
1868 Charles Hartshorne - High Street
1868 Hiram Lloyd - Duke Street
1868 Rowland Smitheman - King Street

Justice of the Peace
1851 Robert Evans - The Dunge

Land Surveyor
1829/35/42 Paul Lloyd (Pigots)
1861/71 William Jones - Dunge House

Librarian
1861 Isaac Burnet

Limemasters & Lime Burners
1828/35/42 John Patten - Benthall
1828/35/42 John Tranter - Benthall
1868 Edward Williams - Benthall

Linen & Woollen Drapers
1828/35/42 Thomas Roberts
1840 Jeremiah Baker
1829/35/42 William Collier
1829/35/42 Isiah John Guest
1840 John Harvey
1829/35/42 Mary Jones
1840 Evans & Son
1840/68 William Perrin
1871 Robert Doughty
1868/71 Thomas Lawrence - High Street
1871 Henry Thomas & Son - Church Street
1885 Mrs Anne Smith - King Street
1868/85/91 Isaac Watts - High Street
1891 John Samuel Smith - King Street
1891 Edward Kenneth Thompson

1868 Moses Smith - King Street
1868 Mary Thomas & Son - High Street

Lloyds Bank 19 High Street
1891 Manager Arthur Clement Downes
1917 Manager J A Downes
1926 Manager John Lyons Du Sautoy
1929 Manager John Edward Shann
1934 Manager Ralph E Piper
1941 Manager J Raymond Nickless

Locksmith
1851 Thomas Collins - Barbers Row

Lodging House - Chapel Street Approx 10 people
1861 Joseph Bradley

Maltsters
1828 Thomas Blase
1828 William Bill
1828 Benjamin Cooke
1828/35/42 Edward Crump
1828/35/42 Charles Davies
1828/35/42 Thomas Gough
1828/35/42 Charles Guest
1828/35/42 John Jones
1828 J Lister & Son
1828 Thomas Perry
1828 Jane Onions
1828 Thomas Onions
1828 John Tranter
1829/35/42 Thomas Birch
1829/35/42 Walker Blaize
1829/35/42 John Burton
1929/35/42 May Lane
1828/35/42 Samuel Matthews
1829/35/42 John Wellings
1840 Thomas Everall
1840/51 Jeremiah Ashwood
1851 Bernard Wilkinson Colley - Queen Street
1851/68 Samuel Davies - Broseley Wood
1868 Stephen Davies - Windmill Malthouse
1868/71 Richard Matthews - High Street
1885 John Burnet & Son - High Street
1891/1916/17 Harry Owen - High Street

Manure Agent
1871 William Burnet - High Street

Marine Store Dealer
1851 Henry Mason - Broseley Wood

Medical Officer
1917 John Goodison Boon - Whitehall

Midwife
1934 Miss Gertrude Jones - 20 Barratts Hill

Miller
1840/51 Jeremiah Ashwood
1840 S Roden - Benthall
1861 Edwin Roden - Benthall
1871 William Appleby - Church Street
1868 Edward Roden - Benthall
1868 Stanyer & Son - Broseley

Milliner/Dressmaker
1851 Miss Griffiths
1851/68 Helen Pugh - High Street
1851 Caroline Stephan - High Street
1868 Mary Ann Burnet - High Street
1868 Miss Greatbach - Duke Street
1868 Hannah Hartshorne - High Street
1885 Mrs Mary Ann Thompson - King Street

Millwright
1871 George Senior - Church Street

Mineral Agent
Goof & Evans - Hockley Bank

Mining Agent
1871 Samuel Bullock - Church Street
1871 William Evans - High Street

Model Girls Pattern Boys
Never absent never late

Motor Cycle Agent/Ironmonger
1926 Edwin Davies - 84 High Street
1929/34/41 Walter Davies - 84 High Street

Motor Engineer/Garage
1917/26 James Davies - King Street Speciality Motor repairs/car hire.Tel: Iron 6
1926/34 James Davies Furniture dealer & Draper - 49 High Street
1934/41 Hadyn Burns - 67 High Street Motor Garage Prop and Inst of

Electrical Engineering Tel: Iron 77
1934/41 James Davies - Avenue Road
1934/41 Ernest Wm Taylor - 4 Church Street Tel: Iron 132
1934/41 William Oakley - High Street Tel: Iron 23

Music Teacher
1916 George Tonkiss - Barratts Hill
1916/17 M Amphlett - Simpsons Lane
1934 Mrs Ford - Hockley Lane

Nail Maker
1840/51 Moses Peters - Duke Street
1829/35/42/51/68 Richard Peters

Newsagents
1885/91 Enoch Nevett - High Street
1929/34 Miss Mary Moore - 26/27 High Street
1941 Charles Owen Jones - 26/27 High Street Tel: Iron 201

Nobility and Gentry
1828/35 Doctor Townsend Forester
1828/35 Lord Forester - Willey Hall
1828/35 F B Harries - Benthall
1828/35 Rev Charles Hartshorne
1828/35 Rev John Williams
1929/35/42 Walter l Lacon - Linley Hall

Outfitters
1934 Joseph Wood - 57 Church Street

Overseer
1916/26 Thomas Jones - 11 Upper High Street Assistant Overseer

Painter
1818/35/42 Thomas Crowder
1861/71 Richard Jones - High Street
1885 James Mason - High Street

Painters & Paper Hangers
1891 James Mason - High Street
1891 Page Bros - High Street
1916 R Thomas - King Street

Parish Clerk
1871 George Langford - Lower Church Street

Pattern Boys Model Girls
Never absent never late

Petrol Service Station
1941 James Davies - Ironbridge Road /Prop.Harry Davies Tel:Iron 6

Photographer/Fancy Repositry
1885 Harry Wright - High Street

Plumbers/Glazier and Painter/Paper Hangers
1828/35/42 Thomas Crowder
1828 John Pritchard
1840/51/68 Richard Jones - High Street
1851 Leonard Crowder - High Street
1871 John Garbett - Queen Street
1868/85/1917 John Garbett - Duke Street
1885/91/1917 James Mason - High Street
1885/91 Page Bros - High Street
1891 Mrs Betsy Garbett - Duke Street
1916/26 Alfred Edgerton Taylor - Cape/High Street
1917 Taylor & Hill - Barratts Hill
1929/34/41 Cecil Transon Harrison - Cape Street

Potters
1828/35/42 Bell & Poole - Benthall
1828/35/42 John Farnall

Post Horses - Licencee
1851 James Mason - High Street

Postmaster/Postmistress
1828 Isiah Guest. Post Shifnal to Broseley at 4.30am
Post arrives from Wenlock in Broseley 3.30am returns same evening
1840 J J Guest
Letters arrive at 8am and despatch quarter before 6pm every day
1828/35 Hannah Guest
1851 Jeremiah Ashwood
1861 Richard Rushton Sub District of Stamps
Letters arrive every morning at 5.30 afternoon 4.30
Despatch at 7.00am and 5.00pm
1885 William Henry Rushton - High Street

1916 Walter Davis
1926 Mrs Mary Eliz Johnston - Simpsons Lane Broseley Wood

Poulterer
1851 John Evans - Broseley Wood
1851 Ann Williams - High Street

Printer
1916 John Dixon - High Street

Private Residents
1861/71/85/91 Edward Glover Bartlam - High Street/Mrs Bartlam
1861 Henry Charton - King Street
1861 Miss Griffiths - Church Street
1861 Mrs Hartshorne - Bank Place
1861 Mrs Humphries - Woodlands Green
1861 Edward Lister - The Cottage
1861 John Hornby Moore - Barratts Hill
1861 William Nicholas - Queen Street
1861/71 John Pritchard Esq MP - High Street
1861 George Potts - Harris's Green
1861 W P Shaw - Church Street
1861 Mrs Thorns - Church Street
1861 Richard Thursfield - Queen Street
1871 Henry Martin Bathurst - Church Street
1871 Rev T Brothwood - Queen Street
1861/71 Rev R H Cobbold - Rectory High Street
1871 Miss Colley - Barratts Hill
1871/85/91 Mr George Davis - Lower Church Street
1871 William Evans Esq - Queen Street
1871/85/1917/26 Wm Francis - Lower Church Street Child Attendance Officer
1871 Mr William Hall - Church Street
1861/1871/85/91 Frederick Hezikiah Hartshorne - Broseley Hall
1871 Mrs Johnson - Barratts Hill
1871 William Jones - Dunge House
1871 Rev Henry Lee BA - Holly House King Street
1871/85/91/1917 Mr Francis Henry Martin - High Street
1871 John Hornby Maw - Barratts Hill
1871 Thomas Greville Thursfield MD - Queen Street
1871 William Nicholas Field House - Queen Street
1885/91 Mrs Nicholas
1871 Mr William Perrin - Chapel Street
1871 George Potts Esq - Harris's Green
1871 John Pountney - High Street
1871 Mr Edwin Prior - The Green
1885 George Baker - The Laurels
1885 Mrs Bartley - Barratts Hill
1885 Mrs Bill - King Street
1885 Henry Boden - Barratts Hill
1885 William Boden - Barratts Hill
1885/1917 Henry Rogers Botwood - The Ferney Church Street
1885/91 Mrs Bowdler - Lower Church Street
1885 Henry Broadhurst - Cape Street
1885 William Burnett - High Street
1885 Thomas Challinor - Queen Street
1885 John Birch Cleobury - Meadow Cottage
1885/91 Thomas Corfield - Barratts Hill
1885/91 Edward Davies - Chapel House
1885/91 Edwin Davis - Thornton Cottage Duke/High Street
1885 Miss Dawson - Alison House Upper Church Street
1885 Rev Samuel Evans - Orchard House High St Congregation Minister
1885/91 Mrs Exley - Hillsden House
1885/91 Joseph A Exley - Rock House, Mrs J Exley 1902
1885 George Gilbert - Cape Street
1885 John Glase - Broseley Wood
1885 Mrs Hill - Cape Street
1885/1916 Stephen Hill - Cape Street
1885 William Hudson - Barratts Hill
1885 Hamnet Hyde-Clarke - Upper Church Street
1885 Richard Alfred Instone - Memorial Cottage The Delph
1891/1916 " " " - Upper Church Street
1885/91/1902 Rev George Flemming Lamb MA - The Rectory Church Street
1885/91 George Langford - Ivy House Pound Lower Church Street
1885/91 George Ledger - Queen Street School Master
1885/91 George Bryan Ledger - Queen Street
1885/91 John C W Lister - High Street
1885 Ben Lloyd - Lower Church Street
1885 William Moore - Duke Street
1885/91 Mrs Potts - The Grange,The Green

1885 Cecil Potts - High Street
1885 James Rowe - Lower Church Street
1885 John Shaw - King Street
1885 John Wiggins - Mill Terrace
1885/91/1917 Ernest Walter Shorting- The Lawns Church Street
1885/91/1902 Charles T Smith - Lower Church Street
1885/91 William Southorn - Broseley Wood
1885/91 William Southorn Jnr - Broseley Wood
1885 The Misses Thorn - Ferleigh High Street
1891/1902 The Misses Thorn - Fifield Barratts Hill
1902/16 Miss Thorn - Fifield Barratts Hill
1885/91 Thomas Watson - Barratts Hill
1885/91 John Wilde - King Street
1885/91 Herbert Wootton - Grove House
1885/91 Edward Bagnall Potts - High Street
1885/1917 Mrs Roden - Holly House
1891/1917 Alfred Arthur Wiggins - King Street/Barratts Hill
1891/1916 Miss Roden - Holly House
1891 John Doughty
1891 Arthur Clement Downes - Orchard House High Street
1891 Miss Edwards - Barratts Hill
1891 George M Garrard - Thornton Cottage Church Street
1891 Stephen Hill - High Street
1891 Mrs Lamb - Bank Cottage 1902 Rev G F Lamb Rectory
1891 George Hornby Maw - Fernleigh
1891/1902 Charles Smith - Lower Church Street
1891 Benjamin Suart - Alison House Church Street
1891 George A Taylor - High Street
1891 Rev Hamilton Vernon - Dunge House Rector St Marys Jackfield
1891/1917 Mrs E H or S Bathurst - Church Street
1891/1917 Thomas Griffiths - Church Street
1891/1917/26 Donald L Prestage - The Laurels Church Street
1891/1902 Edward Oakes Lower - Church Street
1902 Henry Botwood Rogers - The Fernery
1902 James Britton - Barratts Hill
1902 Thomas Richard Burroughs - Woodlands
1902 George Duppa Collins - Half House
1902 Herbert Wilson Cook - Orchard House King Street
1902 George Davis - Thornton House Chapel Street
1902 Mrs Cowley - High Street
1902 Samuel Davis - High Street
1902 William Dyson M B - Alison House Church Street
1902 Gilbert Elliot - Dunge House
1902 John Ibbetson - High Street
1902 Mrs James B Nevett - Barratts Hill
1902 John Pountney - Church Street
1902 Mrs E M Powell - Bank Cottage
1902 Archibald Scott - Chapel House
1902/16/17/26 John Goodison Boon - Whitehall
1902/17 Miss Dixon - Ivy House Pound Lane
1902/17 J A Downes - Fernleigh High Street
1916/17 Arthur Edge - Chapel House
1902/16/17/26 Norman Fox Edwards - Fifield Barratts Hill(1902 High Street)
1902/17 Mrs John Garbett - Fox Street
1916/17 Rev Charles A Howell BA - The Rectory
1917/26 William Instone - Woodlands
1902/16/17 Adam Jones - The Lindens Duke Street
1902/17 Miss Jones - Barratts Hill
1917 Jeffrey Pearce Knight - Dunge House
1902/16/17/26 Mrs Mary Lister - High Street
1916/17/26 Joseph Nicklin - Orchard House
1902 Joseph Nicklin - Cairn House Queen Street
1917 Frederick Meredith - High Street
1916/17/26 Edward Oakes - 5 Barber Street (1902 Lower Church street)
1916/17/26 The Misses Potts - The Deanery Lower Church Street
1916/17/26 Mrs M E Powell - Bank Cottage
1916/17/26 Archibald Scott - Chapel House
1917 Arthur Smith - Folly Farm House
1917 Mrs Southorn -Woodhouse
1916/17/26 Alfred H Thorn Pudsey - Broseley Hall
1902/17/26 Homer Wase - Church Street
1917 John Watkins - Hockley Road House
1902/17/26 Frederick Hezekiah Potts - The Grange
1926 John Watkins - 9 Duke Street
1916/17/26 George H Wilde - The Willows Coalport Road
1917 John B Williams - Coalport Road
1916 Edwin Davis - High Street
1916 Walter Davis - Fairview High Street
1916 Arthur N Dixon - The Downes
1916 J Du Sartoy - King Street
1916 W Edge - Mill House
1916 Rev Robert Gillenders - St Mary's Rectory
1916 George Hurdley - Lower Church Street

1916 Adam J Jones - High Street
1916 Peter Jones - Alison Cottage
1916 Emily Jones - Calcutt House
1916 William Jones - The Mount
1916 Francis Henry Martin - Horton Cottage New Road
1916 George Moore - Queen Street
1916 Isaac Onions - Barratts Hill
1916 John W Price - New Road House
1916 William Scott - King Street
1916/26 Mrs Nellie Worthen Southorn - Simpsons Lane Woodhouse
1902/16 Miss Thorn - Fifield Barratts Hill
1926 Frederick Howells - Queen Street
1926 Wilfred Howells - Hurstlea
1926 Thomas Abberley
1926 Frank Brooks - Ivy House Pound Lane
1926 Edward Brown Charlton - 42 Church Street
1926 Edward Duppa Collins - Half House 12 Church Street
1926 J E Downes Fernleigh - 12 High Street
1926 Mrs Joseph Exley - Rock House
1926 William Garbett - 10 Fox Lane
1926 Mrs Janet Hamilton - Dunge House
1926 Miss Ada Jones - Barratts Hill
1926 Mrs Jane Jones - The Lindens
1926 John Ritchings - High Street
1926 Mrs E M Shorting - The Lawns Church Street
1926 Rev Winnard Alex.Warner - The Rectory
1926 Alfred E Wiggins - King Street
1926 Miss Alice Wilkinson - Chapel House

Professor of Music
1851 Henry Knight Esq - Church Street
1868/71 Charles Roden - Nova Cottage

Provision Dealer
1885 Jonas A Burnet - High Street
1916 Edwin Davies - High Street

Public House See Taverns

Public Officers
1861 William Rushton - High Street Collector of Taxes and Assessor

Rag Man
1868 Thomas Bennett

Railway & General Carriers
1891/1916 R T Smith

Reading Room Victoria Hall?
1917/29/34 Sec. Thomas Jones - High Street
1941 Sec. Norman Ball

Rectors of Broseley
1840 Rev Townsend Forester
1851 Orlando Watkin Weld Forester - Church Street
1851 Rev William Jackson - Broseley Cottage, (Baptist)
1851 Rev William Jones - Chapel Hill (Baptist)

Registrar (Births/Deaths)
1851 Edwin Evans - High Street
1851 Richard Evans - Duke Street
1861 William Pearce
1871 William Perrin - High Street
1885/91 John Dixon - High Street (also collector of Taxes)
1916 William Edge - Mill House
1926/29/34 William Edge - 6 Church Street Tel:Iron 79
1917 Miss Mary J Edge - Mill House
1926/29/34 Mrs Ethel Edge Deputy Reg.- 6 Church Street
1941 John B Dixon - 85 High Street

Relieving Officer
1891 William Edge
1868 W T Jones - Benthall
1941 Bernard S Taylor - 48 High Street Tel:Iron79

Rope, Sail & Tarpauling Manufacturer
1840 James Harrington
1868 John Burroughs - Ladywood

Saddler
1828/35/51 Thomas Richards
1828 Benjamin Davies
1851 Robert Cox - High Street
1861 Robert Smith Cox - High Street
1868/71 Thomas Jones - High Street
1868 Richard Wilkinson - High Street
1885/91 Edward Woof - High Street
1917 William H Saunders - High Street

Salt Dealer
1829/35/42 Samuel Roden - Benthall

Sanitary Inspector
1941 Chris.James Thomas - 29 Church Street

Schools
1829/35/42 Mrs Onions Ladies Day & Boarding School Broseley
1835 William Thomas Day School
1835 Misses Wyke Ladies Boarding Broseley
1891 Arthur Shinn - Alison Villa Middle School
1840 Mary Ann Ball
1840 Wilton George - Master- National School
1829/35/42 William Childs Day School
1851 Henry Martin Bathurst - Barratts Hill - National
1851 Miss Helen Bayliss Ladies Boarding School - Church Street
1855 National School erected, cost £1,600, site given by Lord Forester (mixed /infants) enlarged 1876 to 550 children. Average attendance about 400.
1861 National School Master George Ledger School House - New Road
1861 Sarah Jones - Harris's Green
1871 Greenhalgh - Church Street Ladies Boarding School
1885 Miss Dawson - Alison House Church St. Boarding/Day School
Successor to Miss Hobday
(1885) National School MasterHenry E Wale, Mistress Miss E G Street, Infants Mistress Miss A A L Nevett
1885/91 Mrs Mary Ann Dixon - Ivy House Pound Lane Day School
1916 Miss E A Dixon - Ivy House, Sec to the Schools
1916 National Schools Master Herbert Clark/Mistress Miss A Wilkinson/Infants Mrs Mary Ann Dixon
1916 Legges Hill School Broseley Wood Mistress Mrs A Wiggins
1916 Burks Academy for Boys - The Folley

School Attendance Officer
1891 Thomas Jones - Upper High Street
1917/26/34/41 Frederick Francis - 25 Church Street

Seedsman
1851 Thomas Cowley - 3 High Street
1861/71 Thomas Harvey - Church Street
1885/91 Thomas Norton - High Street
1885/91 Richard Russell - Barratts Hill
1917 John Smith - King Street

Shoemaker see Boots etc

Shopkeepers & dealers in sundries
1828/35/42 William Burnet
1828//35/42 John Davies
1829/35/42 John Instone
1829/35/42 William Millward
1829/35/42 Thomas Pearce
1840 Richard Roden
1840 John George
1840 Henry Long
1840 Francis Oakes
1840 Mary Weaver
1840 M Page
1851 Jeremiah Bill - Broseley Wood
1851/68 John Evans - Broseley Wood
1851/61 Samuel Nevett - High Street
1851/61/71 Richard Powell - Broseley Wood
1851/61/68 Elizabeth Raspass - Barratts Hill
1851 Thomas Speake - Queen Street
1851 Ann Williams - High Street
1861/68 Mary Ann Davis - King Street
1861/68 Elizabeth Everall - King Street
1861 Mary Turner - Quarry Road
1861 James Williams - Workhouse Road
1871 William Barnaby Evans - Broseley Wood
1871 Francis Hartshorne - Broseley Wood
1868 Emma Oakes - King Street
1868 Mary Ann Hartshorne - High Street
1868 Esther Williams - Workhouse Road
1868 Henry Walker - King Street
1868 Eliza & Harriet Pountney - High Street
1885 Miss Julia McCoy - King Street
1885/91 Miss Susan Elizabeth Nicklin - Cape Street
1885/91 Miss Harriet Pountney - High Street
1891 Mrs Charlotte Clark - Upper Church Street
1891 Mrs Mary Danks - Barbers Row

1891 Mrs Mary Mason - High Street
1891 Mrs Caroline Parker - Lower Church Street
1891 Mrs Rebecca Tristam - Broseley Wood
1916 Miss Moore - High Street
1917 Henry Bowen - King Street
1917/26/34 John Edwards - 37 Lower Church Street
1917 R A Instone - Lower Church Street (The Stores)
1917/26/29 Ernest Humphries - Quarry Road
1917/26/34 John Wilkes - 19 Quarry Road
1917/29 John Woollam - Church Street
1917/26/34 Harry Reynolds - High Street
1917/34/41 Ironbridge & Coalbrookdale Industrial Co-operative Society, High Street
1917/26 Mrs Gertrude Oakes - Barratts Hill
1917 Thomas William Parry - High Street
1926/34 Thomas Bullock - 1 Cape Street
1926/41 Mrs Mary Eliz. Johnston - Simpsons Lane Tel:Iron 62
1929 Nellie Bennett - 56 King Street
1929/34/41 William Bowen - 8 King Street
1929 Arthur Leeper - 14 King Street
1929/34 Edwin Oakley - 38 High Street
1929/34 John Wilkes -19 Quarry Road
1934/41Joseph Harvatt - 23 King Street
1934/41 John Thomas Scholfield - Quarry Road
1934/41 Albert Snow - 56 King Street
1934/41 Mrs Constance Mildred Picken - 10/11 Barber Street
1941 R A Instone - 15 Church Street & 81 High Street
1941 Albert G Edgington - The Square
1941 Mrs Ada Edwards - 4 Birchmeadow
1941 Thomas William Parry - 1 Cape Street
1941 Thomas Wm Ed Edwards - 37 Lower Church Street

Small Pox Hospital
Wenlock Municipal Small Pox Hospital
1917/26 Maurice Gepp Medical Officer

Smallware Dealer
1829/35/42 Henry Burnet

Solicitors
1840 John,George,John Jnr Pritchard
1851 George Potts Esq - High Street/The Green
1851 Potts & Nicholls - High Street
1861 Potts & Gordon - High Street
1871 Potts & Son - High Street
1885/91 Edward Bagnall Potts - High Street
1885 Cecil Potts - High Street
1885/91/1916/26 Fred.Hezikiah Potts - High Street
1916/26/34 George Potts - High Street
1917/26/34/41 Potts & Potts - 29 High Street Tel:Iron 40
1929/34 Cyril A Potts of Potts & Potts - High St.Tel:Iron 40
Wenlock Old Age Pension Sub Committee
1929/34/41 George Potts - High Street Tel:Iron 40
1941 Wm Fred.Blakemore of Potts & Potts

Spirit Merchant
1926/29 Charles Edwards (Worcester)Ltd - High Street

Stationer
1851/68/71/85/91 Enoch Nevitt - High Street
1868/71/85/91 James Brian Nevitt - High Street
1868 James Clark - King Street
1916/17 Louisa & Ethel Dixon - The Delph
1917 Miss Mary Moore - High Street
1926/34 Miss Louisa Dixon - 85 High Street
1941 John B Dixon - 85 High Street

Straw Hat & Bonnet Maker
1871 Mary Ann Nevett - High Street

Sub Distribtor of Stamps
1829/35/42 Isiah John Guest

Supervisor
1829/35/42 Jno Wilson

Surgeons
1828 John Ashwood
1828/35/42 William Fifield
1828/35/42/51/68 Richard Thursfield - Queen Street
1829/35/42 J Nicholls & Ashwood
1840 Richard Wyke
1851/61/71 Edward Glover Bartlam - High St(Coroner for Borough 71)
1851/61/71 Frederick Hezikiah Hartshorne - Church Street
1885 Bartlam & Taylor

1885/91 George Duppa Collins - Whitehall
1885/91 George Arthur Taylor (Factory Surgeon)
1916/17 J Goodison Boon - Whitehall Church Street
1926/34/41 J Goodison Boon - Lady Forester Hospital Tel:Iron 2
1917/26/29 Norman Fox Edwards - Fifield Barratts Hill
1868 Thomas Greville Thursfield - Duke Street
1934/41 Sherlock Wm Oliver Hoy - Fifield Barratts Hill Tel:Iron29
1934 Thomas Strahan Hoy

Surveyor
1851 Adam Jones - Church Street
1868 William Jones - Dunge House
1885 George Ledger - Queen Street (Sanitary Authority)
1916 John Broadhurst - Duke Street

Tailors
1829/35/42 John George
1829/35/42 James Johnson
1829/35/42/51 Steven Jones - High Street
1829/35/42 Nathaniel Thomas
1841/61/71/85 Thomas Francis - Barratts Hill (High Street 1885)
1840/51 John Johnson - Barbers Row
1851/61/71 Thomas Davies - The Delph (1868/71 Carvers Road)
1851 Robert Francis -Barratts Hill
1851 Samuel Pountney - Duke Street
1861/71/85/91 James Bryan Nevett - High Street
1861/71 James Smith - Chapel St (68/71Duke Street)
1885/91 Isaac Watts - High Street
1891 Edward Kenneth Thompson
1868 Stephen Jones - Workhouse Road
1916/26/34 E C S White - 48 High Street
1926/34 William N Thompson - Barber Street

Tallow Chandler
1828/40 Richard Evans
1828/35/42 John Jones
1828 Robert Evans
1829/35/42 William Carrington
1851/68 John Humphries - High Street

Tavernes & Public Houses
Albion High Street: 1840-85 Robert Lowe, 1916 Miss E Millward, 1917 Julian Millward 1926 Miss J Millward
Cape of Good Hope Cape Street: 1835-71 Thomas Lane, 1885 Thomas Harley
1902 Thomas Davies, 1917 Harry Russell
New Crown High Street: 1835-61 Elizabeth Yates, 1871 Richard Matthews
1885 John Powis, 1916-17 Miss Florence Powis, 1926 George Fred.Wall.
Crown & Anchor King Street: 1835-40
Dog Church Street: 1835
Dog & Talbot Church Street 1840-61, Church Street: 1871, William Meredith 1885
Duke of Cumberland King/Duke Street: 1840/1851 R T Jones, 1861-85 John Shaw, 1916-26 G Millward
Duke of Wellington 1835 J Leadbetter
Duke of York Church Street: 1840/51/61
1871/85 Ockley Bank, 1902 Richard Evans, 1916/17 Thomas Moore, 1926 Mrs Anne Moore
Duke William 1835 Ellen Cooke
Elephant High Street: 1835//40/51 John Bradley, 1871 Thomas Jones, 1885 Fred Turner, 1917 Mrs M J Millward, 1926 Thomas Parker.
Foresters Arms Church Street/Avenue Road: 1840/61 Eliz.Edwards
1885, 1916/17 Mrs Harriet Britton, 1926 Thomas Smith.
Fox Fox Lane:1835/40/51 Richard Poole
Hand & Tankard Workhouse Road: 1840/71 William Moore, 1885 John Matthews, 1916 Frank Benbow.
Hole in the Wall Carvers Road: 1835/40/85 Noah E Hill,
Kings Head King Street,Broseley Wood: 1835, 1851/61/71 Hannah Rufus,
1885 James D Smith, 1916/17 George Keay, 1926 Henry Starr Southorn.
Lion High Street: 1840, 1885 John Instone, 1902 Ambrose Hancock ,
1917 Thomas Instone, 1926 Archibald George Oswell.
Lord Hill King Street: 1835 A Southorn, 1861 Eliza Weeks, 1885 Stephen Hill,
1916/26 Mrs Marlowe (Ivy).
Lord Nelson Legges Hill Broseley Wood: 1835/40/61

Maypole Woodlands Green: 1835/71 John Morris.
New Inn Speeds Lane: 1835, 1861 William Watkins.
Old Crown Church Street: 1835/40/51 1861 John Reynolds.
Old Red Lion High Street: 1835, 1840 Lion, 1851 Commercial Inn, 1871 Wm Jones.
Pheasant Upper Church Street: Commercial Inn & Posting House:
1835/40/51/61 1871 Samuel Instone, 1885 Mrs Emma Horton & Son,
1902 Miss Lucy Augusta Beard 1916 Mrs Lloyd, 1917 Thomas Smith.
Plough Barbers Row: 1835/40
Royal Oak 1835
Social Club (Broseley) 1919
Spotted Leopard 1835
Talbot Edwin Fletcher Groves Church Street
Crown Barratts Hill 1851
Globe King Street Top of Legges Hill, 1861 Sarah Lloyd.
Victoria Inn & Vetinary Surg. Lower Church St.reet:
1871 Syrus Edmund Onslow, 1885 Clement Fennell.
Wheatsheaf Broseley: 1835 George Lloyd.
Whelps Broseley: 1835 Richard Beard.
Coalport Bridge Inn Swinbach. 1885 Thomas Morris.
Napoleon Inn Woodlands Road, 1916 John Brown.
Elephant & Castle 1916 Mrs Hill.
Seven Stars Fearney Bank: 1916 Thomas R Hill
The Dustpan: 1916
Vaults High Street: 1926 Matthew William Grocott.
Brittania Inn Bower Yard: 1861 Mary Gother-Widow.

Tea Dealer and Druggist
1828/35 Thomas Adams

Teacher of Music
Matthew Amphlett - Broseley Wood

Thatcher
1851 James Dean - Broseley Wood

Tile Maker (Manufacturer)
1861 Maw & Co. Broseley
1885/1929/34/41-William Exley & Sons-The Rock, Tel:Iron 8 Telegram Exley Bros.
1885/91 Milburgh Tileries - Prestage & Co
1891 Holywell Tileries Oakes and Pumford
1929/34 Prestage & Broseley Tileries In 34 Tel: Iron 10 Telegraphic Tileries Bros
1941 " " " " Tel: Iron 36

Timber Merchant
1840/51 John Griffiths - Church Street
1851 Thomas Broadhurst - Church Street
1885 Thomas Morris - Swinbach
1926/29 F.J & E Oakley - 38 High Street Tel:Iron 23 Telegraph OAK-BROSELEY

Tin Man
1861 Thomas Childs - Hockley
1871 William Harris - King Street

Tobacco Clay Pipe Makers
1828/35/42 Richard Legg
1829/35/42 Sarah Roden
1828/35/42 Noah Roden - Benthall and New Inn
1835/42 Samuel Pinner or Pennor
1835/40/51/61/71/85 William Southorn - Broseley Wood
1829/35/42 William Bryan
1829/35/42 John Bradley - Benthall
1829/35/42 John Gethin - Benthall
1835/42 RichardShaw - Benthall
1840 Samuel Roden - (Coalford?)
1840/51/68 Richard Tonkiss - Barratts Hill
1851 Richard Bradley - Broseley Wood
1851 Joseph Southorn - Broseley Wood
1861 /71 Edwin Southorn - Benthall
1885/91/1916 Rowland Smitheman - King Street
1917 Smitheman & Co - King Street
1941 William Southorn & Co Broseley Pipe Works

Tobacconist
1891 Mrs Sarah Ann Clegg - High Street
1916 Richard Hudson - High Street
1926/34/41 George Edward Taylor - 41 Church Street

Transport
1861 Broseley – Chief outlet River Severn

Turnpike Road Trustees
1861 George Hartshorne - High Street

Upholsterer
1851 George Hartshorne - High Street
1891 James Clarke Jnr - Carvers Road
1916/26 Jas Clarke - 35 Church street

Valuer/Appraiser
1851 George Hartshorne - High Street

Veterinary Surgeon
1885 Henry Danks
1916 Herbert Danks - King Street

Victoria Institute
1917/26/34 Secretary Thomas Jones - High Street
1941 Secretary Norman Ball

Water Carriers
1828 To Bristol and all the line of the Severn Ames & Jones from Coalport Warehouse every Springtide.
1828 To Bristol William Devey from Coalport every Springtide
1828 To Shrewsbury William Goodwin from his own house Ironbridge, every Springtide.
1828/35/42 To Shrewsbury & Droitwich Samuel Poole from his own house in Ironbridge every Springtide.
1828/35/42 To Stourport G Lloyd from the Swan every week

Watchmaker
1840 Thomas Blakeway
1917 Henry Powell - High Street
1917/26/34/41 William Roberts - Barber Street (Repairer)
1926/29 Charles James Burns - High Street

Wheelwright
1828/35/42 Robert Griffiths
1829/35/42 Richard Poole
1840/51/61/68 Thomas Broadhurst - Church Street
1851 John Griffiths - Church Street
1851/61 Charles Rowe - Broseley Wood
1861/71 John Porter - Church Street
1885/91 Joseph Garbett - Lower Church Street
1885/91 George Wood - Lower Church Street
1868 Joseph Longmoor - Linley

Wine & Spirit Merchants
1828/35/42 John Lister & Son
1840 Thomas Lister
1851/61/71 Humphrey Charlton - High Street
1871/85/91 John C W Lister - High Street
1885 Richard Instone - Lower Church Street
1885 William Henry Rushton - High Street
1891/1916 Edward Robert Instone - Lower Church Street
1916/17 Slaney & Son - High Street

TAPES

Introduction: I recorded this tape of my father Percy Beddow talking about catching birds. In days gone by birds were kept in cages and bred by many people as a hobby, in these days it is illegal. I have written this piece out as it was spoken in the Broseley dialect, as a matter of interest.

DAD 1995 AGED 81

Talking about birds and his brother Arthur.

Our Arthur had a mule off somebody, I can't think of his name, he could sing. Our Derek came wum one night and said' Ah, Wheer's thee bird Arthur'. Arthur said he's in the cage, Derek said he inna, Arthur said he is, he was singing just - sing from morning till night - Arthur got the cage down, the bird wunna theer, the bloody hawk had had it. The only hawk as ever cum down wum.

I said to Arthur thee wants to catch a sparrow and put im in theer and hang a rat trap on the bottom of it. It didna cum again, no it never cum.

(Conversation interrupted here as a bird appeared in the garden), "that's a gold finch theer, that's no blue tit, I towd thee it was a gold finch, I could do with a gold un. They binna on teasel yet, they dunna cum on teasel till the end of September.

Our Arthur was on the fowl pen, wheer he had his pigeons, an all that, I went down one Sunday morning, there wus nine theer, I said to our Arthur I'll bring a net down this afternoon, ween put it down. I canna mess with it said Arthur. Now thee asna got to, all thees got to do is cover it over with a piece of tin at night, just release the elastics, an in the morning pull em back out again.

Well we got all the birdseed out of the cages, he'd got 3 bantams Arthur had. I could always tell when he caught summat, he'd cum down the road half smiling, - anyway he said Perce pull that net up I amma going to catch nothing, they'n coming every day and they wunna goo in. I said wunna they, I broke em all off, not off, broke em down right by the net, throwed in all the seed. Arthur cum up mythering one afternoon, I said bloody leave it Arthur it inna hurting this afternoon, we'd got the line up by the pigstee.

Thee nowst, he cum up right on taytime, I could tell when he cum - he was half smiling- and said I've had a bit of luck this afternoon, I said I can tell thee ast by thee face. Why, when I went down the garden thur was five bloody goldies in that net, I run back down by the pigstee and pulled the string, I had em, and dust thee know what Perce, they wun 5 cocks, 5 bloody cocks. Well I hadna got any, so I said if they live I'll have one, so he said these't better cum and look tomorrow if I've put that net down right again, so I went down, went down Legges Hill from work on me bike, and then back up when I had me dinner. He cum up, he said them birds un - I said now if thee only sists one or two under it dunna pull it, I said, if there's three or four theer wait until they'n all gawn, they'n buggers for wet seed, bullies bin. He cum up again - there was a goldy under that net this afternoon, it was a cock, I ivered and overed over whether to pull it, an I thought no, Perce said dunna pull it. He wus there waitin when I went down from the button factory - I used to finish at half past three - waitin by the gate, he never said nothing, I thought thees't got summat to tell me, I can tell by thee face. Whats think he said - I caught 5 more goldies this afternoon. Wheer I was buggered, the wire netting was only about a yard high, so the bantams wun gooing in to ate the seed, see, (Arthur had 3 bantams) but the one hen flew over, and wus ating the seed in the net and the goldie wus in the net as well. So I run up in the house, fetched some bread, chocked it on like a landing and called at the bantam chock,chock,chock like a cockerel, calling em, her jumped over the wire.

Arthur said I went back round to the string quick, an I pulled it, I had five more, every one lived, thur was seven cocks and three hens. To breed mules, it has to be a cock goldie and hen canary, I know wheer thur's some. I always had a mule, thee hast to have summat to tutor a young mule, start im off straight away, on the perches, they'n just lying dormant now, there's nothing to break em, you'm buggered. I'd like to get a cock goldfinch.

I really enjoyed that guiness.

Arthur and Percy Beddow, and Eric Corfield with the cage birds 1932

NEIL - 1995

Introduction: This tape is of my brother Neil Beddow who is very interesting to speak to. He talks of local events, past and present, some told to him by people no longer with us. The conversation was quite wide ranging and covered the war, music and mining.

Dad's Aunt Eva had the Fish and Chip Shop that is now, it was the Seven Stars pub, Dad said she had it as a sweet shop, her name on the deeds was Eva Gladys Blake, she was a spinster, she was only there about 2 years. She married Granny's brother Thomas Corfield.

About Dads Aunt Eva, her father was a Police Inspector in Ironbridge, when he was a young copper he actually traced a bloke as far as London, some men had robbed a church and he had followed them, like a Texas Ranger really, gone for miles and miles, there was no jurisdiction then, in them days, they caught up with them and arrested them, sleeping in hedges, walking all the way to places.

Tommy Brookthrustle walked all the way to South Wales for work, when I worked for Lol, me and Eric Griffiths taking logs round on a Saturday morning, we picked Tommy up he was on the back of the wagon, having the crack telling jokes, about him being a ferret and all that sort of stuff, he said that years ago when he was a kid, he walked all the way down South Wales, with his Dad for work, bricklaying or something, to send his mother some money back, they used to walk it and sleep in hedges and haystacks in them days.

Bob Thomas who lived next door, when it was a beer house, or ale house, told me when he was a little lad, some fellow made coffins in my big shed, he was a carpenter or joiner, he used to take him beer on a tray to a little window in the shed.

When he was a little boy his mother took him along the Dead Walls to watch the Shropshire Yeomanry, they came along with their swords swiping the Turks heads off - the targets were called Turks Heads - for practice, he used to come back crying as it had frightened him. They used to hang people along the Dead Walls, there was a stone where the Quakers graveyard is, in the wall there, where the new house is now, it said this is where the hangman's tree stood, Ann has seen the stone but it has gone now.

Bob also told how Cecil Sharpe, there was a house called after him in London, collected folk music throughout the land, the length and breadth of England he went, he came to Broseley, and they said there was no music round here, what he must have done was upset somebody and they gave him nothing, because there obviously was music around here, he remembered him coming to Broseley. These teacher people come here telling me there was no music, Neil said there was, there are photos of Great Grandad playing flutes and banjo's. Perce Roberts used to have dances at the farm there, the Coneybury, they used to have sessions with the flutes, and things, it was quite funny, because Neil was talking to Bob about music, and he said about this Cecil Sharpe, that he remembered him coming.

Bob has been dead about 10 years. The alehouse was open when he was young so you can go back a hundred years, beer houses could not sell wines and spirits. It was called the Unicorn, 24 King Street, and was later Thomas's Paint Shop.

When there was fighting, say somebody on the Fold, there were all miners there in them days, the mothers used to say oh! stop, stop, dunna, stop, take pity on them - then they'd say oh it dunna matter its only Taffy. They didna like em, so they let them get on with it.

It was said that Guest took Broseley miners down Wales to open up the South Wales minefields. They had to walk there, it was a pitiful sight, it must have turned full circle when they came back to Broseley and then went back again in later years.

Where Aunt Beat lived in Perry' Row, where Granny's family the Corfields were born, there is some ground in front of it near Bridge Road, or the Coach Road as it was called then, where cars are parked now, there used to be a small row of kilns there. There also used to be a mill there in the garden of the house opposite the New Inn, it is shown on the old maps of the area. This house used to belong to the Jews, it was a factory at one time, they made dolls faces and mom used to work there, probably during the war, painting these dolls faces, Norah said that she did outwork, but we did go there with her, it could have been to collect this work.

Neil also recalled there being a badger in a cage at the New Inn, seen as he went past on walks to Benthall Edge.

Talking about coal fires, what about the sticks and logs we got, when the wind had been blowing, everybody had a little truck and made trailers, the old and the wise used to go up when the wind had been blowing and the dead branches had come down, there could be some good pickings, apart from that, if the wind had not been blowing you took a rope with a weight on the end and threw it over a dead branch and pulled it till it broke, that's how they used to go 'wooding', old man Gallier and them who'd been in the Great War.

Dad used to go round to Georgie Potters when we were kids, his name was George Harrison he was a hairdresser and barber, in High Street by the Cape of Good Hope pub, he was a cage bird fancier/breeder - a society judge, who became champion of all England with a gold finch, which he exhibited at Crystal Palace in London where he exhibited under the name George Potter, he was an ex miner as well, that's why they were all into cage birds, canaries, they then got onto goldfinches and mules, I remember the old chap telling us stories, he used to be into whippet racing many years ago, down the bottom by Harris's Green, towards the Deerleap, in that long field on the left, by Reeve's cottage, there used to be whippet racing, the miners used to race the whippets and greyhounds there in them days, they bet money too.

They reckon, say somebody was being shaved in his barbers shop, if they got talking about banjo's and that, they would have to forget it, they'd have to wipe the lather off their faces and he'd shut up shop, get the banjo's out and start playing, they'd have to go away and come back another time if they wanted a shave.

The old chap told us that there was once some trouble and someone was after Georgie down by the Cross Keys, and Georgie who was only a little man, was hiding round a corner there in the dark, (the lighting was very poor then,) while whoever was after him had gone by. Another story was of a miner going to work early one morn-ing, when some old lady (she might have been related to the Halls) came out of a house down by the Cross Keys, in a long white night-dress, whatever, and asked what time of the clock, to get up for work, and the man had a heart attack and died.

Dad said when he was a kid he used to go along and listen to Harry Blood, cause he played the banjo, and he was keen on a banjo himself, he watch him playing chords or what ever, but Harry could play a piano, violin, anything, he was noted for his music.

Harry Blood was wounded in the Great War, along with a lot of other blokes. Arthur Harris who looked after the old chaps pigeons lived next door to them when they lived by the phone box there now, in Broseley Wood, he was wounded in the Great War too, he came from away. Bert Garbett, Teddy Burgess, Teddy Storar and Charlie Beddow aged 19, who was killed and has his name on the monument in the Memorial Green, he was dad's uncle, we have his penciled notes here from the trenches.

When old Teddy Burgess was a young man they went on summer camp, in the Cadets, they used to wear red tunics in them days, in 1914, the army was wearing khaki. When they came back, war was breaking out then,

Group of Broseley musicians 1905, William Beddow flute, second from right, back row and his father banjo

they got out a the station in Ironbridge, and they were asking for volunteers, they went and joined the army and went straight to India more or less, after doing a bit of training at Southampton, and were away about 2 years, came back for the Somme offensive, about 1916, he was 16 years old when he was on the Somme battle field, and he'd been in India 2 years, talk about young men being the army, they were all wounded, old man Gallier who lost an eye, Tippin Davies, and him off the Tynning with one leg, Mr Reeves. There was an old joke they used to say 'Gallier used to say Happy new ear to Davies, and Davies used to say Happy new eye to Gallier'.

Bert Garbett was in the Great War, when a German aeroplane was spotted flying over the trenches, they used to go back and drop a message in handkerchiefs to their gunners, and radios etc, and tell them up or down 100 yards whatever. The plane came down, don't know if it was shot down and landed between the lines, the two airmen got out and were running back to the German trenches, him and his mate shot the pair of them with a machine gun, and were court marshalled for doing it, for shooting unarmed officers, it was not supposed to be on, but if they had let them go back they would have known and told the ranges of our side, his punishment was he had to stay in the line until he was killed or wounded, or he could be shot by a firing squad, so he stayed in the line and got wounded, whether his mate shot him or not, I don't know, I'm just guessing, he didn't say.

Bert Garbett, Teddy Burgess - they got wounded and were sent to Ireland. The trouble was on in Ireland, you could go to a pub in Dublin and be drinking with a bloke, you'd walk outside and he'd shoot you in the head, that's how it was in the Irish uprising. Charlie wrote in his little notes home, how different it was being in the trenches, he'd have these letters from home saying how they'd had the most terrific thunder storms, most terrible storms they don't know how they stuck it, he was in the trenches and there was no comparison, he said he never had the cigarettes a neighbour reckoned he had sent him, like a good many of them, they reckon they send stuff but it never gets here, they must have been telling lies.

He met Churchill, he came behind the lines inspecting a bit, they'd built an old shack, he said how ingenious they were, they'd made a fine job making this shack, (a proper Beddows trick), he hadn't been gone long when the damn thing fell down. Harry Blood was mentioned in these notes or letters, he mentioned that he'd seen him, or maybe he had been wounded there, he mentions Charlie in the trenches, but he got hit and was killed and that was it, he was only a young man. One of them from the local shop was in the KSLI in the Great War, he was said to have been a most evil man, he would stand up and blaspheme God, when shells were flying, saying there was no such thing as God.

Deerleap is an old Saxon name, its for hunting deer, you know the valley that runs from the Pitts yard to Lord Foresters, where ever it peters out, they'd run the deer up a canyon and have it all cased in. like they do for horses, and catch the deer in herds, that's what Saxons used to do. It was reckoned that the Romans may have mined in Broseley, on the Deerleap, miners discovered old flanged wheels, very ancient rails that they did not know existed before, they thought they were the first to make them out of iron, they found old workings, wooden rails with wooden flanges on, there were brass fittings on, and wooden shovels, very primitive, it was also reckoned that there were rails on the Birchmeadow, they were iron. Like the Americans used the term railroad, they reckon it was first used on the Birchmeadow, the first ever reference of a railroad was on the Birchmeadow.

END

Introduction: Nell Aston lived at the Mines all her life with her family. They lived near the Mines Spout and she tells of carrying this water for their daily use. She also talks of the potteries and Pitchyard, the local pub.

NELL ASTON AND MRS BATES 1994 (NELL DIED OCT 2002)

Mr and Mrs Clinton had the Pitchyard, Alice Perk's mother and father, they used to do sandwiches, they'd come out with bread and cheese and onions, you could have as much as you wanted, she was very homely, she also made sure they had food in their tummies as well. They used to give things to the men folk for their wives and families as well. Can you remember the Jews, and pottery being made there, our Vera worked theer, they made like a Rockingham china there, a dark brown one, they made teapots, our Vera had left school when er went theer. The old lady Jew, and im lived in the house across the Brook, and his daughter, they lived at 45 the Mines as well.

When they used to have the Pitchyard Show, they had parties for the kiddies, the money raised from the show produce paid for that, one year it was the OAP's, but only on their side of the Brook, the Brook runs underneath there at the bottom of the garden, and separates them, the other year it was for the children, these parties were held at the Floyer Hall, they had their photographs taken in the Pitchyard yard. (Nell said that we went to some of these Xmas parties, but I can't remember that, we must have got in because Arthur and Grandad were members of the committee.)

There used to be a bowling Green in Broseley Wood where Alec Southorn lives now, Beat said about it, it could have been somewhere for the people from the Nap, Seven Stars and the Kings Head, for recreation. The men used to play marbles at the top of the jitty from Simpsons Lane to the top of Quarry Bank on a Sunday, on sandy patch, Nell said they played marbles outside their house at the Mines as well, and they played hopscotch, skipping and jumping, Nell remembered Mrs Robinson who lived in the Clay Meadow, she played the violin and was an artist.

Ted Aston at the Spout, Spout Lane, Benthall, near his home.
He was a brother to Nell

Beat told of when they were young having a yolk round their necks to fetch buckets of water, from the Spout, they went up every day from school, they had to do this before they were allowed out to play, every day. Ted carried no end of buckets from there, and we have. When mom had no water in the tub for washing me dad used to say 'come on you two your mother wants some water for washing' Vera and me, we'd go up and down to the Spout carrying buckets of water and tipping them in the tub. Hazel's husband put the water in for us.

Our Vera used to be in the choir at the Mission in Broseley Wood and the concerts, many a concert, people paid to come in and see it, Beat Leadbetter used to go to the Congregational Chapel when they were children. We used to go to Benthall Church, and on a Sunday morning we used to go to Benthall Schoolroom, and then we'd march up through the Avenue with the vicar's wife.

Dave and Carol put the water in Jakeways house, there was Mrs Deakin, Frank Williams widow, Mrs Owen, Billy Owens wife, Audrey, I think Dave come next, I dunna know.

(Have you done Dora yet, she asked me, I said no I hadn't, I don't like asking people really as I don't know if they will talk for me, most of the people are fine once we get going, like you say its nice to talk, If it can be got on tape and the names put down, you know what area you're talking about.)

Miss Wiggins lived next to the pipe works, her mother was a school teacher, the house was covered with ivy, she used to keep cats, she wore gaiters round her legs, and a shawl round her shoulders, I remember Miss Wiggins, I can just picture her, a little old fashioned piece er wus, Davies's lived in the next house, they were something to do with the Bon Marche.
There used to be a midden or mixen on the Quarry years ago, a place to tip ashes and refuse, there wus a mixen on Coach Road as well I think.

We had some fun in that Kings Head, the owd banjo going on a Saturday night, oh surrey owd mon, we enjoyed that.

If I could get down to the Pitchyard with our Ted and have a couple of glasses, I wus satisfied, I'd say cum on Ted lets go up the road and have a bit of supper, I'll mek a cup of tea, I used to go to the Kings Head on a Friday with our Lil and Ted. I always used the Pitchyard, and me mam and dad, always the Pitchyard, If our Ted could get down to the Pitchyard for half hour with his darts he wus landed.
I remember the Jews being at the works thur, they made teapots and summat. And the Pitchyard, I remember a bit, Mr Clinton lived theer, he used to be a gamekeeper, they used to have a fair down thur, on the piece of ground opposite.
Our Lil worked at Southorns pipes.

Diane's gran used to live in the Broseley Wood, Beat's grandma used to make toffee, and sell it on the market, and Diane said yes there was a candle factory down by the Maypole. (Mary Croudace said her father had a candle factory down by where Raisewells lived by Maypole Green.)

Broseley Discharge Soldiers team, about 1921, that must have been after the 1914-18 war, there's a photograph that shows this.

END

Introduction: This tape is of another Benthall resident, where she talks of her life when she was young. She told of working at the local pottery and the shops and characters about then. She tells of her mother Mrs Hall, a real local character, who did a lot for the community, she was called on to help with births and deaths and was also a staunch member of the Baptist Church.

MAUD WHITMORE AGED 88 1993

My mother was known as Granny Hall, she did all sorts of things, I often say if she was alive today the money she could earn, her'd sit up all night for a shilling a night when they were dying and lay em out.

She was interested in anything, she was a big Baptist. We all went to the Baptist Chapel. If they were getting anything up, like a carnival she would dress all the blasted chapel kids up in one thing or another, she would go to rummage sales and get summat and cut it up and make it up for these kids to go in the carnival, they'd all got to be in it, you see you couldn't put one in without the other, she was so afraid they'd be upset you see, and it used to upset her, she used to teach in the Sunday School. She put a dray in, she was Old Mother Hubbard really, she walked behind this dray, and Harry Evans had all the kids on it. Our Jack would do anything to get out of going on the anniversary, he cuddna bear being on it.

Mother used to be fetched out, I've gone home many a night from work at Benthall Potteries and say, Mam where's me nightdress, and Dad would shout up to me 'Oh ers laid somebody out in that'. Thats as true as I stand ere, our house was everybodies shop. If she'd bin to lay somebody out and was a bit late coming back, Dad would say 'Your a bit late aren't you Nell, its took you a long time today hasn't it' she would say I had to wait a bit, so and so came to see them, he would say 'It inna them you've laid out they've come to see, they've cum to see what that umman has got in her house'.

The Lion has always been a pub that I can remember, our Cliff had it at one time. The Burnt House on the corner of Queen Street, was a workhouse as far as I know and Miss Horton had a shop where the Post Office is now, opposite the Victoria Hall, she sold corn for the folk who had pigeons. There was a library just inside the door on the right hand side of the shop. I remember Grocotts being there, we had their cars for our wedding.

Looking at the race programme, that shop John Rowe, 1 High Street Broseley is where Candlins have their bakery now, it used to be Towlers, it was the last shop I used to call at on my way home, they sold grocery and everything. When we went to work, if I had a penny in my pocket, I used to say to Bella Wall, she worked up here with me, come on Bella lets have a slice of cake for a penny, I often think about them days.

The main road outside here used to be a cart track (this was at Mauds home at Benthall) no pavements or nothing like that, when we used to go to work. Lena Fielding and Alice Gainham, we used to walk where ther'd bin a horse and cart, you know, to walk where it was flat. It was nothing like this is now, no grass verge or anything like that.

The Potteries made everything at Benthall, it belonged to Mr Allen, thats where I worked, the only thing they didn't make was cups, they made jugs, or anything like that, it was all earthen-ware, jugs and teapots and things to keep your bread in, and for the farmers there were cream steins, all earthenware, oh and lamp bases, there were plenty in our garden, I worked on them at Benthall, they were round and had a hole, there were dozens around here, everybody had them, they got throwed away if they were cracked.

The Pottery was at Benthall, I have got some photos, if you go and get that box down there you can see some, we made vases up at the top shop, there was a spinning wheel, of course they're all electric now. Mr Whitmore would sit like that, and this thing would be all around him, and I'd be outside and the rope would be a long way, this rope used to drive this, when you started first this was the first job you did, up the top shop, we used to turn this to make the wheel go round. If you wanted it fast and you got in a temper, you turned it a bit fast, the bloody walls would come down then they'd shout at us. Mr Haynes from Benthall, was at the next bench, he used to make spouts and handles for the teapots, jugs and things, in the next bay was George and me. George used to turn em and I used to stand all day like this, pedalling it down to make this wheel go round, he used to shape them into what shape they wanted, it was an art. The pay was five bob a wick, they thought it was good, five bob was five bob in those days, it was a lot of money. Ooh ha.

We had just the ordinary holidays, Christmas we had a rabbit, if we were lucky cause Mr Allen had the ground, he had the shoot you see, they thought they were giving you the world if they gave you a rabbit. It was interesting.

Benthall school was at the Floyer Hall. The Social Club was where the Pritchards used to live, they used to be in Lloyds Bank Broseley, it was a residential place, Potts lived in it at one time, they were solicitors, I can remember when Potts were there it must have been during the war, the first world war, they had a soup kitchen there, they used to go between the club and the Bank, I've seen them go in taking the basins, Pritchards - the Social Club was their place.

END

Introduction: Another local lady talking about her life as a child and growing up.
She too mentions the Pitchyard and working at the potteries, and the pipe works.

MRS BAGLEY OCTOBER 1992

The kilns at the back of Ken Bryans belonged to the Jews, they made pottery, it had Salopian painted on the front of Ken Bryans building, they made teapots and jugs and things, they used to bring the clay down from Cornwall on the train, to Ironbridge, and then bring it up the bank, they used to stop at the Pitchyard, and used to give the horses, they were two greys they were, who brought the white clay up, they used to give them a bucket of water each, and have a pint and some bread and cheese themselves.

From there they brought it up past our place, across the brook, round by the Cross Keys, right up to Southorns, then our dad used to put it in what we used to call a mixen, it was a wall built around here and there, and round here as well, and here was a square hole which was shut up at first, they put the clay in there.

Then dad had to do what they called 'hug it', then it used to go in a big wooden thing with a wheel in the middle, and then they would open this door, through ther and slide down a piece of board, and dad cut it off with a spade into pieces about like that, for the women to come and fetch it, then the women came and carried it up as they wanted it.

This was for Harry Southorn, the dad, when he started and his sister Miss Hetty, she used to do all the office work. They'd roll the pipes out with their hands and leave so much there, then they used to get moulds then put them pipes in the moulds and shut em down in like an iron case, you know, they used to put the clay pipes in there then close it all up, then they had like a big needle for the stem, then they brought a thing down and it cut it off, then they had a piece in that to clear it all out, then it was ready to put on the board, when they had rolled so many they would pin the board up and it would have to go in the drying house, when they got them out they would trim them up, see they were all cleared ready for going into the saggers, at the old pipe works, Legges Hill.

There was an article in the Journal the other week with Miss Bagley and Ida Humphries in it, Ida is the first one to have worked in the pipe works at King Street, Miss Bagley was one of two sisters, Clara and Annie, they looked after their nephew Bert, Bert Bagley, who used to walk about the place, he was always at our house, we used to feed him, they lived next door to Mrs Hough in the row on Quarry Road, their houses had the backs to the road and faced over the Clay Meadow, and we did. Bert always wanted a fag, my cousin from Leicester used to take him to the pub with them. There's not many of the old ones left now.

When we called at a pub before we got to Worcester, there were all these men sitting round the fire smoking wood pipes, they got talking about clay pipes, so we said the next time we come we'll bring you some clay pipes, and we did, and each year we went they used to be there waiting for us. We took them a box a piece, they used to put their wooden pipes away and smoked the clay pipes when we went in, they had them all out you know, I think Clara Bagley made the church wardens.

Then there was Allens works, they used to make the very big pans, it was next to Mrs Cross's house, which used to be on the corner of the entrance to Lodge Lane, that's been pulled down now, there's a bungalow there now. They made crockery there, but that's been pulled down as well. They made the big water pans and teapots and jugs and that, it was known as the Benthall Pottery. They weren't put into moulds, they used to, what they called 'throwing them', a lump of clay was thrown on the machine and worked it with their hands, marvellous it was to see them doing it. It would spin round all the time, they would start at the bottom and bring it up, I used to work there, I used to put the handles on the teapots. It was a long whitish building with wooden steps up to the doorway. Miss Allen whose family owned the works used to put a party on and a great big Christmas tree at her house for us kids, it was a nice house you know.

END

Introduction: Mrs Blood was one of the first people I taped, she told me of how they lived when she first got married, the local shops about then, local characters and events.

MRS BLOOD FRIDAY 9TH OCTOBER 1992

When I got married, first I lived with his mother, I didn't have a home of my own at all, I lived with er, our Margaret was a baby when we moved in here, I didn't have Freddie, he was born here, at the Birchmeadow houses.

I left er, or er left me, oh! er went an got a home of er own, and left me in the house, it was right by the fish/chip shop, by the phone box thats thur now, Er went to live by Mrs Roden and left me in the house, down Broseley Wood. In Woodlands Road.

I had a part of the house, was me own, thur wus two rooms, I had the one, and er lived in tuther - is muther, thur wus two rooms, thur wus a parlour and a kitchen, Mr Blood and Mrs Blood had the kitchen and I had the front room and a room up stairs, thur wus only two bedrooms. I had eight children there, in one room, then I come down to this one. The Council put me in this, and I had Freddie, I only had Freddie ere, I had nine altogether.

What else dust want to know, - to wash we ad a brewuss down in the bottom, and the coal, the coal wus down thur an all, the coaluss and the brewuss wus down in the bottom, an Mr Blood, thats Harry's dad used to go down some steps when he went to the lavatory, an I used to go through the front door and down some steps down the garden. To dry the washing we went down the garden, but in the winter, I canna remember how I dried them. She was asked if it was clothes lines across the ceilings and on the clothes horse, and on the fireguard if you had one, she said yes, it was. For cooking I had to use the same place as her, we had a range it used to get red hot on the top, we used to boil all the stuff on it. Yes, I used to cook in thur, did my cooking in thur, it only wus a little grate, like that, I remember using the oven plate wrapped in newspaper or a cloth to keep warm in bed.

The children were occupied playing outside, they went to Legges Hill school, ah! they used to goo to Legges Hill school. They used to play marbles and conkers, what else dust wanna know. When Harry did shift work, I took them round the woods for im to have a sleep. Nights afternoons and mornings e used to do, on the dressler at Maws works, thats weer I met im, I kept the dippers gooing, dipping the tiles, carrying the glaze, I used to do all the jobs. I tell you who e used to court before e met me, Mrs Mansell used to keep the Cape of Good Hope, e wus courtin a girl thur, e chucked er up and went with me, and married me.
Archie Dodd went with the other sister, e wus a Broseley lad, I think e married er, thur both dead now. It wus a big pub, I only used to goo in and have a drink with Harry, I dunna know when it wus knocked down, but its all lawn now. Who used to live up thur, Nellie Holcroft, she wus a Burgess, and Norah Jones, they are still thur now, they'n all bin knocked down now, new houses built thur, new council houses along that road, remember Mrs Oakley living thur.

I remember Billy Bowens shop, and Humphries sweet shop, down the bottom, going down Ironbridge bank, Quarry Road. Then over by me thur wus Mrs Garbett, Mr Oakley with the coal, Jim, ad the coal yard opposite me, next door to me wus Mrs Bowen. Ere now, I'm gooin to tell you now, Mrs Bowen the shop, Mrs Harrison, Nellie and Biddy the Irish, then the pub, the Nap (Napoleon), then Mrs Pope - Annie Rickers mother, then Gittings, Jack and Nelly. Then in the garden another Harrison who married Lucy Harvey, can't think of his name now.

The coalman at the yard opposite me wus Jim Oakley, his sister married Norman Ball. He died and his housekeeper carried on for some time but then she went away. Harry Ball wus married twice, his second wife wus Peach, she had a son, Norman. He had two daughters first. Thurs a lot of strangers gone in these shops since I wus married. I remember Roberts's at the Bon Marche (where Downes's shop is now) and Miss Horton, (the Post Office now), and Misses Taylors in the Square (old misery bags). We got our shoes from Sands in the High Street, Mrs Sands is still living thur, wus only im that died, and them two old women that used to bring the magazines round, Mrs Robinson wus the one, and Miss Cox, Mrs Robinson used to paint, and play the violin, lived over Benthall, thur both dead now, both gone. They used to go to the picture house up here, the Elite, one in a wheel chair.

Can't remember the Birchmeadow Chapel, thur wus some people buried thur wunt thur, during the war it wus an ammunition dump, and the Home Guard used it, Mr Hartshorne wus one.

I can remember Mrs Bowen from the shop, when er died, Mr Bowen left that house by me and went and lived in his mothers house by the shop. Mr and Mrs Garbett lived next door to Jim Oakley. Thur wur stables, thur, kids played thur, the stables were for the horses and carts for delivering coal.

Thur used to be stables where Elsie Edwards (Elcock) had er shop in Birchmeadow Road, where Edwards's used to stable thur horses, Teddy Edwards. His mother used to buy rabbit skins, we used to get a penny each for them. She lived in a cottage next to Rowes shop (now Simons butchers - was Traylors) in Barbers Street, they used to dry the skins out. We used to have rabbit for Christmas dinner, very often they poached rabbits in Broseley.

I knowed one woman, I knowed er, dirty owd bugger, in King Street by the Burnt house, er wus a dirty owd bitch, er wus filthy.

Mrs Parry lived near thur, she sold gramophones, needles records and things.

Jinner Evans had a fish and chip shop, it wus by Edwards stables. opposite the entrance to Birchmeadow Road. The fish and chip shop down Broseley Wood as bin thur since I lived thur, Mrs Williams had it, then er husband died and Elwells had it, then Williams had it back again and Harold run it with his wife Joan.

Mrs Bloods daughter Olive, used to work for Evans fish shop, and worked from eight till two or three in the afternoon, cleaning all the house, then eyeing the potatoes, back at night six till ten and eleven o'clock, and worked Saturdays and Sundays for five shillings a week. Gave her mother four and sixpence, and she just had sixpence. Thur wunna much money about in those days, the men were working for little or nothing then, they wus bringing nothing home, very poor them days, I used to work for twelve shillings a week and give my mother six. You can tell, I used to do all that work for twelve shillings a week, this was better than the fish shop job.

The stuff wus cheaper then, than it is today, I can tell you, you could get half a pound of sugar for tuppence then, used to have two pounds for fourpunce, at that time, but now today, we couldn't make the money do, won't go far enough. My husband wasn't giving me much, he wus working his heart and soul out for little or nothing. Our Bob used to sell wood, bundles of wood a penny a bundle, he had to sell 12 so his dad could have a shilling to go to the pub. They used to go wooding, I carried some wood, I lumped some wood when we couldn't afford coal. We used to go blackberrying as well.

END

Introduction: Another local lady talking about her life as a child, growing up, fashions and church events.

MRS HOUGH 1993

Yes that was the Foxholes, we used to get coal out of the Clay Leasow at the same time when Tommy used to come home from work, he worked on the steam roller you know, he worked all over, my grandad used to work the steam roller. I have a photo I was looking at this morning, here's a photo when I worked at Coalport factory, see if you can find me, this was the Metalware. Thats me and Tommy when we were engaged, just look at our clothes. We used to live by the Robin Hood in Ironbridge when I was young, in a row of houses, they are down now, in 1621 they were built. Nearly all the houses have been pulled down now, this black and white house like a manor, should have been kept.

There's a wynde going up by the 'Bird in Hand' my mother used to be a barmaid there. A bloke cut his throat there, he went courting and then her didna want him, so he cut his throat and then he was going to cut hers. I was going up them steps to go into my mother and he came out with all blood down him.

I remember Chippy Reynolds starting up, yes I remember all them on that photo, I remember all that, the Pitchyard was over there, and I lived on the opposite side of the road when I got married, there was only the road between us, on the corner of the lane.

I used to work at the factory making jugs, I used to 'handle and spout' them. Mr Whitmore used to 'throw em' and I used to handle and spout the teapots, this was at Ken Bryans place, the old jew bought it and he lived on the opposite side of the road, under the bank opposite the New Inn, Woolfson his name was. He had a daughter Rebbeca her name was, used to go stark naked down to the Severn and the Spout to have a bath, its the truth.

My granny had nine children, had us four when our dad died, my name was Harris, my granny's name was Northall, you know where the little railway bridge went over, what they called the square, that little cottage was where my mam and dad lived when they were married first, I never knew him he died young. There was a double fronted one by the Toll house, thats where my dads mother and dad lived, my mother went into service. A mon come, owd Mole his name was, he wanted to put us kids in the workhouse, my granny run him down the jitty with a poker saying you aren't having these kids, thats how we all lived at my granny's. She said you dare put your hands on these kids, when we want anything off you we will ask you, my lad wus working at Blesse Hill in the brick and tile works theer, they'n keep us. My mother lived with a man but never married again.

We used to have a pint of thripenny at night, we used to warm it, it was only three half pence a pint, we used to warm it, make a piece of toast and she used to have me in her legs, I'd have this for my supper, a drop of beer and some toast, warmed it in a saucepan, toasted the bread in front of the fire, broke it in bits, we never wanted for anything, it was always plain and good.

Local ladies at the Foxholes getting coal, to the left, back row, 2nd in, my grandmother – her 2 sisters are there too, one to her right and the bigger girl in front in white.

Her'd save up and buy a pig, they used to kill it, Bert Jones dad, he'd kill it and cure it for her, and have the intestines, chittlings and that, he had them, himself. He used to bring the flitiest hams and bacon and hang them up, going up the stairs, it was cured properly with salt petre to keep it, keep for years. Once a week we'd cut a piece ham out and boil it, with cabbage and mashed potato, we never went short of anything to eat.

Me and our Poll went to the Wesleyan Chapel, we were in the choir, this was on Madeley bank, its pulled down now, we always had new frocks for this, you know Phyllis Colley, well er mother used to dress make, er used to make our dresses. Do you remember Mike Evans the preacher, they had a little boy who had just died, well I had to say a piece of poetry on the anniversary, it was called 'The Little Shroud' , 'they put him on a snow white shroud, a chaplet on his head, they gathered many primroses, to scatter on the dead, they laid him in his little grave, it was hard to lay him there'- and I never got any farther, I happened to look up and the mother sitting there and er was cryin, and I could'nt do it, me granny got up out of the congregation and came to me, and dust know what er said to me, 'get up, get up and play it' but I did'nt. I said it the next Sunday, Mrs Evans asked me to say it. Course if I had'nt looked up and seen er crying.

Benthall Wake and Chippy Reynolds fair, two of the young women on the left side of the picture, at the front, are Alice Corfield and Louisa Goodwin, about 1905.

I was saying about Phyllis Colley's mother, do you remember when the hobble skirt came in first, it was a shorter one but very tight. Well I said to Mrs Colley 'how about making me a hobble skirt, so er looked at our Poll and said 'What shall I do', Poll said if you make er one, er'll have it'. So er made me one. Our Polls was a proper dress, pale blue it was, so the morning we got up to go to chapel, we went every Sunday, I thought I don't know how I'm going to get past my granny, any road I did, but er happened to notice, er run me all the way down the shutt, oh dear, with a pair of scissors, er said I'll give thee hobble skirt, ah! I had my hobble skirt. Er was a good old soul, she was very outspoken, granny was. When the relief of Mafeking was, after that war, the one uncle was in, he lived in Aqueduct , er went to all the shopkeepers in the Bridge and begged stuff and give the kids a teaparty on the Lloyds Bank, and we burned old Kruger on a bonfire on Lloyds Bank.

Then I got married, well I could'nt go to my granny's, I suppose she was dead. We lived in Simpsons Lane, Broseley then we came to Cox's Row here. They belonged to a Mrs Cox from Wolverhampton, they were sold by auction and bought by Harriet LLoyd for £300 for the five houses in the row. We come in here, Derek Lloyd lived in one, then he came and said they were going to sell the houses and if we wanted to buy ours we could have it for what they give for it £75. I said where dust think I have got the money from, but I had a policy due with Mr Dentstone the insurance man along the row, so I used it to buy this house.

END

Introduction: Edwin was my mother's brother, he tells stories of local people, and their way of life when he was young. He also talks of his family and the family business.

Edwin Oakley 1993 Aged 85

You know the wicker baskets with wheels on, they used to take the bread round in, he used one of them to go round the town selling teapots, kettles and saucepans, he also sold paraffin, he took paraffin out to people who lived far out. This was John Wilkes, who lived down Quarry Road, we cleared all his rubbish out when he died.

I'll tell you who else used to go round with a little truck on wheels, old Percy Dixon, he lived at the back of the Delph, there was a shop between Instones and the Albion, it was a fish shop not so long ago. He had an ironmongers shop and he sold everything like baths and frying pans and everything you could mention. I'm talking about Percy Dixon now, he used to go round Linley and all those places with this little truck, selling boot laces and paraffin and all that sort of thing, they made a living doing that.

Walter Davis opposite the Memorial, was Tippin Davis's, was working with his father, he worked there till just before the war, then he bought a little business down in Jackfield by the Black Swan, he bought a little shop there and sold groceries, he used to go on a motor bike and side car and take his stuff from Broseley to sell down there. That shop was closed for a long time during the First World War.

Looking at an old program of races, near the back was some mention of horses belonging to Oakleys, there were lots of Oakley's mentioned in the racing events, all known by Edwin and all related. Oakley's came to Broseley about 1810, (according to a recently researched Family Tree).

William and Margaret Oakley lived at Much Wenlock - they had their first child in 1764 and died in 1804 and 1805, their son Edward b. 1766 married a Sarah and they had 7 children all born in Much Wenlock. Perce Roberts mother was an Oakley, she was grandfathers (Fred) sister Harriet and she married George Roberts, their father was William Oakley who was a teacher and haulier from Leighton. Lol had some letters and things off Roberts's of some poetry and everything that William wrote. Dad (Edwin) was a cousin to Perce Roberts, his mother looked very much like granny Oakley to look at.

Mother had a photo taken in Smithy Bank, she had it with the lights out because she had had her teeth taken out, she looks really old on it, she had big long skirts on, she had Bet with her.

(Edwin's wife Lily said she always wanted to write a book, she had been on the stage at the Town Hall in a concert with the British Legion, singing with Norah during the war. We also had a carnival, I was a little Welsh girl).

You know where the club is now, the old Birchmeadow Chapel, there were all old iron graves round it, they were beautiful big cast iron things, I don't know what happened to them, this was in the grounds of the chapel at the front, all to the Onions family. They built the Coalport Bridge, the casting was done by the Onions family, they had a foundry in Foundry Lane, if you look at the Coalport Bridge you will see at the sides the railings are all 'O' shaped, for Onions.

Old Walter Matthews father was a maltser, they used to brew their own beer at the Tankard, a pub.

Thomas Oakley was a grocer, looking at the list of businesses I have we could not find any trace of Oakley's then, this could be about 1840. This book that Roberts's have got did say a date and everything, I have a copy of this book, I will find it for you. It was made into leaflets, the same thing that was the Roberts book. Great-grandfathers name to that was hollowed into the family fireplace.

Cyril Potts lived in the Bank House, Don Potts was a son of the Potts's from the Grange, George Potts was from Benthall, he lived with Mrs Allen from Benthall Potteries, they went to live at Hodge Bower over the river. The Miss Potts' were sisters, opposite the hospital, they had that house built, I remember it being built, not completely but I remember dad taking sand there to do some building work. I remember dad taking sand for the wall around Broseley Hospital too, I was only tiny. Norah said that when she used to go with her mother to Aunt Polly's she remembers her saying that she was one of the first patients in Broseley Hospital.

I used to take trips, day trips, in the little 'Daisy' and 'Felix', I was driving the charabancs to Llandudno when I was 16, we had two charabancs, trips down to Stratford, down to Worcester, and Evesham to see the trees when they were all in flower.

When Mr Jackson the parson came here I fetched him from Bristol, he was a parson at a reform school, a nautical school. When he came here first he brought Harold Spur with him as his batman, he was only a kid.

Looking at the adverts in the race program it had Burns - Jewellers, this was in the building where the Staffordshire Building Society is now, then next to the Town Hall. It was a shoe shop first, then a jewellers after Powells had it, he was a watch maker, Powells later moved to a small shop next to the Crown pub, now the Taverne, where the Washeteria is now, Mrs Powell had sweet shop there, her name was Molly. They were well to do people, Molly Powells grandparents paid for her to go Shrewsbury School, she used to go on the train every morning. Powells had a big jewellers shop in Shrewsbury till just before the war, but he got into some trouble and they sent him away from there and put him in this business here, he was here till he died, he was a timekeeper with the sports.

Dad had a contract with the council, Borough of Wenlock then, to sprinkle the roads up and down the High Street, and Church Street, all the way round to keep the dust down, not only the dust but the horse manure as well. It was nothing but horses then, because of the mud on the roads in the rainy season, from the Elephant pub to the Bon Marche there was a causeway, this was stone sets in the road, like square blocks of stone set in the road, they were raised so that you could walk across the street without getting your feet wet.

Told by Edwin but not on the tape:

He remembered the General Strike in 1921, and watched a flying machine from Smithy Bank.

There was an ammunition dump down Dark Lane - used for the mines explosives, it was brick built with an egg shaped steel door, cased in wood.
Jack Cross drove horse and cart for Instones, grain was ground on their own premises about 1918/19.

There were carnivals in 1911, during the reign of Edward V11, he watched a big procession from Smithy Bank.

He said the railway wall down by Ironbridge/Broseley Station was built by Jack Doherty, he was three then, he was born in 1908.

One of Frederick Oakley's charabancs about 1925

Chippy Reynolds shop was where Masons used to be, there was a hand pump on the wall for water. There was a water pump at the top of Hockley.

Some famous coach driver with a 4 or 6 in hand horse coach, who took them into the Lion Hotel yard (at Shrewsbury) at full speed, quite a feat. Gerald Instone had an uncle who could do this too, blowing his horn to clear the way.

George Harrison (Potter) High Street - Hairdresser and bird cage fancier breeder - a society judge who became champion of all England with a gold finch, which he exhibited at Crystal Palace at London, where he exhibited under the name of George Potter. Hezekiah Potts 1917/26 lived at the Grange, Harris's Green.

END

Introduction: Jack Oakley was my mother's cousin, he tells of local events, characters, shops in the town, and the family businesses.

JACK OAKLEY 1992 AGED 89

We started talking about High Street, near the top of Barratts Hill, where the Cape of Good Hope pub was some years ago. Where Jackson Avenue is now used to be a private house belonging to Howell's, and its gardens. They were lovely gardens, lovely apple trees. Then up from Barratts Hill, there were Reynolds next door, in the old buildings, then Georgie Potter the barber. The other side was a field that belonged to Grandad Oakley at one time. How many of the Oakley's were there, there was Jack, Fred, Ted and Will. They took Will in when they had the firm, but the firm began to decline.

Oakley's have been here for years, one used to be a school teacher at Barrow, he was a very clever man, exceptional, one Oakley , I forget who he was, but Arthur Davies, out of Broseley Wood told me about him. When I was a lad, he was a brilliant man.

He said Oakley's had always been a Broseley family. Granddad (Fred) was brother to Ted Oakley in Broseley Wood with the coal, that was his brother Edwin that was. Jim Oakley was Edwin's eldest son, George, and old Will in Ironbridge - he lived just over the Free Bridge, he lived with his son over there, Edward. There are thousands of Oakley's about somewhere, oh my goodness, they'll never run out, they are everywhere, all over the world. I was talking to a chap in the Foresters Arms one night, they were on holiday, he said he was at a do in London the other night, talking to 2 or 3 chaps, and I said I was going to Broseley, one of the chaps said I was born in Broseley, it was our David in the police.

Our Grandad started a big business, Grandad Oakley. He had his own coal trucks, Ted Oakley Coal Merchant. The yard was Swan Street, High Street, Carvers Road. He bought Potts coach house, stables, he bought them.

Grandad had the house and the yard built in Swan Street, and the sheds. He had traction engines, timber horses, everything, he had everything.

Every summer there was haymaking in the fields down the Dark Lane. Will Oakley come and he didn't know much about it, he was just a clerk at Coalport, he didn't make a success of it. It's all gone now, there's only Lol's left and that's his own. Will had the garage, yes, he worked it himself, he give it all away, he sold it away cheap to Roberts', and Will left £2,000 in his will. He made a mess of it.

The Victoria Hall was a big billiard hall, there were 3 or 4 big tables in it, it used to be a good club, the only club in Broseley. It was run by a committee, four shillings a year, men used to play crib, old men. Card tables in there and seats all round to watch the billiards, it was very good. After the war it seemed no men didn't go much, they didn't want to go there, and the lads spoilt it, they knocked it about and spoilt it, so it was closed.

It was closed for a long time, then Parr opened it, he thought he owned it, because he lived here. (We are in the flats by the Victoria Hall taping this). Next door was Bert Jones the butcher, then Parr moved in and he had a coal yard here.

The Town Hall dropped to pieces, I was on the committee when that closed. It had been knocked about that much. It belonged to the church, it was called the church hall really, there was only the parson and the clerk as was any scholars to look after it. Charlie Jackson run it and he made a mess of it, he let Haydn Burns put a petrol tank under it. He let dances go and never had the money for it, kids knocked it about and everything. Walter Summers had it for years for the Old Tyme Dances and never paid him a penny, Walter and Kitty.

Miss Horton's shop belonged to Stevie Hill before her, he used to have it before her, they used to call him 'glass' he was that sharp, he was a funny little chap, he kept the Elephant pub as well. It was sold after he died to Miss Horton, then Wood's from Cannock had it.

Leslie was born at the Villa, in Carvers Road, we moved there some time after we married.

We had a lot of shire horses, they were used for fetching coal from the pits and the station at Ironbridge, taking carriages out and brakes. They used to run the brakes to Church Stretton and the Wrekin. The carriages and brakes belonged to Grandad Oakley, when he got old he turned it over to his three sons, Jack, Ted and Fred, but Will Oakley was taken in with them to run it. Edwin (Ted) Oakley had a scrap yard at 38 High Street, they also had a shop there which sold groceries and sweets etc.

Massey's had a shop opposite and they sold groceries, corn etc. an old man and his son lived there, the old man used to walk to the Meadow at Buildwas for half a pint every night and walk back, all his life.

Broseley was full of pubs, there was the Foresters Arms, then the Dog and Talbot and the Old Crown in Church Street, until a few years ago this was Fellowes grocery shop, the Dog and Talbot was next to Bert Meredith Blacksmiths. The Old Crown opened at 6 o'clock in the morning, they would have a drink sometimes going to work. They smoked clay pipes and twist. Then there was the Pheasant, the Duke of York, the Hand and Tankard at the very top of Carvers Road, then there was the Hole in the Wall that was in the corner here (at the back of the Spar Market now) run by Patsy Foye, we lived here in the first house, Fred lived in the other and Ted lived in the third, the old places, it was great. The Vaults was next and then the Albion, the Albion, the Elephant, the Lion, the Crown and the Social Club, the Cape of Good Hope was run by Harry Russell and his wife. This went to nothing as the trade dropped off, there was no work around here. Then there was All Nations (Prince of Wales?) along King Street, our Bill used to live there, he married Dorothy Scott. No, it was called the Prince, they used to say 'back of the Prince'. Then there were all the houses knocked down behind there. Kenyons Bakery was next along the street, Mrs Kenyon used to serve in there, dressed in her long dress and white apron. Then there was the old Cumberland on the junction of King/Duke Street, by the garage, then the Kings Head, next to that the Seven Stars, this was closed and opened up as a fish and chip shop in 1924, it had a good reputation as one of the best chip shops about. Continuing down Woodlands Road there was the Napoleon, then the Maypole, the next pub was the Cross Keys in Simpsons Lane, then the Pitchyard on Bridge Road (Coach Road), now the New Inn.

Every summer there was hay-making in the fields

Old Dick Hudson was the barber, charged a penny, he was there for a life time was old Dick. Kids used to go to Oakleys for a free hair cut, if they did have a penny they kept it and went to Oakleys, the chap who looked after the horses cut their hair, he cut them with the horse clippers, it didn't take a minute to get it off, they used to leave a big fringe on, when they went to school old Nobby Clark their school teacher said 'you've been to Oakleys again'.

Grandad had a nice van built, and two horses and Flooky Sargeant used to drive it a lot, he'd start at 8 o'clock from here and then start back the next morning at 4 o'clock. Bring the letters back, they done that many a time, it called at all the Post Offices gooing to Wellington. Yes, they started to go at 6 o'clock and spend the night in Wellington, a long night. The streets used to be dirt tracks then, if you used to park your wagon years ago they told you to move, you were blocking the road if the bus come. I don't know what they'd say if they came back now.

Always had an outing on a Saturday, the brakes and waggonettes, everything. They went to the Wrekin, Church Stretton, Haughmond Hill at Shrewsbury. By gum, they enjoyed that, they had their tea, cakes and everything. Yes they had a good time, there were a lot of them. There was nothing else for them in them days, they climbed up to the top of the Wrekin. They didn't do much at all, they had fields to play in, teachers used to play games with them, there was nothing else at all, only make their own fun you see. And then they used to have their Anniversary, always had an anniversary, they looked after the kids then, they were very nice.

George Dean was one of the last policemen. PC Edwards, Algy Edwards was here at one time when I was a lad. He was a good policeman, he was very fair, yes very fair, he used to loose you off if he caught you doing anything, he'd give you a smack with a stick, he'd tell you off, ah, he'd frighten you to death almost. We had two or three but they didn't stop long, then Jack Penny come. He was here a long time, lived by the Lord Hill in the first house, in that garden, yes. There was a big house by the Lord Hill on Duke Street. Albert Leadbetter lived there when I was young, he had a blacksmiths shop down Church Street, by Will Edges, on the corner, he lived there a long time.

The first shop was Instones, Edward Instone, (a brother to R A Instone), opposite Wedges house. Then Fellowes shop, Mrs Taylor had a little shop opposite in the house. Then Wedges, well it was Onions' first then they all died off, they lived down Barratts Hill in a little farmhouse, and had a couple or three cows in the Deer Leap. Marriatte and Mary Onions used to take the milk out, an inspector was after them so he (the father) took the milk one morning, he went one way and the inspector followed him, and the two girls went off the other way with the milk. When he caught George, his was full of water, he'd followed the wrong one. He thought he was going to catch him, old George said what do you want, There you are said the inspector, oh, its water, George said yes I carry water, the milk has gone the other way. There was some characters in Broseley, they got up to some tricks then, there were some characters. They'd be sitting all around the monument when it was up, ah, they all sat on it, smoking their pipes and spitting out, oh they used to.

They all had their seats round the monument, the old blokes, every day, and on the back the writing on the wall was 'they rest from their labours'. The school teacher told us one morning, he said ' yes, look for the writing on the wall, its on the wall in proper figures, in stone, 'they rest from their labours' and they surely do. They never worked, no, not them, they didna work, they did not work, no. Oh there's bin some characters.

Ther's bin some pubs in Broseley, they used to have racks, to put the church wardens on when they wanted to smoke, then they used to put them back. They didna drink pints hardly, if there were two or three they had quart jugs and a glass each and keep tipping it out, what they called Broseley drinking. They didna use the pints much, they had quarts, there wasn't much else for them to do only drink.

If you had to go anywhere you had to walk, I've walked to Bridgnorth many a time, we used to walk it, it's all changed, by gum it has all changed. We used to have a polishing room for all the harness, we had a man polishing harness regular, and a man cutting shafts, used to be there at 6 o'clock cutting shafts. Albert Knocks dad, was up here every day. The horse brasses were polished, the men who drove the horses thought a lot of them, they looked after it they did, oh ah, they were good horse men, they looked after them, they were good horses they were, you couldn't mix them, enthires and the shires, no they never had one, dad never had one, only one mare and she was no success.

END

Introduction: Dennis talks about the Broseley Horticultural Society started in 1937, this covers the shows, the people involved, and the events and outings organised through the years.

DENNIS WILLIAMS: BROSELEY HORTICULTURAL SOCIETY

First show as such was Broseley Coronation Fruit and Vegetable Show in 1937. President then was Lord Forester, Chairman His Worship the Mayor of Wenlock Mr Shorting, Vice Chairman W Andrews, he lived in Duke Street, opposite the Crusaders Club, Treasurer Dennis Ridley of Lloyds Bank, Tommy Goodall of Swan Street, Assistant secretary Billy Ball, Committee: Jackson, Collins, Howells, Broadhurst, Cross, Minton, Jakeways, Evans, Boden, Tarte, Fletcher, Tommy Instone, Ward, Instone, Griffiths, Madeley, Cis Hough, Pountney, George Potts.

That's actually the foundation, that's when they were thinking about shows. They actually showed fruit and veg. and Chrysanths in the early shows. Right back in April there was the Daffodil Show, then they would go to the Rose Show, then to the Coronation Show, mainly fruit, and then the Chrysanthemum Show later on, early Chrysanths and late Chrysanths, there were about 5 or 6 shows a year.

The show before Chrysanths was the fruit and veg, the Handicrafts joined up with the Arts and Crafts in 1947, Coronation Flower, Fruit and Vegetable Show at Broseley School, the first one was at the Town Hall. These were the programmes, Miss Potts, Captain Collins, Mrs Hoy, Major Howells, Edith Pargeter, Broadhurst, Jakeways, Birch, Mrs Carlisle, Mrs Hamilton, Mrs Prestage, W Andrews, Jane Nicklin, Major General Ward, Colonel Hayward, Councillor Jones, S Moreton, W Roberts, Salter, W S Ball, J Roberts, G F Wall, Mrs Tom Instone, Mrs Whitmore, Tommy Goodall, 1947.

That's when they gave prizes, these people supported it a long time, they don't give prizes now, its too expensive. Morrells of Shrewsbury, Reeves Amateur Gardening, Dixons of Edinburgh, the first two gave medals and diplomas, Dixons a gift voucher £1. They used to write around to different nurseries etc and they would get the advertising of their names. Dobies of Edinburgh, Ryders, Cuthberts veg seed, Davies' garden spade, John Dixon mechano set, Jackson 10/6d, quite a lot of money then. (Dennis wasn't with the society then, he joined in 1950's and has been with them a long time.)

It was called the Broseley and District Horticultural Society before the Arts and Crafts joined them you see. The Annual Show was called the Coronation Flower, Fruit and Veg Show as a memorial to the coronation of H M King George V1 and Queen Elizabeth.

There were a lot of allotments in Broseley at one time, some at Bridgnorth Road. We are struggling now because there are no allotments, or gardens as such. Others were Chapel Lane, there was a lot of ground by the Chapel, where Jack Boden lived. Mr Roberts had a garden there. This gives some idea of what sort of shows there were, well they are still the same today. A collection of vegetables, 6 varieties kidney potatoes, 5 round, 3 plates of 5 potatoes named, spring onions, shallots large and small, 3 beetroot, 3 parsnips, 3 carrots, kidney beans, peas, green cabbage, red cabbage, cauliflower, cabbage lettuce, 2 marrow's, 6 tomatoes, stick celery, 4 leeks, 6 pears, 6 desert apples, 6 cooking apples, plums, mixed fruit, 6 chrysanths - any variety, 4 vase cut flowers, 5 vases sweet peas, 6 roses, 6 asters, 3 vases annuals, 6 dahlias, 4 stocks, 4 carnations, cut flowers decorative etc.

Schedules haven't changed much, they are basically the same, they specialise more, its mainly veg and chrysanths now its gone the other way about, its mainly Chrysanth Shows. People taking part in these shows were very dedicated to preparing their exhibits, they dressed each chrysanthemum, curling and placing the petals most carefully. Washing and cleaning the fruit and vegetables after they have sorted for best shape, size and condition, ready to show it. It took some time to prepare the exhibits and get them to the place where the show was being held, and lay out each class.

The Society had a 'Question Time' in Broseley in 1961, I was with them then. Miss Thorn-Pudsey suggested it, it was held at the Elite Cinema or Bladen Club on 23rd April 1961 and the BBC actually came there, Freddie Grisewood was in the chair, and Lord Sourbut and Alan Gimmell. The secretary did all the organising and they finished being entertained at the Cumberland Hotel.

Old English Fairs were held at the Lawns, Broseley in 1957. There were stalls, entertainment, music and period costume parade. Admission was 1/-d, if bought before the date it was 9d. Financially we just try to pay our way, mainly through the efforts of the arts and Crafts, they are the back bone now, they run a big draw Chrysanth and Arts/Crafts Show in September. The Arts/Crafts secretary is Dennis's wife, Mrs Brookes the schoolteacher passed it on to her, said she would make a likely deputy. I went to the Annual General Meeting to see what the procedure was, when Bill Forester resigned as secretary. I went to see about getting lime, which as a society they got reasonably cheap, and I was roped in and have been there ever since, 1958 that was. The first trip I went on was before I was secretary, in the 1950's, I remember it very well, they went to Bodnant Gardens in North Wales, beautiful grounds, it was a Sunday trip which needed careful planning, if you please, very careful planning, because when we got there the place was shut. So we learnt lesson one very quickly. You wouldn't believe it would you, a coach load of us. Any way Colonel Boon said I'll see what I can do, so he had a word with his Lordship and said he was very sorry but we hadn't checked on it, so he let us in. We were very lucky. Ever since then we always write and confirm. We have had lots of outings since then.

It has changed a lot lately, we don't have the monthly meetings now, they got that there was only the shows to talk about each month, so we decided to develop it into evening shows, and general interest, a social evening really. The interest is for the members not just the committee, this year we are running 3 outings. We have been to the main rose gardens in the country which is at St Albans, that's their headquarters, and the Royal National Society Gardens, there's acres and acres of roses there, we have been to Woolmans Chrysanth nursery as well.

Mainly what we do now, is the stately homes, the best of both worlds there, the crafts people see all the tapestries, pictures and the house, we see the gardening people and the exotic gardens. We have about 180 members, a lot of them are just interested in the gardens, the outings and shows. The number of exhibitors you can almost count on your fingers. Its the same in most societies, its the older ones that keep it going. You have got to be dedicated, when you get older you can't do the digging etc. which is needed. Keeping the kids football off the veg was a must, or there was trouble. We've got two very good rose growers, there's John Jones, they've wittled the shows down to two now, and as long as we can keep those two going, we can keep the rose show going. And believe it or not I think it's the only one in Shropshire.

There is now the Rose Show and Chrysanth Show and the Arts and Crafts. They combined in about 1937. Became the Coronation Broseley Horticultural and Arts/Crafts Society. The schedules are separate.

This is secretary Bill Foresters last report: He felt that we had experienced another successful year and thanked the members for their help during the year, concluding, Mr Forester stated that he would have to give up his position of joint secretary, as he had not got the time to do the work. So then came in muggins, this was in 1958. Jack Sweetland was treasurer. We used to run a Garden Fete and dance, dances at the town Hall. The shows used to be at the Town Hall, then they went to the school, and then the Victoria Hall. The date the Town Hall was pulled down is not really clear but Dennis has a wooden bowl that was carved by Ern Harris out of the original oak out of the roof of the Town Hall that was built in 1779 the same year as the Ironbridge, taken down in 1964.

END

MISCELLANEOUS INFORMATION ABOUT BROSELEY

A WIDE VARIETY OF GENERAL INFORMATION FOR USE IN MY BOOK

Most of this information has been taken from the books and reference drawers at the Records Office Shrewsbury.

1558/1906 – Property Broseley High Street, formerly butchers, opposite the part of the Memorial Green on which the Pritchard Memorial stands:- 2 houses, formerly one, malthouse etc, warehouse etc, opposite the Delph in High Street, 3 cottages opposite the Delph.

1595 – Broseley Church, licence for burial ground.
Amies – pre 1614
29 Sept 1618 – Old Broseley Church, sums paid Richard Old for seats in new building.
1622 – Broseley Woodlands –Coalmines in Childs Woodlands.
1630 – The Lodge (farm) old hunting lodge for Royal Chase at Shirlott
1632 – Mention of a glass making in Broseley, there is a glass house yard on a 1840 map, in Cockshutt Lane.

Broseley Church – 1645, sale of kneelings. 1723 Citation in case over new gallery. Presentation to chapel by Prior and convent of Wenlock on nom. Of Lady of the Manor 1322. 1618 - Persons compounding with Richard Old for seats in his new building. 1794 – New gallery, particulars of pews 1840, plans of old and new buildings 1845. 1880 Churchyard, title of land as addition.

1665 – Raddle Hall, Church Street – much later became 3 cottages
1670 – Map of Broseley
1678 – Title, Broseley Manor from 1678.
1700 – Benbow claimed to make glass in Broseley

Early 18th century Broseley Hall, and White Hall Church Street
Middle 18th century The Crown, High Street

1709 – Hurstlea, Queen Street
1726 – Lampers Lane (meadow)
1727 – The Lawns, Church Street. Home of John Wilkinson
1730-1883 Burgess Lists. Also 1770-1821 and 1770-18824.
1746/52 – Broseley Windmill Deeds (Ashwood).
1750 - Coneybury Foundry – New Road was owned by Banks and Onions.
1752 – Broseley, Lutwyche Estate, lease of land.
1755-1984 - Monumental Inscriptions.
28th November 1755 – Isaac Wyke aged 79.
1758 – Land in Fiery Fields and part of the Butts
1759 – Red Church, Old St Marys by Francis Turner Blythe, Broseley Hall.
1759 – Lease of land and buildings Bradelys Green.
1759 – Clench acre, piece of waste land, lease Purcell to Hartshorne.
1761 – Cherry Tree Hill, land lately fenced in – leased for brickworks.
1770/1865 - St Marys Jackfield.

1779 –	Edwin Bathurst	Earthenware Manf. Benthall Pottery
	John & Edward Burton	Farmers and brick makers.
	Joseph Currier	Shopkeeper
	John Duckett	Timber merchant
	Brittania Inn	Mary Gother vict.
	John Gother	Joiner
	Hiram Hill	Lime burner
	Joshua Instone	Blacksmith
	Leopard Inn	John Jones
	Warren Taylor Jones	Earthenware Manf. Posenhall, Benthall
	John Patten	Lime burner and barge owner
	Ann Pitt	Farmer
	Thomas Pitt	Farmer Posenhall
	Edward Roden	Farmer and corn miller
	Mary Roden	Farmer
	Noah Roden	Tobacco Pipe Manf.
	James Shepherd	Maltster

24/6/1785 – Lousy Bank alias The Green Yard, 3 houses and blacksmiths shop (mines and ironstones).

1788 – Penelope Guest , aged 56
1794/5 – Extracts re new gallery.
1801 – Population 4,832
1801/19 – Friendly Society.
1807 – Baptist Church – A lease by ministers/trustees to Abraham Wyke with permission to open the Bottom Pit and mine coal under land belonging to the chapel, but not the graveyard or the minister's garden.
1809 – Miscellaneous burial and birth certificates.
4 Nov 1815 – William Thursfield died 13 April 1815, His widow Elizabeth formed a partnership with Richard Hodges Gwyn – dissolved 31 Dec 1825
31 Dec 1823 – Dissolution of partnership between Abraham Wyke, surgeon, apothecary and man midwife, and John Nicholls Ashwood same as above – partnership formed May 23 1817

Broseley Census 1831:

	Broseley	Benthall	Barrow
Area acres	1,550	770	2,290
Houses inhabited	1,012	121	76
Houses-families	1,029	123	76
Houses-buildings	2	-	-
Houses-uninhabited	93	13	0
Occupation-Agric.	43	4	48
Families Trade Manf.	387	42	2
Other	599	77	26
Person-Males	2,158	252	163
" Females	2.141	273	188
	4,299	525	351

1831/1860 – Samuel Roden
1832 – District Report Book ND acknowledges report of cholera at Jackfield.
1833 – Receipt to Broseley Board of Health.

Broseley Hall – Rental 1834/sale 1913.
1835/37 – Birchmeadow Particular Baptist Chapel, Register of births. Some names Barnet, Adams, Roper, Jones, Harvey, Davies, Griffiths, Davis, Taylor, Mason and Smith.

1840 - Toll was paid to pay for the new Ironbridge Road, the first coach was about 1840.
The Tollgate opposite Coneybury Foundry were the offices of the first furnace and last kept by William Oakley when it ceased in 1903.

1840 – Particulars of pews in the late Parish Church.
1840 Map – Glass House Yard, Cockshutt Lane.
Workhouse, Mill Lane.
Windmill Malt House, Mill Field.
Meeting House/Chapel, Chapel Road.

1840 – Copy of bond of consecration and deed of separation for Broseley Cemetery and petition to consecrate
1842 – Broseley Friends Meeting House.
1843 – Broseley Conservatives – Gain and loss of Con. and Radical parties
1843 – Faculty for taking down and rebuilding Parish Church. Plans of old and new churches
1845 – List of new proprietors and occupiers, plans of old and new church/accounts.

7/2/1845 – Draft conveyance piece of land for school.

Feb 7 1845 – Draft conveyance Fran. Blithe Harries and William Edgerton Jefferies to the Rector and Church Wardens a piece of land as to a site for the erection of a school in Broseley

April 14 1847 – Sale of notice for Hand & Tankard, the house adjoining and two houses at Hockley
14 April 1847 – Particlars and sale of Lion Inn in Bros.
1848 – Account of money spent repairing Highways Broseley
June 24 1848 – Benthall Female Friendly Society – General release and indemnity on division of funds to trustees and treasurer
May 1 1849 – Thomas & Edwin Broadhurst – Wheelwrights
1851/1899 – Property at Fearney Bank
1854 – National School, land for site conveyed by Francis Blythe Harries to Rector and Church Wardens- sale of Broseley School premises. Foundation laid. Building the following year costing £1600, attendances 300.

1856/1910 – Quarter Sessions: register of convictions, certificates of dismissal transmitted to the Clerk of the Peace.
1858 – Insurance policy for Reading Rooms

1860 – Builders, King Street, co partnership agreement Rowland and Thomas Smitheman.

27/2/1865 – Rev Osborne Gordon and others to Henry Whitmore and others, Mines of coal and ironstone in Broseley – tracing.

1867 – Severn Valley Railway Co.
1870 – Probate, Roberts, Pitts Yard
1871 Census:
The Victoria Inn – James Rowley 36 Cleobury North/Eliza Rowley 32 Caughley
Butcher-Humphrey Legge 38/Sarah Legge 39 –Barratts Hill Broseley
Marine Store Dealer +Furrier – Thomas Bennett, Barratts Hill
Edwin Southorn 50, Tob.Pipe.Manf. Speeds Lane.Employing 8M – 31 F – 1boy
Butcher –James Cartwright 71, King Street
Police Officer-George Nolley 30, King Street
Publican and grocer –Emma Oakes 50, Ferney Bank

24 May 1871 Tenancy agreement re shops, new Town Hall Broseley. Rector and Churchwardens of Broseley and Thomas Lawrence.

1872/1935 – Broseley Gas & Coke Co.
1872/1908 – Broseley Gas Co.
1873/4 – Crown Inn High Street, deeds.
1874/5 – Papers re Hole in the Wall
1876 – Bakers Shop/Oven and messuages at King Street, and 2 pumps.
Abstract of title from 1801 (Kenyons?)

1876/1920 Cottages – Carvers Road
1876/86 – No's. 8/11 and messuages Legges Hill for sale. (1832 particulars/rent book)
1877 – Onions, Lower Downs.

28/9/1877 – Conveyance 'Cape of Good Hope' sold to John Shaw Innkeeper for £1,175, and grocers shop on the North side adjoining the inn and 3 cottages adjoining on South side of High Street and King Street on the west. 4 houses with a wash house: Emma Harries, Wm Beddoe, Geo.Halford, Edward Amplett, 2 houses Richard Carter and Edwin Bates.

8/61878 – Holly House £450, Edward Roden.
1878-9 – Chapel Terrace, papers re Richard Jones
1878 – Crown Inn
1880 – Addition of land to churchyard
1881 – Population 4,458
1881 – Draft agreement for sale and purchase Major General Charles Vanbrugh Jenkins and Broseley Local Board. A piece of land in Broseley for a cemetery 1885 – Copy of agreement as to road to cemetery
1885/91 - Meeting Room for Brethren High Street
1885 – Deeds and papers re land near Down Well Bros. For a site for water tank, Gen. C V Jenkins and Bros. Local Board.

1885 – Sale 3 houses and cottages, Maws furniture.
1885 – Down Well, land for site water tank.
1887-97 – Coneybury Farm papers re cottages, receipt for deeds.

1888 – Broseley Bank (Pritchards) taken over by Lloyds.
1889 – Property near Hole in the Wall, Carvers Road. 2 houses at 1847, papers re 1874/5.
1889/93 - Sunday School/ bills etc.1893 including rejoicings on marriage of the Duke of York

1890 – John Doughty , roofing tiles advert.

31 Dec 1891 – Vouchers for year for Mission School Room

1891/3 - Broseley Wood School
4/12/1891 – Mission School, Sycamore Road, Broseley Wood.
26/11/1892 - Samuel Tonkiss – tile maker, probate.
8/2/1892 – Broseley Wood School, Legges Hill.

1893 – Bills to the Rejoicing Committee/Old Peoples Committee/Royal Wedding Committee (5/8th July).

Forester Hospital Broseley – See also Lady M A Forester 1892/7

1896 – Broseley National School
1896 – Forester family, papers re improvements to Broseley National Schools.

20 Feb 1896 – Report to Town Clerk from Mr Wyatt re Broseley Water Supply.
24 June 1896 - Plan of Broseley Water Supply by Mr Wyatt
17 July 1896 – Plan showing ground on which trial borings are proposed.
18 August 1896 – Letter Mr Thursfield to Mr Mear of Inett Farm re Fiery Field /water.
Sept 3 1896 – 2 letters from Town Clerk to Mr Potts: Fiery Field Water/Broseley Water supply.

12/5/1896 – Letter from W L Hutchinson of Nottingham to Potts & Potts about water supply on the Forester Hospital site.

1897 – Minutes of meeting re site at Town Hall, valuation/report on site (B.Hosp.)

7/6/1898 – Letter from Thursfield to Potts about the Forester Charity. 4 maps of proposed sites for the hospital, 1-3 for Broseley, 4th for Wenlock.
1899 - Letters and plan.
1899 – 'Alison House', Partnership dissolved Holt and Jacobson (Dr).

1900 - Copy draft agreement for the sale and purchase of 6 houses and smithy and garden etc in Broseley. C E Jenkins with Rt Hon C T W Baron Forester. Plan Hospital site.

30th July 1901 – Copy declaration by E B Potts as to land at Bros. To be bought by Lady Foresters Charity Trustees as the site of a cottage Hospital.

1901/48 – Broseley Charity Commission Accounts.
1902 – Dorcas Society.

1902 – Benthall Stoneware Company. Wm J Legge & others to Benthall & Ironbridge Pottery Co.Ltd for purchase of the clay tobacco pipe and pottery manufacture for £2000.
1903 - The Tollgate opposite Coneybury Foundry were the offices of the first furnace and last kept by William Oakley when it ceased in 1903.

Nov 5 1903 – Letter to Potts & Potts re: Broseley Sanitary Authority & Water Supply
Nov 11 1903 - Letter to Potts from Clerk to Oakengates U C re joint water board 2 rough plans. Edward V11 Session 1904. Bill to constitute a Joint Water Board Oakengates, Dawley and District.

1904 – The Batches, papers re sale.

1904 – Application to fix a telephone pole on a field side between Lord Forester's property and James Davies premises in King Street, Broseley.

1905 – Lord Forester to Howard McLean. Terms of lease and leasees covenant for a rifle range at Benthall Edge for 21 years.

Congregational Chapel – Minute Book 1912/27.
Papers re sale and closure 1961/67.

15/4/1917 – A troop ship was torpedoed, lost at sea. Buried just off Greece. (Derek Roberts.)
1918 - Chantry House
22/9/1920 – Lord Forester to Abr. Woolfson, John F Rowe, and Harold George Cleveland – Buildings and premises formerly used as tobacco pipe manufactury at Pitts Yard in parish of Benthall.

Benthall & Ironbridge Pottery Co.Ltd 3 draft agreements to Mrs & Miss Southern.

1920 – Feb. Draft lease – Lord Forester to C R Jones & Sons, land, mines, coal and clay at Ladywood, Broseley.
1920 – Receipt for deeds, Beggar Hill.
1920 – Oct. Lease Lord Forester to Broseley Tileries Co. Mines of coal, slack and clay in Broseley.

22/9/1920 – Lord Forester to Abr. Woolfson, John F Rowe, and Harold George Cleveland – Buildings and premises formerly used as tobacco pipe manufactory at Pitts Yard in parish of Benthall.

Broseley Capacity Engineering - Sold by Forester to C.E & Co (Smitheman & Potts) 1922, sold by them 1931/2 to Instone & Lloyd. Assigned to Bagley 1931, conveyance to Massie 1931.

1923 – Willey Estate to Broseley Lawn Tennis Club, declaration of trust & contract for purchase of piece of land at Duke Street, Broseley
1926 – Doctor and Surgeon – John Goodison Boone, Norman Fox Edwards.

1917/26 – Hezekiah Potts solicitor, The Grange, Harris's Green.

St Leonards Mission School Broseley Wood – Services 1928-46, 1955-65, 1966/71
St Leonards Mission Church Broseley Wood – Services Registers 1928-46, 1955-65, 1966-71. Minutes 1956 – 59.

1929-Amalgamation of business W Southern & Sons and Ironbridge Pottery Co.
Nellie Worthen Southorn widow, 16 Legges Hill, Ethel Mary Southorn Spinster, John Fred.Rowe, Laurels Cottage Benthall Ironbridge Pottery Co. John Raleigh Aqueduct.
Joint Business now carried on (with dwelling house) at 16 Legges Hill in her occupation and two cottages adjoining. 1930- Sale between Wm John Legge of Madeley, Nellie Worthen Southorn Widow, John Fred.Rowe, John Raleigh-partnership of 1 business Clay Tobacco Pipe Man.(Wm Southorn & Co) and the

Ironbridge Pottery Co. as one business and Benthall and Ironbridge Pottery Co.Ltd. of Benthall, Broseley.

1929 – Lease Lord Forester to Benthall & Ironbridge Pottery Co. Pottery manft land at Benthall, mines of clay and sand.
1929/30 Trusteeship of the property of Mrs Elizabeth Gray 20-22 Church Street.

Kelly's1937 – Rapid Repair Service, J Aston Boot Repairers 88 High Street, Bros.
Albert Stanley Snow, 56 King Street, Bros.

1917/41 - Broseley Wood (Mission
7/5/1944 – Sunday morning, a Thunderbolt aeroplane from USA base at Atcham crashed in Joe Robert's field on Coach Road, now Bridge Road. (I was aged 8 and in isolation in my bedroom with Scarlet Fever).
31/8/1954 – 75 children admitted to Madeley Modern School from Broseley
1961/67 – Congregational Chapel, Duke Street Sale, correspondence re closure and sale.

Broseley Church – When taking down the church in 1844 the foundations were found of another church. In 1201 the church or chapel of Burwardsley was valued at £6.13s.4d. per year. In 1535 burials were allowed to take place at Broseley instead of Wenlock which was customary, the oldest gravestone in the church dates 1628.
The church of St Milburgh at Wenlock covered a district of its whole southern frontier.
The Manor of Broseley stood within its boundaries. The church or chapel which was founded in the 12th century, was founded as subject to the Mother Church of Wenlock, demolished in 1844. Registers go back to 1570, printed and indexed from then to 1750.

Benthall Church – St Bartholomew. In the parish of Wenlock, appears to have been built prior to 1221. Rebuilt in 1667 after bad damage in Civil War. Was built on foundations of the medieval chapel. Remains of the original settlement survive in a field behind the Hall.
(Broseley 'A guide through and early industrial town' and Directories).

Broseley Beam Engine.

Coneyberry, alias Conniborough House, deeds re seats in Broseley Church

Back Alley near Albion

Potteries – Messrs Bell & Lloyd, John Lloyd then his nephew Mr E Bathurst, his son succeeded him then sold to Mr Allen

Old Pitchyard works – little is known, only that they stood where the Pipe Works of E Southorn were. The numerous saggers found in cottage gardens show they must have continued for some considerable time.

Mintons of Stoke, Maw & Co of Benthall, Hargraves and Craven of Jackfield and Mr Bathurst of Broseley have each produced beautiful encaustic tiles.

Broseley and Benthall – 2 large earthenware manufacturers Mr John Bell and John Thursfield (Quaker) Barrow has large manufactory carried on by Thomas Turner Esq under the name Shropshire Porcelain Manufactory. (From Universal Brit.Direct. compiled about 1789.
Salopian Monthly - General

Reference books used Cooper & Co Broseley, Salopian Shreds /Patches. Quarter Sessions. Post Office Directory of Shropshire. 'Bygones 1881. Shropshire Feds of WI. Shropshire Village Book. Gazetter of Shropshire.
Drawer at Shrewsbury Records Office with Information Cards re Broseley

REFERENCES:

Shrewsbury Records Office.
John Randall's Book on Broseley,
Various Directories including: Slaters 1868, Kellys 1885, Robsons 1840, Pigotts 1829, The Shropshire Gazeteer, Lewis's Topographical, the Salop Directory 1828, Shropshire Directory 1835, Tibman & Co. Shrewsbury, Gregory 1824, Shropshire, Slaters, Cassey 1871, Villages around Bridgnorth 1861.
Clay Tobacco Pipes Shire Album 37 by Eric G. Ayto
How Broseley Pipes Were Made – reprinted from the Shrewsbury Chronicle Friday August 12th 1932.
Victoria County History.
The Archaeology Newsletter Vol 5.
Tobacco Pipes of Broseley, Shropshire by D.R. Atkinson.
The Clay Industries by John Randall.
Silver Screen Memories by Fred Brown.
Benthall Hall – The National Trust.
Catalogue of Mines by Ivor J. Brown.
The Darby's of Coalbrookdale by Barrie Trinder.
Broseley Pipeworks – Clay Tobacco Pipe Museum.
Ironbridge – History and Guide by Richard Hayman and Wendy Horton.
Welcome to Broseley – a brochure of the town, produced by several local people, and sponsored by Bridgnorth District Council Rural Development Commission, Broseley Forum.
Broseley – Broseley Parish Council and Broseley Society.
Birchmeadow information and Victorial Hall from documents from Bridgnorth District Council re: my book research.
Letters/correspondence sent to newspapers in 1862 in Shrewsbury Chronicle about Water Supply (Broseley) – Shropshire Records & Research Office.
Information from a book by Miles Taylor.
Many books and leaflets which I have read about Broseley mostly from the Records & Research Office, Ironbridge Gorge Museum Trust, some Broseley Leaflets, reference books in Broseley Library and information given to me by local people.

Again I wish to apologise for any information in my book which I have used but not credited to any other person, this is because I cannot remember the source after such a long period of time of my research.